American

Sketches

*Great Leaders, Creative Thinkers,
and Heroes of a Hurricane*

———◆———

Walter Isaacson

Simon & Schuster
NEW YORK   LONDON   TORONTO   SYDNEY

Simon & Schuster
1230 Avenue of the Americas
New York, NY 10020

First Simon & Schuster hardcover edition November 2009

SIMON & SCHUSTER and colophon are registered
trademarks of Simon & Schuster, Inc.

For information about special discounts for bulk purchases,
please contact Simon & Schuster Special Sales at
1-866-506-1949 or business@simonandschuster.com.

The Simon & Schuster Speakers Bureau can bring authors
to your live event. For more information or to book an event,
contact the Simon & Schuster Speakers Bureau at
1-866-248-3049 or visit our website at www.simonspeakers.com.

Designed by Paul Dippolito

Manufactured in the United States of America

1   3   5   7   9   10   8   6   4   2

Library of Congress Cataloging-in-Publication Data is available.

ISBN 978-1-4391-8064-8
ISBN 978-1-4391-8345-8 (ebook)

To Cathy and Betsy, as always

Contents

7. JOURNALISM

9. NEW ORLEANS, MON AMOUR

American Sketches

My So-called Writing Life

On the Bogue Falaya with Walker Percy,
photographed by Jill Krementz

I was once asked to contribute an essay to the *Washington Post* for a page called "The Writing Life." This caused me some consternation. A little secret of many nonfiction writers like myself—especially those of us who spring from journalism—is that we don't quite think of ourselves as true writers, at least not of the sort who get called to reflect upon "the writing life." At the time, my daughter, with all the wisdom and literary certitude that flowed from being a thirteen-year-old aspiring novelist, pointed out that I was not a "real writer" at all. I was merely, she said, a journalist and biographer.

To that I plead guilty. During one of his Middle East shuttle missions in 1974, Henry Kissinger ruminated, to those on his plane, about such leaders as Anwar Sadat and Golda Meir. "As a professor, I tended to think of history as run by impersonal forces," he said. "But when you see it in practice, you see the difference personalities make." I have always been one of those who feel that history is shaped as much by people as by impersonal forces. That's why I liked being a journalist, and that's why I became a biographer. As a result, the pieces in this collection are about people—how their minds work, what makes them creative, how they rippled the surface of history.

For many years I worked at *Time* magazine, whose cofounder, Henry Luce, had a simple injunction: Tell the history of our time through the people who make it. He almost always put a person (rather than a topic or an event) on the cover, a practice I tried to follow when I became editor. I would do so even more religiously if I had it to do over again. When highbrow critics accused *Time* of practicing personality journalism, Luce replied that *Time* did not invent the genre, the Bible did. That's the way we have always conveyed lessons, values, and history: through the tales of people.

In particular, I have been interested in creative people. By creative people I don't mean those who are merely smart. As a journalist, I discovered that there are a lot of smart people in this world. Indeed, they are a dime a dozen, and often they don't amount to much. What makes someone special is imagination or creativity, the ability to make a mental leap and see things differently. In 1905, for example, the most knowledgeable physicists of Europe were trying to explain why a light wave always appeared to travel at the same speed no matter how fast you were moving relative to it. It took a third-class patent clerk in Bern, Switzerland, to make the creative leap, based only on thought experiments he imagined in his head. The speed of light remains constant, he said, but time varies depending on your state of motion. As Albert Einstein later noted, "Imagination is more important than knowledge."

The first real writer I ever met was Walker Percy, the Louisiana novelist whose wry philosophical depth and lightly worn grace still awe me when I revisit my well-thumbed copies of *The Moviegoer* and *The Last Gentleman*. He lived on the Bogue Falaya, a bayou-like, lazy river across

Lake Pontchartrain from my hometown of New Orleans. My friend Thomas was his nephew, and thus he became "Uncle Walker" to all of us kids who used to go up there to fish, capture sunning turtles, water-ski, and flirt with his daughter Ann. It was not quite clear what Uncle Walker did. He had trained as a doctor, but he never practiced. Instead, he worked at home all day. Ann said he was a writer, but it was not until after his first novel, *The Moviegoer,* gained recognition that it dawned on me that writing was something you could do for a living, just like being a doctor or a fisherman or an engineer.

He was a kindly gentleman, whose placid face seemed to know despair but whose eyes nevertheless often smiled. I began to spend more time with him, grilling him about what it was like to be a writer and reading the unpublished essays he showed me, while he sipped bourbon and seemed amused by my earnestness. His novels, I eventually noticed, carried philosophical, indeed religious, messages. But when I tried to get him to expound upon them, he would smile and demur. There are, he told me, two types of people who come out of Louisiana: preachers and storytellers. It was better to be a storyteller.

That, too, became one of my guideposts as a writer. I was never cut out to be a pundit or a preacher. Although I had many opinions, I was never quite sure I agreed with them all. Just as the Bible shows us the power of conveying lessons through people, it also shows the glory of narrative—chronological storytelling—for that purpose. After all, it's got one of the best ledes ever: "In the beginning . . ." The parables and narratives and tales in the Bible always seemed more compelling than the parts that tried to decree a litany of rules.

My parents were very literate in that proudly middlebrow and middle-class manner of the 1950s, which meant that they subscribed to *Time* and *Saturday Review,* were members of the Book-of-the-Month Club, read books by Mortimer Adler and John Gunther, and purchased a copy of the *Encyclopaedia Britannica* as soon as they thought that my brother and I were old enough to benefit from it. The fact that we lived in the heart of New Orleans added an exotic overlay. Then as now, it had a magical mix of quirky souls, many with artistic talents or at least pretensions. As the various tribes of the town rubbed up against each other, it produced sparks and some friction and a lot of joyful exchange, all ingredients for a creative culture. I liked jazz, tried my hand at clarinet, and spent time in the clubs that featured the likes of reedmen George Lewis and Willie Humphrey. After I discovered that one could be a writer for a living, I began frequenting the French Quarter haunts of William Faulkner and Tennessee Williams and sitting at a corner table of the Napoleon House on Chartres Street keeping a journal.

Fortunately, I was rescued from some of these pretensions by journalism. While in high school, I got a summer job at the *States-Item,* the feistier afternoon sibling of the *Times-Picayune.* I was assigned the 5 a.m. beat at police headquarters, and on my first day I found myself covering that most awful of stories, the murder of a young child. When I phoned in my report to the chief of the rewrite desk, Billy Rainey, he started barking questions: What did the parents say the kid was like? Did I ask them for any baby pictures of him? I was aghast. I explained that they were grieving and that I didn't want to intrude. Go knock on the door and talk to them, Rainey ordered.

To my surprise, they invited me in. They pulled out photo albums. They told me stories as they wiped their tears. They wanted people to know. They wanted to talk. It's another basic lesson I learned: The key to journalism is that people like to talk. At one point the mother touched me on the knee and said, "I hope you don't mind me telling you all this."

Almost twenty-five years later, I recalled that moment in the most unlikely circumstance. Woody Allen had been hit by the furor over the revelation that he was dating Soon-Yi Previn, the adopted daughter of his estranged consort, Mia Farrow. He invited me to come over to his apartment so that he could explain himself. It was just the two of us, and as soon as I opened my notebook, it became clear how much he wanted to talk. At one point, when I asked if he thought there was anything wrong with this set of relationships, he replied in a way destined to get him into the quotation books: "The heart wants what it wants." After more than an hour, he leaned over and said, "I hope you don't mind me telling you all this." I thought, as his psychiatrist might have, No, I don't mind. This is what I do for a living. I get paid to do it—amazingly enough.

When I went north to Harvard, I drove up with cases of Dixie beer piled in my beat-up Chevy Camaro, so that I could play the role of a southern boy, and I reread *Absalom, Absalom* and *The Sound and the Fury*, so that I could channel Quentin Compson while avoiding his fate. The most embarrassing piece I have ever written, which I fear is saying a lot, was a review of a biography of Faulkner for the *Harvard Crimson* that I attempted to write in Faulkner's style. (No, it's not included in this collection.) Not surprisingly, I was never asked to join the *Crimson*, but I did join the *Lampoon*, the humor magazine. Back then the *Lampoon* specialized in producing parodies, such as one of *Cosmopolitan* that had a fake foldout of a nude Henry Kissinger. It was thus that I learned, though only moderately well, another lesson that is useful when traveling in the realms of gold: that poking fun at the pretensions of the elite is more edifying than imitating them. I also began, for no particular reason, to gather string and write a chronicle of an obscure plantation owner, then no longer alive, named Weeks Hall, who had, earlier in the century, invited a wide variety of literary figures and creative artists to be houseguests at his home, which he called Shadows-on-the-Teche. From that I learned the joys of unearthing tales about interesting and creative people.

During the summers, I tended to come back home to New Orleans to work for the newspaper. I liked to think that I had the ability to drive into any small town and, within a day, meet enough new people that I would find a really good story. I pushed myself to practice that every now and then, with mixed success. If I were hiring young journalists now, that would be my test: I would pull out a map, pick out a small town at random, and ask them to go there and send me back a good story in forty-eight hours.

On one such outing through southern Louisiana, I wrote a set of articles on the life of the sharecroppers on the sugarcane plantations along Bayou LaFourche. The pieces showed the effects of my having read James Agee once too often, in that they tried too hard to be lyrical and literary, but they did help me get an even more interesting job the following summer. Harry Evans, who is now well known as an author and a historian, was then the hot, young, crusading editor of the *Sunday Times* of London. He gave a talk in which he lamented that America was no longer producing as many literary journalists in the mold of Agee. Without even a pretense of humility, I put together a packet of my sharecropper pieces and sent them off to him in London, asking for a summer job. I heard nothing, promptly forgot about my impertinent request, and thus was a bit baffled when months later a telegram arrived at my dorm (an occurrence almost as unusual then as it would be today), saying: WILL HIRE FOR LIMITED TERM AS THOMSON SCHOLAR. It was signed by someone I had never heard of, but I soon realized it was an offer from the *Sunday Times*. The "Thomson scholar" bit was because Harry needed a way to get around the unions in hiring someone like me, so he made up a fellowship and named it after the paper's then-owner, Lord Thomson. I scraped up the money to buy a cheap ticket on Icelandair to London.

It was the summer of 1973, and the Watergate scandal was unfolding. Harry had created an investigative unit known as the Insight Team, and he put me on it under the mistaken impression that, since I was an American, I bore some resemblance to Woodward and Bernstein. My first big assignment was to go up to Dundee, Scotland, where the mayor, quaintly known as the Lord Provost, was suspected of having Nixonian tendencies. When I arrived at the airport, I cockily presented my *Sunday Times* press credential at the car counter only to be told that I was not old enough to rent one. Too embarrassed to tell my editors, I hitchhiked to my hotel.

Over the next few days, I was able to meet a lot of local characters and get them to talk. I pieced together a tangled web involving secret land purchases combined with nefarious adjustments to zoning laws. The article I wrote so baffled and unnerved my editors that they sent in reinforcements in the person of the most amazing journalist I have ever known, David Blundy. He was wild-eyed, boisterous, thrill-seeking, conspiratorial, and so excessively lanky that he looked like an animated cartoon character. One night when we returned to the hotel, the desk clerk mentioned that someone was in our room. David uncoiled himself into full alert mode, assuming that it must be some thug hired by the Lord

Provost, and barked to me that I should take the elevator and he would take the stairs. The point of this eluded me, but I did as I was told. We arrived at the sixth floor at the same time. David flung open our door and, since he was a chain-smoker, immediately collapsed on the floor wheezing from his race up six flights of stairs. The interloper turned out to be a television repairman who scurried out of the room leaving various parts strewn on our floor.

I subsequently partnered with David on stories involving the troubles in Northern Ireland, Morocco's war for the Spanish Sahara, and a ring of traders violating the sanctions against Rhodesia. He was exhilarated by danger. Once in Belfast he insisted that we go cover a demonstration, when I was quite content to stay at the bar of the Europa Hotel. He showed me that even though the street clashes might seem violent and bloody on television, just a half block away things were calm and safe. Journalism required an eagerness to get up and go places. While we were out, a bomb went off at the Europa Hotel. Blundy insisted that this should serve as a lesson for me. I agreed. But when he was killed a few years later by a sniper's bullet in El Salvador, I gave up trying to fathom the meaning of the lesson he wanted me to learn.

At the *Sunday Times,* I learned that I was not cut out to be a Woodward or a Bernstein. I tended to like people too much to relish investigating them. Perhaps that's the flip side of finding it easy to meet strangers and get them to talk. For example, one week I was sent to cover a fire at an amusement center, known as Summerland, on the Isle of Man, in which fifty people had died because of chained exit doors and other lapses. I ended up meeting Sir Charles Forte, the chief executive of the company that owned the park. He was very open, indeed vulnerable, as he discussed the mistakes that had led to the tragedy. It made for a good story, but it could have made for a really great story if I hadn't decided to downplay some of what he told me. My instinct to be sympathetic got the better of my instincts as a journalist.

I learned from Harry Evans's example that it was possible to be crusading and investigative while also retaining access to the people you cover. With his engaging manner and skeptical curiosity, he could be both an outsider (he was from Manchester) and an insider (he was knighted), as the occasion warranted. Every now and then, this lesson would be reinforced for me. For example, my first week covering the 1980 presidential campaign of Ronald Reagan for *Time*, I wrote a piece that looked at the facts he used in his stump speech, ranging from taxation levels to how trees caused pollution, and declared many to be dubious. I thought I would be shunned by the campaign staff on the plane the following week. Instead, I was invited to the front to ride with the candidate. There's a phenomenon common to many people in public life. Bill Clinton's mother described it when she said that if he walked into a room of a hundred people, ninety-nine of whom loved him and one who was a critic, he'd head over to that one to try to convert him. I found that true of Henry Kissinger as well. Like a moth to flame, he is attracted to his critics and feels compelled to convert them.

My stint at the *Sunday Times* helped me win a Rhodes scholarship, in part because members of Rhodes selection committees tend to be, not surprisingly, quite anglophilic. My panel was thus probably overly impressed by bylines in a British newspaper. The interviews took place in a French Quarter hotel, and I was spending my Christmas break shucking at a nearby oyster bar where, fortunately, nobody had any idea what a Rhodes scholarship was. Since my dream at the time was still to be a "real writer," I was quite intimidated when I saw that Willie Morris was on my selection panel. I paid no heed to one of the other judges, an Arkansas law professor who was about to launch an unsuccessful campaign for Congress. Years later, Bill Clinton surprised me by recalling the questions he had asked and the answers I had given. He also told George Stephanopoulos that I would go out of my way to be tougher on him as a journalist, now that I realized he had been on my selection committee. He knew that the remark would get back to me, and he probably calculated it as a bit of reverse psychology. In any event, I ended up having to oversee *Time*'s coverage of his amazingly messy second term, and my thoughts about him are reflected in the review of his memoirs included in this collection.

Before leaving for Oxford in 1974, I had an offer to be a summer intern at the *Washington Post*. This should have been an irresistible treat, since Watergate was coming to a climax. I was, however, still in the throes of my "real writer" obsession. So I decided instead to take a job as a stevedore on a derrick barge unloading ships in the Port of New Orleans. I assumed that kind of job would provide me, like it had Mark Twain, with a cast of characters for my intended Great American Novel About the River. Indeed, it did—or would have had I been Twain. In the bottom left drawer of every desk I've had since then lies the manuscript of my unfinished novel, set on the derrick *Terence* with Captain Coon and his colorful crew. Every decade or so, I pull it out, polish it up a bit, then reread it to remind myself that I am not, in fact, a "real writer." The world will have to make do with *Huckleberry Finn*.

At Oxford I studied philosophy, politics, and economics; combined with my history and literature concentration at Harvard, that prepared me to be a journalist and biographer, but not much else. My adviser there was a lively but wise professor named Zbigniew Pelczynski, a Hegel scholar who had been active in the Polish underground during World War II. Once again, I was exposed to the specter of Bill Clinton. Pelczynski assigned me a paper on how democratic undercurrents can be manifest in authoritarian regimes, which I promptly dashed off. He was not impressed. There was a better paper that had been written by a star student of his a few years earlier, and he made a copy of it for me. I probably knew the author, he said. No, I said glancing at the name. But he's from Arkansas and you're from Louisiana, Pelczynski pointed out. I allowed that not everyone in Louisiana knew everyone in Arkansas; indeed, I suspect I let my petulance show by declaring that I'd never known anyone at all from Arkansas, ever.

Bill Clinton's paper, on democracy in Russia, was in fact far better than mine, which made this professor's pet from Arkansas seem all the more annoying. Almost two decades later, in 1992 when I was a national affairs editor at *Time*, I got a call from Pelczynski. Reporters were asking him to talk about what Clinton was like as a student, he said, and he was wondering if he should give them copies of the paper. I was puzzled for a moment. What paper? I had long since forgotten about the essay. But once I recalled it, I realized that it could be explosive. It no doubt included some sentences that, taken out of context, or perhaps even in context, would cause Clinton big problems, especially since Republicans were already criticizing him for going to Russia as a student. A journalistic dilemma: Do I tell a well-intentioned old professor to show reporters a paper that could disrupt Clinton's candidacy? After a few moments of reflection, I replied that I didn't know what he should do, but if it were one of my papers, I would want him to ask me first before releasing it. So Pelczynski said he would ask Clinton what to do.

That left a second journalistic dilemma. If I could find the paper, *Time* would have a great scoop. Should I? I called my father in New Orleans. "Go down to our basement workshop," I asked him, "and look in a white chest of drawers just behind the table saw and see if you can find an essay on Russia by Bill Clinton." A few minutes later, my father came back to the phone sounding upset. During one of the many New Orleans floods that afflicted our basement even before Katrina, that chest and its contents had been destroyed. My mother had thrown it out. I was disappointed, but part of me—the side of me that made me a less-than-tough reporter—was relieved. A journalistic dilemma had been averted.

A few years ago, after Bill Clinton left office, I visited Pelczynski in the Oxfordshire cottage where he had retired. He pulled out a scrapbook containing Clinton's paper. Also there was a telegram sent during the 1992 campaign from Betsey Wright, who was part of Clinton's ever-busy damage control team. It thanked Pelczynski for asking whether he should release the essay, and it urged him not to. I reread the paper and, this time around, found it rather good. I suggested to Pelczynski that he send a copy to the Clinton Library. Historians should have some things that eluded journalists at the time.

Under Pelczynski's spell, I considered becoming a philosopher. Well, not really a beard-stroking philosopher, but at least pursuing an academic career in the field. I had written my Oxford dissertation on an aspect of John Locke's view of property, and I decided to send it to two philosophy professors I'd had at Harvard: John Rawls and Robert Nozick. This was an inspired approach, since they held opposing views on Locke's notion of property, so one of them would likely find my analysis interesting. On my way home after finishing Oxford, I went to call upon each to see which might want to take me under his wing as a doctoral candidate. Both of them—Rawls somewhat more politely than Nozick—let me know, based on reading my Oxford dissertation, that the world of philosophy could make do quite well without my services. Thus I went back to the New Orleans *States-Item,* which was then in the process of being absorbed into the *Times-Picayune.*

I was assigned to cover City Hall, a job made easier because Mayor Moon Landrieu, who was dedicated to integrating the power structure of the city, hired Donna Brazile to be an assistant and the guardian of his door. Most of the old politicos resented having a young black woman controlling their access to the mayor. But I found her sassy attitude refreshing, and I used to pump her for gossip and information. A key to journalism is spotting people like Donna, who are always completely clued in. Star reporters like Woodward and Bernstein never reveal their sources. I subscribe to a thirty-year statute of limitations. Donna gave me some of my best stories.

Thanks to my job, I was able to rent one of the apartments in the Pontalba Buildings, which flank Jackson Square. They are owned by the city and the state, and I put myself on the waiting list to get in. One day, the city council president told me he had gotten me bumped to the top of the list. He also gave me a blue light, which baffled me at first until he explained it was a police light that I could put on my dashboard so that I could park illegally in the French Quarter. These were the days before press ethics had evolved into a refined theology, so I accepted his largesse.

My final chance to be lured away from the writing life came when I got a call from a man named Cord Meyer, who had worked in some mysterious capacity for the U.S. embassy in London and spent a lot of time getting to know the American students at Oxford. It turned out that he was with the CIA, and he arranged for me to meet a colleague of his by the swimming pool of the New Orleans airport Hilton hotel. It all seemed very cloak-and-dagger exciting until the recruiter began stressing that they did not, of course, want me to be a covert agent but rather an analyst at headquarters. If he had pushed the former prospect, I might have accepted on the spot, and this would be a much different book.

That same week I also met with an editor at *Time* who had been dispatched to venture forth from Manhattan and find young journalists from "out there." New Orleans had just held a mayoral primary featuring twelve candidates, each quirky in a delightfully different way (one of them was married to the founder of Ruth's Chris Steak House and campaigned, wearing a gorilla suit, on the platform of buying a gorilla for the Audubon Park zoo). I had gone around to every ward leader and made them fill out a chart of how many votes each candidate would get in each of that ward's precincts. With that and a bit of luck, I was able to predict correctly the exact order and vote percentages for all twelve candidates. When the *Time* editor arrived in town, the paper was touting my feat in its promotional ads. He offered me a job, which I accepted over the CIA one. My last act at the newspaper was to write a column predicting the runoff. This time I didn't go around interviewing every ward leader, because I was cocky enough to think I knew enough on my own. I got it wrong. Another lesson.

I was the only reporter from "out there" who had been found by this wandering editor, and when I arrived at the Time-Life Building I was brought like a proud catch to the thirty-fourth floor to be presented to the top boss, Hedley Donovan. Donovan proclaimed how pleased he was that they had found someone from "out there," because far too many of the people at the magazine had gone to Harvard and Oxford. By the way, he asked, where did I go to school? I thought he was joking, so I just laughed. He repeated the question. The editor who had found me gave me a nervous look. I mumbled, "Harvard," in a drawl that I hoped made it sound like Auburn. Donovan looked puzzled. I was whisked away. I do not recall ever being brought to meet him again.

As it turned out, the people I got to know and work with at *Time* over the years actually did come from a diverse array of backgrounds, rich and poor, rural and urban. There was a tendency that afflicted many of us who made it into the national media to forget our roots and become more likely to attend a Council on Foreign Relations meeting than a Rotary Club lunch. So when I became editor of *Time,* we organized a three-week Greyhound bus trip across America, on old U.S. Highway 50, which forms the Main Street of scores of towns across the nation's midsection. My fellow *Time* journalists on the trip included the children of a train engineer from Ohio, a rent-to-the-poor businessman from

Arkansas, a Boys Club executive from the Stuyvesant Town housing project, a dockworker's son from Mississippi, a domestic worker from Harlem, and a bus driver from Long Island. We dropped in at chicken-processing plants and bowling alleys, Kiwanis Clubs and PTA meetings, Pentecostal churches and cheap bars that cashed checks on payday. We did a similar trip a few years later using a boat to go down the Mississippi, starting in Hannibal, Missouri, and climaxing in New Orleans. As explored in works ranging from the *Odyssey* to *Huckleberry Finn* to *Route 66*, there's a fascinating mix of engagement and detachment that comes from being on the move, stopping as a stranger in a new place for an adventure, and then moving back onto the road or the raft, leaving all complexities behind. Journalists and writers are particularly drawn, I think, to that mix of engagement and detachment.

During my early years at *Time*, I was assigned to work under the national affairs editor, Otto Friedrich, a wry man with a bushy red mustache who seemed perpetually amused by himself. He taught me a wonderful insight about journalism and later biography: Obscure facts and pieces of colorful detail, even though they may seem trivial, provide the texture and verisimilitude that make for a great narrative. It was something that Plutarch noted at the beginning of his *Lives:* "Sometimes a matter of lesser moment, an expression or a jest, informs us better of their character and inclinations, than the most famous sieges." Friedrich had expanded on the notion in a piece he titled "There Are 00 Trees in Russia." The "00" referred to the way a newsmagazine writer sticks in "00" or "TK" as a placeholder for a fact and then lets a researcher fill it in.

From Friedrich, who wrote books on the side, I learned that writing biographies and histories could be a satisfying accompaniment to a day job in journalism. When covering the 1980 Reagan campaign, I was struck by the bug-eyed bevy of people who showed up on the fringes of rallies and handed out leaflets purporting to expose the insidious nature of the East Coast foreign policy establishment. The leaflets were filled with charts and arrows about the Trilateral Commission, the Council on Foreign Relations, the Rockefellers, the Bilderberg Group, Skull and Bones, and various banking cabals. I asked my *Time* colleague Evan

Thomas about it, under the theory that as an East Coast preppy he could decode it. Eventually we began to talk about writing a book that would explore the reality and myths about "the establishment."

We sketched it out in a summer cottage in Sag Harbor on Long Island. I'm a night person, and would try to stay up until 5 a.m., at which point I would hand over my notes to Evan, who got up around then. We'd go to the beach in the afternoon. We came around to the dual approaches that were at the core of our work at *Time:* Tell the tale through people, and make it a chronological narrative. We selected six men who were at the core of the so-called establishment (Dean Acheson, Averell Harriman, Robert Lovett, John McCloy, Chip Bohlen, and George Kennan), and we traced chronologically their interwoven lives through prep school, college clubs, Wall Street, the foreign service, cold war statecraft, and the Vietnam War.

We took our outline up Madison Street in Sag Harbor to Amanda Urban, who had recently become a literary agent, and she sent us farther up the street to Alice Mayhew, who was an editor at Simon & Schuster. She heard us out for a few minutes, grasped the idea immediately, and said that she had always wanted to publish such a book and it should be titled *The Wise Men.* And so it was.

We were concerned that academics would dismiss our book as being too (or "merely") journalistic, so we immersed ourselves in presidential archives and relied heavily on what real historians reverentially call "the documents." That proved useful after one of our early interviews, in which McGeorge Bundy denigrated our thesis that there was anything that could be called an "establishment" group. Then Evan found, in the Lyndon Johnson archives, a memo by Bundy titled "Backing from the Establishment," which detailed the behind-the-scenes role our characters played and urged Johnson to create an advisory group of them that would offer support for the Vietnam War.

But I also became convinced of the benefits of journalistic legwork, not just archival research, in writing contemporary history. For example, the daily letters that Lovett wrote Harriman provided a wealth of archival documentation, but by the late 1950s, when long-distance telephoning became common, they were abruptly replaced in the files by cryptic phone messages saying such things as "call me regarding Laos." It thus helped to be able to interview the players with a reporter's notebook in hand.

That was all the more the case when I set out to write a biography of Henry Kissinger. I learned that many of the documents in the archives had been written more for the purpose of posterior-covering than for historical accuracy. (His aide Winston Lord told me that Kissinger sometimes had aides write three versions of meeting memos: one for the archives, another for Nixon, and an accurate one for Kissinger.) So it helped to go out and ask the players what truly lay behind the official memos. As Kissinger himself once pointed out: "What is written in diplomatic documents never bears much relation to reality. I could never have written my Metternich dissertation based on documents if I had known what I know now."

Kissinger, it turned out, was not excessively thrilled by what I wrote, and he let me know. Over a two-day period, as he read the just-published book, he dictated a flurry of letters declaring various points I made to be "outrageous." Some were hand-delivered from his office on Park Avenue to the Time-Life Building by a mildly amused L. Paul "Jerry" Bremer, who was then Kissinger's young associate and later had the slightly easier job of being America's viceroy in Iraq. At one point Kissinger confronted his close friend Henry Grunwald, who was Editor in Chief of Time Inc., and thus my boss. Grunwald told Kissinger that he considered my book to be fair and straight down the middle. Kissinger paused and then grumbled, with that ironic sense of humor that saved him, sometimes, from pomposity, "And what right does that young man have to be fair and straight down the middle about me?"

Perhaps as a reaction, I decided to do my next book on someone who had been dead for two hundred years. I picked Benjamin Franklin, because I felt the country was becoming too ideologically and politically polarized. Franklin was the founder who helped the others find common ground and practical solutions. He realized that tolerance and compromise would be the new nation's key civic virtues. These were ideals I felt could use a little exalting at the time. Instead of doing it by preaching, I again felt it was better to convey these ideals through narrative biographical storytelling.

One of the things that struck me about Franklin was that he was an avid and serious scientist. We sometimes think of him as a doddering old dude flying a kite in the rain, but his experiments produced the single-fluid theory of electricity, which was the most important scientific advance of the era, and the lightning rod, which was the most useful invention. Whether he was charting the Gulf Stream or recording botanical designs, he loved science and would have considered as philistines those who took no interest in it. In our age, however, many supposedly educated people feel comfortable joking about how they are clueless about science and intimidated by math. They would never admit to not knowing the difference between Hamlet and Macbeth, but they happily concede that they don't know the difference between a gene and a chromosome or between the uncertainty principle and relativity theory. I wanted to show that science—even for a nonscientist like myself—could be fascinating and creative and imaginative. Once again, the best way to convey that message was through the narrative of a person, in this case Albert Einstein.

Those of us who write history used to have a variety of sources. There were wonderful diaries, such as the one that Secretary of War Henry Stimson kept during World War II, but those have disappeared due to laziness, time pressures, and the fear of subpoenas. We also had letters—those of Franklin and Einstein each fill more than forty volumes—but in the age of telephones and e-mails, these, too, have pretty much disappeared. There was a glorious period of the Kennedy-Johnson-Nixon years when we had secret tape recordings, but this delightful practice was discontinued after it brought Nixon down. Nowadays, policymakers are wary of keeping notes, writing honest memos, or sending e-mail. Everything can be subpoenaed by congressional committees. I wish there were a way we could convince Congress to pass a law giving privacy protection to e-mails and other such material except when a court orders that they are truly needed for a serious criminal case; they could then become part of the archival record open to historians after twenty-five years. But that's unlikely. The only new resource historians will have are the great journalistic books—such as those by Bob Woodward, David Sanger, Jane Mayer, Barton Gellman, Rajiv Chandrasekaran, Steve Coll, George Packer, Thomas Ricks, Michael Gordon, and many others—that pry out from the powerful players what really happened behind the scenes. If print journalism and the business models for newspapers collapse in the Internet age, these will soon disappear as well.

"All biography is autobiography," Emerson says, and I suspect I have projected some of my own sentiments on the subjects I profile. That is particularly true of Franklin. A successful publisher, journalist, and marketer—and a consummate networker with a techie curiosity—he would have felt right at home in the information revolution and as a striver in an upwardly mobile meritocracy. I could relate to that. My daughter once pointed out the obvious, that in writing about Franklin I was writing about an idealized version of myself. Yes, I admitted, but what about Einstein? That, she noted, was me writing about my father. Indeed, my father is a kindly, Jewish, distracted, humanistic engineer with a reverence for science. Einstein was his hero, just as my father has been mine. At that point I asked my daughter what she thought I was doing when I wrote about Kissinger. That's easy, she said. You were writing about your dark side.

One topic that has always interested me, throughout my various journalistic and writing endeavors, is the impact of technology on our lives. In 1989, I went to Eastern Europe to cover the unraveling of the Soviet Communist empire. When I got to Bratislava, in what was then Czechoslovakia, I was put in the Forum Hotel. Because it was where foreigners stayed, it was one of the few places to get satellite television. One of the maids asked if I minded my room being used in the afternoon by schoolkids, who liked to come watch MTV and the other music video channels. I said sure, and I made a point of coming back early so that I could meet the students. But when I came in, they weren't watching MTV. They were watching CNN, which was showing the unrest at the Gdansk shipyard. I realized that the collapse of authoritarian regimes was inevitable because they would eventually be unable to control the free flow of information in a digital age.

I saw something similar ten years later in Kashgar, an oasis town in western China across the Gobi desert from the rest of the nation. In the back of a small coffee shop on an unpaved street, three kids were sitting around a computer. I asked what they were doing. They were on the Internet, they said. I asked to try something and typed in "time.com." The screen said "Access denied." I typed in "cnn.com." Again, access denied. One of the kids elbowed me aside and typed in something. CNN popped up. He typed something else. *Time* popped up. I asked what he had done. "Oh," he said, "we know how to go through proxy servers in Hong Kong that the censors are clueless about." As I watch that region of western China erupt in occasional protests coordinated on Twitter and Facebook, and as I see the same happening in Iran and elsewhere, I realize that digital technology will do more to shape our politics than anything since Gutenberg's introduction of the printing press to Europe helped usher in the Reformation.

I have also watched, with much joy and some trepidation, the effects of technology on journalism and writing. When I first came to the *Sunday Times* of London, reporters still typed their stories on paper and handed them to typesetters. There was a room on a different floor that held what was called "the new technology"—word processors that could send stories directly into type. But the typesetters' union had blocked the implementation of the system. Because I had used computers and word processors at college, I tried out one of the idle *Sunday Times* machines. In protest, and as a warning shot, the typesetters' union called a "chapel meeting," meaning they all stopped work as the newspaper neared deadline. It was my first taste of the Luddite tendencies harbored by some in the newspaper business.

In the early 1990s, even before the advent of the World Wide Web, I was struck by the rise of online communities such as the Well. We did a *Time* cover story called "Welcome to Cyberspace," and it was clear that we were seeing a fundamental transformation of media. Until then, information tended to be packaged by large companies and handed down to a mass audience. Henceforth, there would also be another model: Communities would be built online in which participants created and shared information among themselves, peer to peer. When I was put in charge of "new media" for Time Inc., our group focused on creating communities and discussion groups online, rather than merely using the Net for cheap electronic distribution of our magazines. *Time* and its sister publications struck partnerships with CompuServe, Prodigy, and the fledgling AOL to create a variety of online bulletin boards and discussions about our articles.

The Web changed things. We were no longer confined to the walled gardens carved out of the Internet by the commercial online services. It became easy—too easy—to put our entire magazine online. The idea of community got downgraded to a few "comments" sections at the bottom of pages. Users were no longer treated as members of our community; instead, they were surfers who glided by while glancing at our articles.

At first we thought that users might pay for such privileges, but once we helped develop the idea of banner ads, young account executives from Madison Avenue came rushing to our door with bags of money to pay for as many user eyeballs as we could muster. So we got seduced by Stewart Brand's mantra that "information wants to be free, because it is now so easy to copy and distribute," while ignoring the second part of his formulation, which is that "information wants to be expensive, because in an Information Age, nothing is so valuable as the right information at the right time." There is a tension between the two parts of his concept, one that we must still resolve.

The new technology offers wonderful possibilities for the so-called writing life. I hope, for example, that my next book will be written with an electronic reading device, such as a Kindle or a Sony Reader, in mind; I want to integrate my words with music and pictures and voices. I think journalism can thrive in the digital realm as well. It will be deeply enriched by citizen journalists and bloggers, while traditional journalists will benefit from magical new ways to distribute what they produce. Even old-fashioned print may benefit. Paper, after all, is a very good technology for the storage, retrieval, distribution, and human browsing of information. Imagine if we'd been getting all of our information on electronic screens for four hundred years, and then some modern-day Gutenberg came along and took the words and pictures and put them onto nicely designed pages that we could read in the bathtub or bus or backyard. We'd be impressed. We might even declare that paper was such a good technology it would replace the Internet someday. At the very least, paper will, I think, find an enduring niche as a pleasing and convenient complement to electronic forms of information distribution.

However this future evolves, we will have to answer a pressing question: How will writers (or anyone else who creates content that can be digitized, from movies to music to apps to journalism) make a living in an era in which digital content can be freely replicated? That is now my greatest worry as I contemplate the so-called writing life that I hope to continue—and that I hope my daughter and all future generations will continue.

For three hundred years, ever since the Statute of Anne was established in Britain, there has been a system under which people who created things, such as books or articles or music or pictures, had a right to benefit from copies that were made of them. Because of this "copyright" system, we have encouraged and rewarded three centuries of creativity in various fields of endeavor, and this has produced a flourishing economy based on the creation by talented individuals of intellectual property. Among other things, this allowed all sorts of people, ranging from Walker Percy on down to me, to make a living at the so-called writing life. May the next generation enjoy that delightful opportunity as well.

1. FRANKLIN AND OTHER FOUNDERS

———◆———

Franklin and the
Art of Leadership

Benjamin Franklin would, I think, have been pleased, even tickled, by the election of Barack Obama as president. He believed that America's foundational virtue, the key to creating a pluralist democracy, was tolerance—the humility to allow people of different faiths, backgrounds, and ethnic origins to be equal participants in the nation's civic life.

Franklin was a very practical man, and I wrote my biography of him partly to celebrate the idea that a healthy democracy requires pragmatic people who can find common ground during times of great partisan division. I hoped that more politicians would emerge who were sage and sensible, and I came to believe that Obama was the most like Franklin of all our national politicians. I suspect that Franklin would appreciate the way that Obama held true to certain core values while displaying a willingness to be practical and bridge partisan divides. He would also approve of Obama's leadership style, which involves doing a lot of listening and being able to work collaboratively with strong characters. (When it comes to a Team of Rivals, with all due respect to the cabinets of Lincoln and Obama, nothing can top the founders.) So when Newsweek *asked me to write about Franklin for its January 2009 issue commemorating Obama's inauguration, I wrote the following essay.*

When Benjamin Franklin was a young printer just starting to keep shop in Philadelphia, he formed a self-improvement club of his fellow tradesmen that was designed to help them become civic leaders. To that end, he made a chart of twelve virtues that he would try to perfect, such as industry and frugality, and each week he proudly showed off his progress to the other members of his club.

One member, noting Franklin's too-evident pride, "kindly" informed him that he had left off a virtue that he would do well to practice. What was that? Franklin asked. Humility, the friend replied. Franklin later conceded that he was never quite able to master that virtue, but he wryly noted that he learned to fake it very well. "I cannot boast of much success in acquiring the *reality* of this virtue," he wrote in his *Autobiography*, "but I had a good deal with regard to the *appearance* of it." He soon came to realize that the pretense of humility could be just as useful as the reality of humility: It caused you to listen to the people around you and show respect for their opinions, which was the essence of the system of democracy based on mutual tolerance that he and his friends were trying to forge.

Each of America's founders displayed different leadership skills. George Washington had unassailable rectitude and stature. John Adams and his cousin Samuel had great passion and fealty to principle. Thomas Jefferson and his protégé James Madison displayed elegant creative intelligence. Franklin had many leadership strengths that are quite akin to Obama's: He was inventive, pragmatic to the core, and had a wry wit that warmed rather than wounded those around him. But most importantly in those tumultuous years, he was sage enough to bring passionate people together, to lead them by listening to them. He was able to unify people by displaying the humility, or at least the pretense of humility, that is so lacking during eras of hyper-partisanship but remains the essence of liberty and democracy.

Franklin used his club to launch a procession of civic-improvement schemes. The first was a lending library, which began when he suggested that members pool their books at the clubhouse and expanded when he came up with the idea of raising money to acquire new books that public subscribers could borrow. The Library Company of Philadelphia, which is still in existence, was incorporated in 1731, when Franklin was twenty-seven. The motto he wrote for it—"To pour forth benefits for the common good is divine"—reflected his civic leadership creed that the best way to serve God was to serve his fellow man.

In raising money for the library, he learned what became his first rule of leadership: It's easier to accomplish things if you don't worry about getting the credit. Instead of saying that the library was his idea, Franklin recalled, he "stated it as a scheme of a number of friends." By using this method, he avoided arousing any jealousy, and "in this way my affair went on more smoothly, and I ever after practiced it on such occasions." For example, when he decided to propose creating the town's first volunteer fire company, he did so in an essay that he pretended had been written by an old man of his acquaintance. Of course, given that he admitted that he never mastered the virtue of humility, Franklin took satisfaction in noting that, even if you allow others to take credit, eventually people will learn of your role and respect you all the more. "The present little sacrifice of your vanity will afterwards be amply repaid," he said.

Like Obama, Franklin's leadership instincts led him to be a uniter. Another of his leadership maxims was "The good men may do separately is small compared with what they may do collectively." He drew the nation's first editorial cartoon, which showed a snake cut into pieces labeled with the names of the colonies and a caption urging "Join, or die." After he retired as a printer, he spent almost seventeen years as an envoy in London trying to hold together the British Empire, which he likened to a "fine and noble china vase . . . that, once broken, the separate parts could not retain even their share of the strength or value that existed in the whole."

The challenge for leaders who are uniters by instinct is to know when a chasm has become unbridgeable and it is necessary to take a stand on one side or the other. For Franklin that moment came in 1775, when he sailed home to Philadelphia just as the Revolution was beginning. Franklin kept his views private until he had a chance to consult with his son William, a loyalist whom the king had appointed to be royal governor of New Jersey. Franklin told his son that he had decided to come down on the side of the rebels in favor of independence. William replied that he would remain a loyalist; Franklin coldly cut him off and barely spoke to him for the remainder of his life. When finding common ground was no longer possible and the time had come to take a stand, Franklin did so both politically and personally without flinching.

The Continental Congress decided to put him on a committee to write a declaration explaining why the colonies were seeking independence. It was back in the days when Congress knew how to appoint really good committees: Franklin and Jefferson and John Adams were on it. They knew that leadership required not merely asserting values, but finding a balance when values conflict. We can see that in the deft editing of the famous sentence that opens the second paragraph of the Declaration. "We hold these truths to be sacred . . . ," Jefferson had written. On the copy of his draft at the Library of Congress we can see the dark printer's ink and backslashes of Franklin's pen as he changes it to "We hold these truths to be self-evident." His point was that our rights would come from rationality and the consent of the governed, not the dictates and dogma of any religion. Jefferson's draft sentence went on to say that all men have certain inalienable rights. We can see Adams's hand making an addition: "They are endowed by their Creator" with these inalienable rights. So just in the editing of one half of one sentence we can see how Franklin and his colleagues struck a unifying balance between the grace of divine providence and the role of democratic consent in the founding values of our nation. How stark the contrast is with eras when politicians and the media use religious issues—school prayer, public placements of the Ten Commandments or Christmas crèches—as ways to polarize people.

The clause at the core of the Declaration's opening sentence—"a decent respect to the opinions of mankind requires that . . ."—makes it clear that it is designed as an act of public diplomacy. So Franklin, despite now being seventy and suffering from the gout, embarked on a treacherous secret wartime crossing of an ocean ruled by enemy warships to enlist the French to our cause. His writings and scientific experiments had made him world-famous, and he was particularly beloved in France, where his theory relating lightning to electricity had first been proved. Franklin knew that the art of global leadership required adroit backroom diplomacy involving balances of power, and he wrote masterly private memos to the French foreign minister explaining how the strategic interests of the new United States could align with France and its Bourbon-pact allies against Britain. But he also knew that America's might in the world would come from a public diplomacy that sought to enlist people to the new nation's ideals. So when he arrived in Paris, he built himself a printing press and started publishing the inspiring documents and declarations that explained America's values of liberty and equality, values that were welling up among the French masses and intellectuals as well.

After his return to Philadelphia, he became, at eighty-one, the elder statesman at the Constitutional Convention. During that hot summer of 1787, the rivalry between the big and little states almost tore the convention apart. Their dispute was over whether the legislative branch should be proportioned by population or by equal votes per state. Finally, Franklin arose to make a motion on behalf of a compromise that would have a House proportioned by population and a Senate with equal votes per state. "When a broad table is to be made, and the edges of planks do not fit, the artist takes a little from both, and makes a good joint," he said. "In like manner here, both sides must part with some of their demands." His point was crucial for understanding the art of true political leadership: Compromisers may not make great heroes, but they do make great democracies.

The toughest part of political leadership, however, is knowing when to compromise and when to stand firm on principle. There is no easy formula for figuring that out, and Franklin got it wrong at times. At the Constitutional Convention, he went along with a compromise that soon haunted him: permitting the continuation of slavery. But he was wise enough to try to rectify such mistakes. After the Constitutional Convention, he became the president of a society for the abolition of slavery. He realized that humility required tolerance for other people's values, which at times required compromise; however, it was important to be uncompromising in opposing those who refused to show tolerance for others.

During his lifetime, Benjamin Franklin donated to the building fund of each and every church built in Philadelphia. And at one point, when a new hall was being built to accommodate itinerate preachers, Franklin wrote the fund-raising document and urged citizens to be tolerant enough so "that even if the Mufti of Constantinople were to send a missionary to preach Mohammedanism to us, he would find a pulpit at his service." And on his deathbed, he was the largest individual contributor to the building fund for Mikveh Israel, the first synagogue in Philadelphia. So when he died, twenty thousand of his fellow citizens came out to march in his funeral procession, which was led by ministers, preachers, and priests of every faith as well as the rabbi of the Jews.

God of Our Fathers

Every July, Time *does a "Making of America" cover story that explores a major figure in our nation's history. In 2004, the subject was Thomas Jefferson. In light of the many debates over church-and-state issues, during which partisans on both sides were prone to invoke our founders, I used the opportunity to explore how Jefferson and his avuncular soul mate Benjamin Franklin dealt with the deity and their own deism in our founding documents.*

Whenever an argument arises about the role that religion should play in our civic life, such as the dispute over the phrase "under God" in the Pledge of Allegiance or over the display of the Ten Commandments in an Alabama courthouse, assertions about the faith of the founders are invariably bandied about. It's a wonderfully healthy debate, because it causes folks to wrestle with the founders and, in the process, shows how the founders wrestled with religion.

The only direct reference to God in the Declaration of Independence comes in the first paragraph, where Thomas Jefferson and his fellow drafters of that document—including Benjamin Franklin and John Adams—invoke the "laws of nature and of nature's god." (The absence of capitalization was Jefferson's, though the final parchment capitalizes all four of the nouns.)

The phrase "nature's god" reflected Jefferson's deism—his rather vague Enlightenment-era belief, which he shared with Franklin, in a Creator whose divine handiwork was evident in the wonders of nature. Deists like Jefferson did not believe in a personal God who interceded directly in the daily affairs of mankind.

The first use of the phrase "nature and nature's god" by one of the founders comes in a rather improbable place: a hoax written by Franklin in 1747 about a fictional woman named Polly Baker who is on trial for having five illegitimate children. In her speech to the court, she defends herself by claiming that she was merely obeying "the first and great Command of Nature and of Nature's God, *Encrease and Multiply*." (Not only did the court acquit her, Franklin writes, but one of the judges married her the next day.)

In his first rough draft of the Declaration, Jefferson began his famous second paragraph: "We hold these truths to be sacred and undeniable . . ." The draft shows Franklin's heavy printer's pen crossing out the phrase with backslashes and changing it to "We hold these truths to be self-evident." Our rights, he felt, derive from nature and are secured by "the consent of the governed." Franklin was particularly fond of the idea of "self-evident" truths, which was a phrase used by his close friend David Hume, that giant of the Scottish Enlightenment. According to Hume's two-pronged fork, self-evident or analytic truths are ones that we derive from reason alone, in contrast to synthetic truths that we induce by doing experiments or gathering empirical data.

Later in that same sentence, however, we see what was likely the influence of John Adams, a more doctrinaire product of Puritan Massachusetts. In his rough draft, Jefferson had written, after noting that all men are created equal, "that from that equal creation they derive rights inherent & inalienable." By the time the committee and then Congress had finished, the phrase had been changed to "that they are endowed by their Creator with certain unalienable rights." For those of us who have toiled as editors, it is wonderful to watch how ideas can be balanced and sharpened through the editing process (and also how even giants have trouble knowing whether the word is *inalienable* or *unalienable*). The final version of the sentence weaves together a respect for the role of the Almighty Creator with a belief in reason and rationality.

The only other religious reference in the Declaration comes in the last sentence, which notes the signers' "firm reliance on the protection of divine Providence." Most of the founders subscribed to the concept of providence, but they interpreted it differently. Jefferson believed in a rather nebulous sense of "general providence," the principle that the Creator has a benevolent interest in mankind. Others had faith in a more specific doctrine, sometimes called "special providence," which held that God has a direct involvement in human lives and intervenes based on personal prayers.

In any event, this phrase was not in Jefferson's original draft, nor in the version as edited by Franklin and Adams. Instead, it was added by Congress at the last minute. Like the phrase "under God" in the Pledge, it got tucked into a resounding peroration and somewhat broke up the rhythm: ". . . for the support of this Declaration, with a firm Reliance on the protection of divine Providence, we mutually pledge to each other our Lives, our Fortunes, and our sacred Honor."

In the Constitution, the Almighty barely makes an appearance, except in the context of noting that it was written in "the year of our Lord" 1787. (Jefferson was ambassador to France at the time, so he missed the convention.) A tale, perhaps apocryphal, appears in Ron Chernow's biography of Alexander Hamilton and elsewhere. When a Princeton professor chided Hamilton for the founders' failure to invoke God or the Christian religion in the document, Hamilton is said to have replied, "We forgot."

There was an interesting dispute at the Constitutional Convention, however, when Franklin, of all people, stepped in at one of the most contentious moments and moved that they open each session with a prayer. In a passage destined to become famous, and to be the epigram on Vice President Richard Cheney's Christmas card one year, the eighty-one-year-old sage argued, "The longer I live, the more convincing proofs I see of this truth—that God governs in the affairs of men. And if a sparrow cannot fall to the ground without his notice, is it probable that an empire can rise without his aid?"

Though Franklin believed in God, his deist leanings had generally led him to eschew personal prayers seeking divine intervention and rely instead on the doctrine of salvation through good works here on earth. During the French and Indian War, he had irreverently written to his brother that he calculated that forty-five million prayers were offered in all of New England seeking victory over a fortified French garrison in Canada. "If you do not succeed, I fear I shall have but an indifferent opinion of Presbyterian prayers in such cases as long as I live. Indeed, in attacking strong towns I should have more dependence on works than on faith."

So the question arises: Did Franklin make his proposal for prayer out of a deep religious faith or out of a pragmatic political belief that it would encourage calm in the deliberations? There was probably an element of both, but more of the latter. He thought it useful to remind this assembly of demigods in Philadelphia that they were in the presence of a God far greater than themselves, and that history was watching as well. In order to succeed they had to be awed by the magnitude of their task and be humbled.

Hamilton warned that the sudden hiring of a chaplain might frighten the public into thinking that "embarrassments and dissensions within the convention had suggested this measure." Franklin replied that a sense of alarm outside the hall might help rather than hurt the deliberations within. Another objection was raised, that there was no money to pay a chaplain. The idea was rejected. On the bottom of his copy of his speech, Franklin appended a note of marvel: "The convention, except three or four persons, thought prayers unnecessary!"

The one clear proclamation on the issue of religion in the founding documents is, of course, the First Amendment. It prohibits the establishment of a state religion or any government interference in how people should, or should not, freely exercise their beliefs. It was Jefferson, the original spirit behind the Virginia Act for Religious Freedom, who emphasized that this amounted to a wall between two realms. "I contemplate with sovereign reverence," he wrote after becoming president, "that act of the whole American people which declared that their legislature should 'make no law respecting an establishment of religion, or prohibiting the free exercise thereof,' thus building a wall of separation between church and State."

Colonial America had seen its share of religious battles, in which arcane theological disputes such as the one over antinomianism caused Puritans to be banished from Massachusetts and have to go found Rhode Island. They had even experienced a wave of ecstatic revivalism, the Great

Awakening, in which preachers such as Jonathan Edwards breathed fire and brimstone about "sinners in the hands of an angry God."

The founders, however, were careful in their debates and seminal documents to avoid using God as a political wedge issue or a cause of civic disputes. Indeed, that would have appalled them. Instead they embraced a rather vague civic religion that invoked a rather depersonalized deity that most people could accept.

So it is difficult to know exactly what they would have felt about the phrase "under God" in the Pledge or about displaying the Ten Commandments in a federal courthouse. It is probable, however, that they would have disapproved of people on either side who used the Lord's name or the Ten Commandments as a way to divide Americans rather than as a way to unite them.

The Opinions of Mankind

When George H. W. Bush went to war against Iraq in 1990 after its invasion of Kuwait, he and his secretary of state James Baker diligently courted other nations to support the effort. The coalition they assembled included fighting forces from thirty-four different countries. It was a triumph of diplomacy, and it was based on convincing the international community that we had shared values. When his son George W. Bush went to war with Iraq in 2003, he showed less of a desire to court the international community. I believe that, more than any nation, our foreign policy (and even our wars) are motivated by values and ideals—and it's a shame when we don't take care to assure that the world understands and supports us. I took the opportunity of July 4, 2004, to write an op-ed piece for the New York Times *reminding readers that the Declaration of Independence itself was, fundamentally, a public diplomacy document designed to "let Facts be submitted to a candid world."*

Amid all the hot dogs and fireworks, it's useful to reflect for a moment on precisely what we are celebrating on the Fourth of July. Yes, we all know that the day is about independence and an aversion to colonialism, but what was that sacred parchment to which our founders affixed their John Hancocks really all about, and why is it relevant today?

By July of 1776, the Continental Congress had concluded not only that the American colonies ought to be independent but also that they needed a declaration explaining why. So they appointed a committee to draft one. It may have been the last time Congress created a truly great committee; among its members were Thomas Jefferson, John Adams, and Benjamin Franklin.

Jefferson, who got the honor of writing the first draft, was very direct in his first sentence about the motivation for the document. "A decent respect to the opinions of mankind" required them to explain what they were doing. So the Declaration is, in effect, a great propaganda document or, to put it more politely, an exercise in public diplomacy designed to enlist other nations to our cause.

If you are trying to persuade people to join with you, there are three general methods. You can coerce them with threats, convince them by pointing out their own interests, or entice them by appealing to their ideals. Those who run businesses, or have teenage kids, know how each of these approaches works.

One can imagine the founders trying the first tack on France and other European nations in 1776. We are breaking away from Britain, they could have said, and you're either for us or against us. If you're against us, your ships are not safe near our shores, your future trade is at risk, and you might as well forget about the fur trade and navigating on the Mississippi if we win.

Or, they could have used the second tack. The Bourbon-pact allies, they could have pointed out, had been fighting England off and on for four centuries or so, and the best way to shift the balance of power would be by detaching England from its colonies and forging treaties of friendship with America.

Instead, they tried the third tack. They appealed to the values and the ideals of potential allies.

Because they were Enlightenment thinkers, the drafters of the Declaration, particularly Jefferson and Franklin, began by positing basic premises, an analytic approach that reflected the philosophical methods of John Locke and the scientific method of Isaac Newton. People were created equal, they postulated, and they had certain unalienable rights. From this premise they deduced what this meant for the role and the legitimacy of governments. "To secure these rights, governments are instituted among men, deriving their just powers from the consent of the governed." A nice concept.

In order to make the document a reality, we had to get France in on our side in the Revolution. Even back then, the French were a bit difficult, so Congress sent Franklin, by then in his seventies, to woo them. He wrote some brilliant balance-of-power memos appealing to France's interests, but then he did something unusual. He began appealing to France's ideals as well. He built a press at his house on the outskirts of Paris, and there he printed the Declaration and other inspiring documents from America to show the French that we were fighting for the ideals of liberty and aversion to tyranny that were welling up in their country as well. It worked. France joined our cause and helped make sure that we won.

These are the same values—liberty and aversion to tyranny—that we still share with the French and our other natural allies in the world today. But unlike the founders, we are not as willing to court the hearts and minds of others. Rather than caring for the opinions of mankind, President Bush jokes, "Call my lawyer," when the concept of international law is raised, and Defense Secretary Donald Rumsfeld saw little need to distribute the Geneva Convention rules to American soldiers dealing with prisoners.

Machiavelli famously advised his prince that it was better to be feared than loved. By that standard, the United States is doing well in the world. Alas, fear is not a formula for winning a war against terrorism and the spread of dangerous weapons. We need allies who will want to help us because they share our values. That will require leaders who display a decent respect to the opinions of mankind.

It was the appeal of America's values—and the vision of statesmen like Jefferson and Franklin who were willing to engage in a war of ideas—that helped to win our independence. Likewise, it was the appeal of America's values—and the vision of wise leaders who were willing to engage in a war of ideas—that assured victory over communism in the cold war. Both of these generations realized that ideas had power—and that this power of America's ideas would prove even stronger than our weapons.

Now we are losing the war of ideas and ideals around the world. That failure would dismay our founders, for they knew the power of those self-evident truths that they proclaimed 228 years ago: that people are entitled to liberty, and that their rights should be guaranteed by governments whose legitimacy comes from the consent of the governed. These were inspiring ideals then, and they remain so today. The founders had the pride to realize that they could enlist legions to this noble cause. But they also had the humility to realize that this required "a decent respect to the opinions of mankind."

Best Supporting Actor

Whenever I am stymied while writing a biography, I pick up one of David McCullough's glorious narratives and reread a chapter. The rhythm of his sentences, the telling details that spice his storytelling, and the easygoing authority of his research inspire me to try to march in his footsteps. My biography of Kissinger came out, unfortunately, the same year as his on Truman. I remember being at a bookstore for a signing, with no customers showing any interest in me. Finally, a sweet, elderly lady came up and asked me to sign a book. It was McCullough's Truman. *I politely told her that I hadn't written the book. She said she knew. I pointed to a pile of unpurchased Kissinger biographies and said, "I wrote that book." "But I don't want a book on Kissinger," she said firmly, shoving me McCullough's book. "I want this one on Truman." So, I agreed to sign it. I hesitated over whether I should sign my own name or McCullough's, but finally decided to sign my own.*

Academics, with some notable exceptions, have shied from writing narrative biography. Imposing a narrative and focusing on individuals can, they argue with some justification, do damage to historical complexities. This has opened the realm of narrative biography to some truly great nonacademics, such as Doris Kearns Goodwin, Robert Caro, Evan Thomas, Jon Meacham, and, above all, David McCullough. His biography of John Adams came out in 2001, as I was working on my Franklin book, and I reviewed it for Time.

John Adams is hot these days. First came the eerie parallels to the Bushes: A competent but uninspiring vice president succeeds a charismatic president, serves only a term, is defeated by a liberal southerner, but lives to see his son and near-namesake restore the dynasty by winning the electoral vote but not the popular vote against a populist from Tennessee.

Now comes something even more exciting for his reputation: America's most beloved biographer, David McCullough, has plucked Adams from the historic haze, as he did Harry Truman, and produced another masterwork of storytelling that blends colorful narrative with sweeping insights.

Alas, though Adams had the same prickliness as give-'em-hell Harry, he's just not quite as lovable or colorful. From a family of Puritan farmers, Adams was honest and solid, but he could be argumentative, vain, stubborn, cantankerous, and despairing. Though smart and well read, he had neither the ingenuity of Franklin nor the brilliance of Jefferson nor the grandeur of Washington. In *John Adams*, McCullough does not try to exalt Adams nor polish him up; instead, he shows how his ability to be sensible and independent made him an important element in the mix of talents that created a new nation.

Among those who gathered in Philadelphia in 1776, Adams was one of the first to advocate independence. A disputatious trial lawyer, he gets much of the credit for winning the vote for such a declaration, and he saw more clearly than others its historic significance, though he was slightly off in choosing which of the two votes on the proposal would be remembered. "The second day of July," he wrote to his wife that week, "ought to be solemnized with pomp and parade, with shows, games, sports, guns, bells, bonfires and illuminations."

The following year, Adams was sent by Congress as an envoy in Paris, where he worked with Franklin and later Jefferson. With both he developed intense relationships that mixed admiration with disdain. They were more polished and popular than Adams, and certainly less Puritan in their approach to the pleasures of Paris. After the war he became America's first ambassador to England, where he again proved stiffly reliable but devoid of the courtier's charm that counted for so much in the world of European diplomacy.

If Adams's rigidity and propensity to argue made him a mediocre diplomat, they also made him rather unsuited for his next job, vice president. His first initiative was to tie up the Senate for a month debating what title of address should be used for President Washington, which tarred Adams as a closet monarchist and made him a target of mockery for those too timid to take on Washington directly. He ended up having little influence with the president or with Secretary of State Jefferson.

Adams's great goal was to keep American politics nonpartisan and to prevent a division into what were then called "factions." In that he failed. When Washington retired after two terms, the election of 1796 became the first between two parties: Jefferson leading what were then known as the Republicans, and Adams the unenthusiastic choice of the Federalists. Indeed, it was only because of the advent of party politics, and the Federalists' ability one last time to scrape together enough electors, that Adams was able to win his one term.

Nevertheless, Adams governed in a responsibly nonpartisan way. The great issue of the time was the threat of war with France, which was interfering with American shipping and whose agents were demanding bribes and tributes. The Republicans, admirers of the French Revolution, advocated peace; the Federalists, spurred by Hamilton and Washington, spoiled for war. Adams defied his party, conducted a delicate multichannel diplomacy with Paris, and ended up averting both war and the rise of the ambitious Hamilton as a military leader.

McCullough's triumph is that he uses the story of Adams to show how human the founders were, with their friendships and rivalries, grand philosophies and petty jealousies. Though Adams may pale compared to his compatriots, his complex relationships with each of them make the men on marble pedestals seem more real. Adams regarded the "old conjurer" Franklin with awe, then disgust, then anger, and finally grudging admiration. Jefferson won his affection and then betrayed him, but they ended their lives with a remarkable series of letters; both died on the same special day, July 4, 1826, each determined to make it to the fiftieth anniversary, with Adams gasping on his final day, "Thomas Jefferson survives."

Adams is also outshone by his beloved family. The book's most memorable character is his outspoken, sharp-penned wife, Abigail. Her deep and eloquent love for her husband, passionate beliefs on slavery and women's rights, and deft letters skewering Franklin and Jefferson and Hamilton make her worthy of a McCullough biography of her own.

Likewise, Adams at times pales when compared to the brilliance of his son, John Quincy Adams. Lest the comparison with the Bush family go too far (Bush père has been said to refer to his son as "Q"), McCullough tells how the younger Adams was brilliant and intellectually focused as he traveled on his own while a teenager to Russia, Finland, Germany, and other European countries during his father's stint as a diplomat. By the time the real Q was seventeen, his father had made sure he had translated Virgil, Tacitus, Cicero, Aristotle, and Plutarch, and understood geometry, algebra, and Newton's new calculus.

With such a cast, McCullough ends up with an interesting literary device: a great and flavorful drama told through a focus on a quirky costar. What makes the tale so revealing is that, through the perspective of Adams, the heroes of our founding become more human and their historic triumphs more nuanced. The result is more than a biography of Adams: It is a rollicking ensemble drama featuring a collection of giants put into perspective by their relationship with an honorable, intelligent, and somewhat stiff man who deeply loved his family, his farm, and the nation he helped create.

A Delicate Balance

To me, the most important lesson to be found in the crafting of our Constitution is the importance of balance. It's easy to hold passionately to your values. It's harder, and less glorious, to realize that legitimate values sometimes conflict with one another, and they have to be balanced. This is not a talent that is exalted on talk radio or cable news shows. But the need to calibrate a proper balance among opposing principles is evident in every issue we face today, from abortion to health-care reform to affirmative action. It is at the core of what we do in our seminars at the Aspen Institute. Benjamin Franklin was a master at that delicate and underappreciated art. Professor Richard Beeman, in a book published in 2009, showed how he and others created some near-perfect balances, and one failure, in 1787. I reviewed it for the New York Times.

We like to think of our nation's founders as men with unwavering fealty to high-minded principles. To some extent they were. But when they gathered in Philadelphia during the summer of 1787 to write the Constitution, they showed that they were also something just as great and often more difficult to be: compromisers. In that regard they reflected not just the classical virtues of honor and integrity but also the Enlightenment's values of balance, order, tolerance, scientific calibration, and respect for other people's beliefs. On almost all issues that they faced—with one very big exception—this art of compromise served them well. As Benjamin Franklin, that ultimate Enlightenment sage, conveyed in both his actions and words at the convention, compromisers may not make great heroes but they do make great democracies.

In *Plain, Honest Men*, Richard Beeman, a professor at the University of Pennsylvania who has taught and written about America's founding for forty years, offers a scholarly yet lively account of the Constitutional

Convention that emphasizes the craftiness and craftsmanship that went into each of the compromises. This saga has been often told, most recently in David O. Stewart's novelistic narrative *The Summer of 1787,* but Beeman's work is distinguished by a gently judicious tone that allows us to appreciate, and draw some lessons from, the delicate balances that emerged out of that passion-filled Philadelphia crucible.

The first major balance the framers had to strike was the extent to which they were going to retain a confederation of thirteen sovereign states or create a true national government—or concoct some magical combination of both. At the outset, Edmund Randolph of Virginia put forth a plan that, in Beeman's words, "amounted to an entirely new conception of the fledgling American government, a revolutionary step that would render the governments of the individual states distinctly inferior to that of a new 'national' government." In the ensuing weeks, the convention diluted the sovereignty of the national government so that to some degree it was balanced by the sovereignty of the states in their own realms. Nevertheless, the principle remained that the national government's power came not from an agreement among sovereign states but from, as proclaimed by those wonderfully simple yet profound opening words, "We the people."

This balancing act led the delegates to face another: Should every state get an equal vote in the new national legislature or should their votes be proportional to their population? Beeman notes that "James Madison believed from the outset that the fight to create a system of representative government in which ultimate sovereignty resided in the people of the nation as a whole rather than in the states would depend on creating a national legislature based on the principle of proportional representation." This created a power struggle between the big and little states. Eventually it was resolved by the compromise of having a Senate with equal votes per state and a House of Representatives proportioned by population.

That led to a third great compromise, one that would bedevil the nation for the next seventy-five years. If the apportionment was to be based on population, southerners argued, then slaves should be counted. No one was proposing that slaves (or for that matter women) be allowed to vote; the question was whether they should count as part of a state's population. Madison, a slave owner from Virginia, proposed that slaves be counted, mainly because, according to Beeman, "he wanted to send a clear signal to his more militant Southern colleagues . . . that the new national government need not threaten their interests." Northern opponents countered that such a provision would reward the increased importation of slaves. James Wilson of Pennsylvania proposed a purely mathematical compromise: Slaves would be counted as "three-fifths" of a person for the purpose of calculating representation. In a document that was designed to "secure the blessings of liberty to ourselves and our posterity," it was a stark case of compromise becoming divorced from principle.

One of Beeman's scholarly contributions is that he raises by a notch the role of South Carolina's Charles Pinckney, a man whose vanity and inflated claims of credit caused both contemporaries and later historians to give him less than his due. Most histories of the convention rely heavily on the famous notes taken by Madison, but apparently he could barely abide Pinckney and avoided recording much of what the South Carolinian said. On the day that Randolph proposed his plan for union, Pinckney offered an alternative plan, which Madison mentioned in two bland sentences and never described. As it turned out, Pinckney's version included much of what ended up in the final document—including the idea of counting slaves as three-fifths of a person. He also helped to assure that the final document required all states, even ones that banned slavery, to return fugitive slaves to their owners.

The framers were able to do all of this while assiduously avoiding use of the word *slave*. Clearly they were discomforted by the disjuncture between their principles and their pragmatism. Here Beeman seems almost too judicious. On the one hand he warns against presentism, the mistake of judging people of the past by the standards of the present; on the other hand he says that "we cannot avert our eyes from the magnitude of the evil." Then, when it comes to the central question of whether it would have been possible to achieve a constitutional union without making such odious compromises, he hedges: "Perhaps we should not overestimate the commitment of the lower South delegates to the union.

We will of course never know." He is, of course, right that we will never know. But since he is in a far better position to make an assessment than we are, it would be nice to know what he believes.

Beeman's judiciousness, however, usually serves him well. He is able to avoid the overemphasis some historians place on the economic interests of the framers while still showing when they were motivated by parochial and personal concerns. For example, the Virginians shared with other southerners the desire to protect slavery, but they were more willing to stop the importation of new slaves (thereby increasing the value of the ones they already owned) than were delegates from Georgia and South Carolina, where rice and indigo farming created a greater demand for them.

More important, Beeman captures the nuances and complexities of the compromises that the framers made. Knowing when to stand firm on principle or when to find common ground with your fellow citizens is the most important, and also the most difficult, activity in a democracy. There's no simple formula for it. That is why it is so useful to have narratives, especially authoritative and readable ones like Beeman's, showing how the men who gathered that summer in Philadelphia struggled so hard, and in most cases so wisely, to get the balances right.

2. STATECRAFTERS

———◆———

McGeorge Bundy,
the Brightest

The relationship between intelligence and greatness is tricky. Indeed, it seems at times that the correlation is weak. McGeorge Bundy had a sharp intellect and a formidable mental processing power. But like Robert McNamara and other whiz kids who became part of what David Halberstam dubbed "the best and the brightest," he lacked the proper doses of sagacity, common sense, and humility when it came to the Vietnam War. I interviewed Bundy a few times at his New York University office when I was working on The Wise Men. *His smile and his attitude when talking about his elders, such as John McCloy and Robert Lovett and Averell Harriman, betrayed a touch of condescension. These banker types, who got us through the cold war, were perhaps not as brilliant as Bundy. But he was not, as it turned out, quite as wise as they were, as I gently tried to convey in this obituary for* Time *in 1996.*

His laserlike intellect radiated from behind his clear-rimmed glasses with an intensity as hot as his smile was cold. Had he been half as smart, he might have been a great man. Instead, McGeorge Bundy came to personify the hubris of an intellectual elite that marched America with a cool and confident brilliance into the quagmire of Vietnam.

The early 1960s will be remembered as a moment when meritocracy and patrician elitism enjoyed a celebrated cohabitation, the rise and then fall of which Bundy came to symbolize. The scion of a foreign policy establishment whose members unabashedly viewed America's leadership role (and their own) as a sacred destiny, Bundy became the epitome of the well-intentioned arrogance that David Halberstam grandly captured in *The Best and the Brightest*. Born in Boston, a descendant of the Lowells, he was educated at Groton, where he displayed his admixture of smoothness and sharpness. On his college-board exam he refused to answer the essay questions on summer vacations or favorite pets, instead writing on how inane the topics were; although an initial grader flunked him, the supervising grader gave him a perfect score, the same he had gotten on his other entrance exams.

At Yale (Phi Beta Kappa, Skull and Bones) he wrote a noted essay, "Is Lenin a Marxist?"; an editorial in the *Yale Daily News* calling for abolition of the football team; and a scholarly paper arguing for America's entry into World War II: "I believe in the dignity of the individual, in government by law, in respect for the truth, and in a good God; these beliefs are worth my life and more; they are not shared by Adolf Hitler."

He went on to Harvard as one of the exalted group of scholars called the Society of Fellows, joined the navy by memorizing the eye charts after being rejected for poor vision, then returned to Harvard, where he taught the course on U.S. foreign policy. His lecture on Munich each year, in which he mimicked the players, drew standing-room crowds; he fervently conveyed his realist's belief in the dangers of appeasement and the role of military force in diplomacy.

On a flight down to Palm Beach, Florida, after his 1960 election, John Kennedy mused that he wished he could make Bundy his secretary of state, but he was "too young." Instead he became national security adviser, transforming the job into the powerful fiefdom it has been ever since. It was a heady time as Bundy, Defense Secretary Robert McNamara, and others exuberantly conceived limited-war options and counterinsurgency theories. Their intellectual firepower dazzled much of Washington, though Sam Rayburn did grumble to an awed Lyndon Johnson, "I'd feel a whole lot better about them if just one of them had run for sheriff once."

Throughout the Kennedy years, Bundy took a detached, centrist position on Vietnam. But early in 1965, President Johnson, who proudly called Bundy "my intellectual" but liked to humiliate him by making him give briefings while Johnson sat on the toilet, sent Bundy on a fateful fact-finding trip to Vietnam. He arrived just as the Vietcong launched a direct attack on an American base in Pleiku. Bundy got on the phone with the White House to urge retaliation, then traveled to Pleiku. For once in his coldly rational life, his response was emotional.

The report he wrote became a seminal document in America's escalation of the war: "The situation in Vietnam is deteriorating, and without new U.S. action defeat appears inevitable. . . . There is still time to turn it around, but not much. . . . The international prestige of the U.S. and a substantial part of our influence are directly at risk." And so a new policy, dubbed by Bundy "sustained reprisal," was born. "Well," Johnson said, "they made a believer out of you, didn't they?"

For a while after he resigned in 1966, Bundy continued to support the war. "Getting out of Vietnam is as impossible as it is undesirable," he told Johnson at a meeting of elder statesmen in late 1967. But when the elders assembled again the following March, Bundy told Johnson there had been "a significant shift" in their thinking. The meeting marked the disintegration of the cocksure knights of the cold war, and along with them America's sense of moral hegemony.

In the ensuing years, Bundy epitomized a fascinating subspecies of fallen statecraft wizards—including his brother Bill and Robert McNamara—who seemed sentenced to wander in a purgatory where they sought to expiate their Vietnam sins and exorcise memories of being in cars surrounded by chanting protesters. "Mac is going to spend the rest of his life trying to justify his mistakes on Vietnam," commented his closest friend, Kingman Brewster, who was named president of Yale in 1963 after Kennedy talked Bundy out of accepting the job. Bundy became president of the Ford Foundation (which in a different world would have come later, after being secretary of state), wrote a thoughtful tome on the relationship between the atomic bomb and diplomacy (with scant mention of Vietnam), and headed a Carnegie Corporation project studying nuclear proliferation.

In 1986, when Evan Thomas and I were writing *The Wise Men*, a history of American cold war diplomacy, Bundy told us that there was no such thing as the establishment. If so, it was Bundy as much as anyone who brought about the end of an era in which foreign policy was entrusted to a noble club of gentlemen secure in their common outlook and bonds of trust. As his successor, Walt Rostow, recalled thinking at the end of the 1968 meeting of elders that Bundy helped convene, "The American establishment is dead."

Kissinger and
the Roots of Realism

*My biography of Henry Kissinger portrayed him as being a brilliant
analyst with a fingertip feel for global power balances. But I also tried
to show that his furtive and manipulative style arose from a lack
of appreciation for the openness and values and idealism that are a
strength (not a weakness, as he felt) of America's democracy. His 1994
tome* Diplomacy *sweeps through four centuries of statecraft to provide a historical justification for his realist approach. I found myself
impressed, as I described in this review written for* Time.

Both fans and foes of Henry Kissinger, whose ranks rival each other in
fervor, have long agreed on one thing: He is brilliant at analyzing national
interests and balances of power. If only he would step back from his
corporate consulting and fashion-set socializing, they say, he might produce the grand tome that secures his place alongside George Kennan
among the great diplomatic thinkers of our time.

Now he has, and it will. In *Diplomacy,* a sweeping portrayal of historical forces that begins with Cardinal Richelieu and ends with the
challenges facing the world today, Kissinger makes the most forceful case
by any American statesman since Theodore Roosevelt for the role of
realism and its Prussian-accented cousin realpolitik in international
affairs. Just as Kennan's odd admixture of romanticism and realism
helped shape American attitudes at the outset of the cold war, Kissinger's
emphasis on national interests rather than moral sentiments defines a
framework for dealing with the multipolar world now emerging. He has
produced one of those rare books that are both exciting to read and destined to be classics of their genre.

I should make it clear that I come to this book as an interested party.
Two years ago, I wrote a biography of Kissinger, for the same publisher,

which many of his detractors, and some of his putative friends, said pulled too many punches, and which his fervent defenders (himself among them) decried as too harsh. My conclusion was that Kissinger had a remarkable feel for the interplay of national interests but that he failed to appreciate the strength America derives from the openness of its democratic system. His strategic and tactical brilliance made possible the United States' rapprochement with China, but his secretive style and disdain for the moralism that undergirds America's sense of mission led to a backlash from both the left and the right against détente with the Soviet Union. *Diplomacy* reaffirms both my respect for his brilliance as an analyst and my reservations about the low priority he places on the values that have made American democracy such a powerful international force.

The world, Kissinger writes, is entering an era when many states of comparable strength will compete and cooperate based on shifting national interests. America has never felt comfortable with such balance-of-power arrangements. So to understand what lessons history may hold for this new order, Kissinger maintains, we should study the diplomatic dances that began in Europe 350 years ago—a topic that, perhaps not coincidentally, is Kissinger's area of academic expertise.

Cardinal Richelieu, the first minister of France at the time, developed the concept of national interest while working to prevent the revival of the Holy Roman Empire, which he deemed a threat to France's security even though both were Catholic. No longer were national interests to be equated with religious or moral goals. During the eighteenth century, balance-of-power diplomacy was perfected by England, an island state with a security interest in preserving equilibrium on the European continent.

In discussing the century of relative stability after the Congress of Vienna in 1814, Kissinger draws on his published doctoral dissertation on Metternich and Castlereagh (*A World Restored*, 1957) and an academic paper he wrote on Bismarck. (Like a good professor, he footnotes himself.) One difference between the earlier works and *Diplomacy* is that Kissinger now puts slightly greater emphasis on the role of justice and values. "The Continental countries were knit together by a sense of shared values," he writes. "Power and justice were in substantial harmony."

This relationship between moral concerns and national interest, Kissinger argues, is the dominant theme in American foreign policy. There are the idealists, who believe that spreading American values should be the nation's motive force, and the realists, who emphasize national interests, credibility, and power. Kissinger is unabashedly in the realist camp.

Kissinger casts Nixon as a realist, the first in the White House since Theodore Roosevelt. To support this contention, he quotes from Nixon's annual foreign policy reports, which Kissinger himself wrote. But as Kissinger admits, Nixon placed a picture of the unabashed idealist Woodrow Wilson in the Cabinet Room and repeatedly proclaimed the altruism of American policy. It amounted to a combination that Kissinger rather disparagingly calls "novel" but which seems to me quintessentially American.

"By the beginning of the last decade of the twentieth century," Kissinger writes, using a typically grandiloquent phrase to say "by 1990," Wilsonian idealism "seemed triumphant." This does not please him. He concludes his book with sentences of pro forma praise for America's idealism followed by sentences that begin with "But." In the end, the buts win: "American idealism remains as essential as ever, perhaps even more so. But in the new world order, its role will be to provide the faith to sustain America through all the ambiguities of choice in an imperfect world."

Kissinger is probably right that the end of the cold war has made Wilson's emphasis on exporting American values "less practicable." Instead of engaging in a moral showdown with a rival superpower, the United States will have to participate in a balancing act with Europe, Japan, China, and others. The irony may be that his emphasis on national interests and power balances may turn out to be more politically palatable now than when he had the chance to put it in practice in the midst of the cold war and Vietnam.

He's Back!

In one sense, this 2002 piece, which I wrote for the New Republic, *was quickly outdated. It was about President Bush asking Henry Kissinger to cochair the 9/11 Commission. A week later, Kissinger backed out of the assignment because he did not want to have to disclose information about the clients of his consulting firm. Nevertheless, this piece does make some points, which I think remain valid, about what happens when a power player starts looking at the possible judgments of history.*

In 1975, back when Iraq's greatest enemy was the shah of Iran, Secretary of State Henry Kissinger testified before a congressional panel investigating the covert aid that America had given to the Kurdish opposition in northern Iraq. In what was already becoming a pattern, the United States had suddenly abandoned the Kurds, leaving them to be decimated, and Kissinger was asked why. "Covert action," he replied, "should not be confused with missionary work."

The answer was revealing in many ways. It showed his dark humor, aversion to sentimentality, keen understanding of the role that realism must play in a messy world, and somewhat less keen appreciation for the role that morality plays in sustaining the policy of a democracy. It also showed his instinctive discomfort with investigative panels that rummage through the secrets of American statecraft. As he once grumbled about a CIA director: "Every time Bill Colby gets near Capitol Hill, the damn fool feels an irresistible urge to confess to some horrible crime."

Now Kissinger has been called upon to chair such an investigation, this time a very public one, into the policies and lapses leading up to the 9/11 terrorist attacks. For the new commission to succeed, it will need two traits above all: intellectual rigor and brutal public candor. The first comes naturally to Kissinger. The second, however, has not, to put it delicately, always been one of the foremost distinguishing characteristics of his three decades on the world's stage. Therein lies his challenge, and his opportunity.

The picture of Kissinger standing in front of the White House last week reminded those who have made a pastime of observing him that he still tends to elicit exclamation points—He's back!—that are laden with many conflicting emotions. He has won the Nobel Peace Prize and been slurred as a war criminal. He is widely respected as the greatest foreign policy intellectual since George Kennan, and a celebrity to boot, but the mere mention of the two dominant foreign policy endeavors that attach to his name—Vietnam and détente—can cause convulsions on both the Left and the Right. His selection was thus a surprising one. But for many reasons it could turn out to be an inspired one.

For much of his early career, Kissinger courted the patronage of powerful politicians, an attribute that would not serve him well in his current assignment. But he has also been, first and foremost, a student of history. At age seventy-nine, he is now looking to secure his rightful place in the pantheon of American diplomacy, which should impel him to protect his independence and intellectual integrity. In the first book he ever wrote, back in 1957, he quoted Napoleon's assessment of the Austrian statesman Metternich that "he confused policy with intrigue." Now he has the opportunity to make it less likely that history will say the same of him. Indeed, he made clear that this was his goal (and set quite a high bar for himself) when CNN's Wolf Blitzer asked him about a *New York Times* editorial that questioned his capacity to display integrity and independence; he pledged that he would produce a report that would make the paper apologize.

Aiding him in this endeavor will be his feel for how events in one corner of the globe can reverberate in another. He understood how the opening to China in the early 1970s would affect relations with Russia, and from this he built a policy framework that protected the possibilities of American global influence after the debacle of Vietnam. Useful as well will be his intuitive sense, drawn from his days on the Harvard faculty, for the way entrenched bureaucracies operate. His healthy skepticism about how they resist creative thinking led him to challenge government agencies, including the CIA and State Department, that he felt were overly concerned with preserving their prerogatives.

His career also shows a recognition that raw intelligence data is useless unless put into a conceptual framework. The annual foreign policy reviews produced by the State Department before he became secretary were amalgams of mushy clichés and unconnected sentiments. He famously insisted, sometimes by throwing early drafts on the floor in a tantrum, on sharper thinking (and an unusual dose of intellectual honesty) that connected the dots of intelligence assessment into a rigorous analysis of global threats.

Kissinger's worldview has tended to be more nuanced than the for-us-or-against-us approach that, at least in rhetoric if not always in practice, has come from the Bush administration. He has worked as an unsentimental realist with regimes in the Middle East, ranging from the Saudis to the Syrians. He has also been a strong internationalist who recognized the need for tending to alliances and lining up multilateral support. In early September, in an oblique criticism of some of the thinking at the Pentagon, he wrote a column arguing that the United States had an obligation to "rest our policies on principles" that were developed through consultations with other nations rather than unilaterally asserting "an unfettered right of preemption." But when Bush a few days later echoed these Pentagon unilateralist sentiments in a challenge to the United Nations, Kissinger sent out a revised version of the column praising the president for "defining the challenge as of a magnitude requiring cooperative action by the world community."

Kissinger has long had a complex relationship with the Bush family and its advisers, which could make his commission interesting. When he visited China in 1971 after the opening of relations, he was not candid with the UN ambassador at the time, the elder George Bush, whose efforts to prevent Taiwan from being expelled were then undermined. In his autobiography, Bush aimed one of his rare disapproving comments at Kissinger.

When Donald Rumsfeld became President Ford's chief of staff in 1974, he sought to dispel the perception that Secretary of State Kissinger, rather than the new president, was running foreign policy. (Kissinger had made the mistake, when the press asked him why Ford had been brought into a meeting with the Soviet foreign minister on arcane arms control issues, of quipping, "We felt the need to get some technical competence into the discussions.") Rumsfeld even insisted that Ford, rather than Kissinger, conduct all the press briefings at a NATO summit, which caused Kissinger to threaten to resign. The following year Ford made Rumsfeld defense secretary and Dick Cheney the chief of staff, and Kissinger was convinced that the two men were behind the decision to make him relinquish his title of national security adviser, which he had held in addition to being secretary of state. Again he considered resigning.

When Ronald Reagan challenged President Ford for the Republican nomination in 1976, Kissinger became the whipping boy for conservatives and neoconservatives who felt he sacrificed moralistic fervor in his pursuit of détente with the Soviets, a relationship with China, and secret understandings as part of the endgame in Vietnam. Their wedge was to force a vote at the convention on a platform plank, pointedly named "Morality in Foreign Policy," which denounced détente and "secret agreements." Kissinger wanted Ford to fight the plank, but Cheney successfully persuaded the president to let it quietly slip by. At the same time, Rumsfeld was able to convince Ford, over Kissinger's objections, to abandon efforts for a new arms control agreement with Moscow, in order to take that contentious issue off the table as well.

Kissinger was a key player four years later in trying to arrange for Ford to be Reagan's running mate, rather than the elder George Bush. Ford made the plan contingent on Kissinger being appointed as secretary of state, and Reagan refused. The only role that Kissinger played in the Reagan administration was a precursor to his current task: He was made the chair of a bipartisan commission on Central America. "They give me all the good ones," Kissinger privately complained. Despite his desire to return from the wilderness where he had been banished by conservatives, he did permit the final report to include a recommendation that future aid to El Salvador be made contingent on curbing human rights abuses there.

A question now being asked about Kissinger, as he takes over his new commission, is the same as the one posed in 1974 after Nixon resigned. "Will he move to a more open style," Richard Holbrooke wrote back then, "or will he remain the elusive, manipulative, brilliant diplomatist of recent years?" During his government career, Kissinger's greatest weakness was his aversion to the openness that makes the conduct of American diplomacy more sloppy—but also provides its democratic underpinnings at home and moral authority abroad. From the invasion of Cambodia to the opening with China, Kissinger (taking his cue from Nixon) tended to operate with great secrecy. But he subsequently showed, when writing memoirs that were at times surprisingly candid, that he understands the need for the public to be educated.

For him to burnish his reputation for history will require, fortuitously, the same thing that will make his 9/11 Commission successful: a willingness to be open, forthright, and accountable to the public. He is capable of being analytically brilliant and intellectually honest, even brutally so. He is also capable of deciding that it is now in the nation's interest, and his own, to apply that analytic rigor with an unflinching candor. In doing so, he would show his appreciation for the fact that democracies draw strength, not weakness, from giving people the unvarnished truths that they need.

Kissinger Reappraised

Kissinger's realism made him wary of transformationalists in the Woodrow Wilson mode who would crusade in foreign lands to make them safe for democracy. The best realist foreign policy president of our time was George H. W. Bush, who helped orchestrate a calm landing for the end of the cold war and conducted a war against Iraq with carefully limited aims. Ironically, one of the most transformationalist, crusading presidents was his son, who embraced a democracy agenda for the Islamic world after 9/11. Although I had questioned Kissinger's realism in the past, the younger Bush's policies made me yearn for just a dash more realism in the foreign policy balance. That is reflected in a new introduction I wrote for the 2005 reprint of my Kissinger biography.

Three decades after he left office, Henry Kissinger continues to exert a fascinating hold on the public imagination as well as intellectual sway over the nation's foreign policy conversation. The longevity of his influence—and of his celebrity—is greater than that of any other statesman in modern times. He remains the most prominent foreign policy intellectual in the world, his advice sought by corporate and political leaders, his rumbling voice a regular on the airwaves, his byline stamping frequent analytic essays.

Partly this prolonged prominence is due, as even his detractors concede, to the power of his intellect. Nowadays, policy discussion too often tends to be polarized, partisan, and propelled by the type of talking points that work well on cable TV shows. Even people who disagree with Kissinger tend to be impressed by the rigor, nuance, depth, and unsentimental sharpness of his arguments. His writings and pronouncements combine historical axioms with timely insights to produce the same mixture of sweep and specificity that distinguished his memoirs.

Now that global politics is no longer oversimplified by the clarity of the cold war, Kissinger's approach of understanding and emphasizing balances of power has become even more relevant. Likewise, his fingertip feel for the world's webs of interdependence—how an event in one corner of the planet will reverberate in another—has become more important in an era of complex globalization.

Despite his continuing prominence, however, he has been oddly absent from any official role in government. From the time he left office at the end of the Ford administration through the terms of the younger George Bush, there have been three Republican presidents in office for almost twenty of the last thirty-two years. Yet none appointed Kissinger to any high post. Why?

The answer says as much about the political changes in the Republican Party, and in the country, as it does about Kissinger. Kissinger represents a conservative internationalism that is rooted in realism, realpolitik, power balances, and pragmatism. In this book, I have described how the opponents who did him most harm were not those on the dovish left or liberal Democratic side, but rather the neoconservatives or highly ideological Republicans who saw America's global struggle in crusading, values-based, moral, and sentimental terms.

Ronald Reagan, as readers of this book will see, ended up being Kissinger's most wounding ideological adversary. Although Reagan at various points considered having a rapprochement with Kissinger, in the end he was excluded from the administration. More importantly, Reagan's approach to foreign policy—as a crusade for freedom rather than as a quest for a stable balance of power—came to define the Republican view.

This was especially true after September 11, 2001, during the George W. Bush administration. Some Kissingerian realists, most notably Brent Scowcroft and to some extent Lawrence Eagleburger, went public with their skepticism of a crusading foreign policy. Kissinger likewise had qualms, but he expressed them in a hedged, nuanced, subtle way.

That was typical for two reasons. First, his views are invariably rather nuanced, and the complexities he saw involving Iraq and the greater Middle East were typically subtle, smart, and filled with ambiguities that turned out to be prescient. The world is a complex and dangerous place, and Kissinger's great strength as an analyst (and his weakness at fitting in with more ideological conservatives) is that he is not very good at oversimplification. In addition, he is instinctively averse to open and outright challenges to those in power. This is particularly true when it comes to conservative Republicans, because he knows that their distrust of his ideological fervor is what has kept him exiled from office.

This relates to a core argument I make in my biography of him, one that is, I think, even more valid today. I contend that Kissinger was one of the few realists—as opposed to idealists—to shape American diplomacy. In that approach he was a master. He had a feel for power relations and balances of power, for spheres of influence and realpolitik relations. He brilliantly created a triangular structure involving the United States, Russia, and China, and that architecture preserved the possibility of America's power and global influence after the debacle of Vietnam.

On the other hand, he did not always have the same feel for the role that idealistic values—sentiments he would call them—play in allowing a democracy to operate openly and with sustained confidence at home and abroad. Nor did he fully appreciate, I argue, that the openness and messiness of America's democracy is what gives strength, not weakness, to its foreign policy. He was thus—under Nixon's dark tutelage—too fond of secrecy, and too much in need of it.

Kissinger was not exactly thrilled by this argument when my biography came out, even though he had given me many interviews. I think he was surprised that its critique came from the conservative side as much as from the liberal side. I also suspect, given the fact that he is not known for his thick skin, that he would probably be outraged even if he reread his own memoirs, on the grounds that they are not favorable enough.

For a while after the book came out, he didn't speak to me. Then, after I became editor of *Time,* he was invited back to an anniversary party featuring all who had been on the cover. The phone rang and his distinctive voice came on to say, "Well, Walter, even the Thirty Years' War had to end at some point. I will forgive you." (He did allow that his loyal wife, Nancy, was partial to the Hundred Years' War.) Since then, we have worked together on various projects, including a Middle East program at the Aspen Institute.

In our recent conversations, Kissinger has contended that he has always recognized the role of values in forging a sustainable foreign policy. For him there is a balance that must be struck between a nation's interests and its ideals, and that balance is best struck unsentimentally.

In his 1994 tome *Diplomacy*, Kissinger traces the balances made in foreign policy, including that of realism and idealism, from the times of Cardinal Richelieu through chapters on Theodore Roosevelt the realist and Woodrow Wilson the idealist. Kissinger, a European refugee who has read Metternich more avidly than Jefferson, is unabashedly in the realist camp. "No other nation," he wrote in *Diplomacy*, "has ever rested its claim to international leadership on its altruism." Other Americans might proclaim this as a point of pride; when Kissinger says it, his attitude seems that of an anthropologist examining a rather unsettling tribal ritual. The practice of basing policy on ideals rather than interests, he pointed out, can make a nation seem dangerously unpredictable.

In fact, America's idealism and realism have been interwoven ever since Benjamin Franklin played an ingenious balance-of-power game in France while simultaneously propagandizing about America's exceptional values. From the Monroe Doctrine to Manifest Destiny to the Marshall Plan, the United States has linked its interests to its ideals. This was especially true during the cold war, which was a moral crusade as well as a security struggle.

Kissinger's realist power approach during the 1970s succeeded at building a worthy framework for stability, but it failed to sustain political support from either end of the political spectrum, was not fully compatible with the sentiments that permit sustained international engagement in a democracy, and therefore tended to encourage an unhealthy secrecy.

Today, however, the questions facing the American polity may be from the reverse side: Have we tilted too far in the idealistic direction? Do we need a bit more Kissingerian realism and subtlety? Has the nation's international approach, in its zeal to spread freedom, become so driven by a sense of moral mission and crusading spirit that it could now use a sobering dose of caution, pragmatism, realism, cold calculation of interests, and traditional conservatism?

In answering these questions, I think it is crucial that we appreciate the role of the Kissinger conservative realpolitik tradition in the context of his forty-year struggle against what he regarded as the sentimental idealism of both crusading neoconservatives and moralistic liberals. An understanding of Kissinger and of his sense of global dynamics is just as relevant now as it was in the aftermath of Vietnam and at the end of the cold war.

James Baker, Wise Man?

The appointment of James Baker to cochair the Iraq Study Group gave me a chance, in this essay I wrote for the Los Angeles Times *in 2006, to look at how a power player, especially one so adroit and velvety, goes about shaping a historic legacy. I had done the same with Kissinger when he was briefly considering cochairing the 9/11 Commission. But the issues for Baker were different. The legacy he wanted was that of a Wise Man, but this quest collided with the younger President Bush's instincts to treat him like a family political retainer.*

James A. Baker III has one great goal left as he hones his legacy: trying to make sure that the words "American statesman" appear in his newspaper obit before the words "Florida recount." That's one reason why he's eager to make the findings of the Iraq Study Group, which he cochairs, sagacious and bipartisan enough to ensconce him firmly in the pantheon of "The Wise Men," those polished gents of a more statesmanlike era for whom sagacity was synonymous with bipartisanship.

I applaud the instinct, and not merely because I once coauthored a book with that title, which celebrated the clubby cold-war coterie that included Dean Acheson, Averell Harriman, Robert Lovett, and John McCloy. After they had grayed into elder statesmen, they were summoned back to advise Lyndon Johnson on what to do about the Vietnam War. At first they suggested that he should stay the course, but by early 1968 they had come to the pragmatic conclusion that the United States had to disengage. Throughout their careers and into their dotage, they were above all practical and realistic, beholden to no ideology or partisan agenda.

The question facing Baker is whether he will end up being remembered as a latter-day Lovett, the most emblematic of the old Wise Men, or whether he will fall on the other side of a subtle divide and instead be seen as more like Clark Clifford, who was a skilled statesman but remained a Wise Man wannabe because he could never quite shake his reputation as a partisan wheeler-dealer and manipulator.

By heritage and breeding, Baker most resembles Lovett, a Republican banker who served as Harry Truman's undersecretary of state and defense secretary. They had similar, indeed intertwined, backgrounds as scions of patrician Texas families. In the 1890s, Lovett's father and Baker's grandfather helped build the Houston-based railway law firm then called Baker, Botts, Baker and Lovett; James Baker is now a senior partner at that firm. Like Lovett, Baker approaches issues with a cool yet vinegary pragmatism. Problems are meant to be solved, usually with a blend of firmness and negotiability that is devoid of emotion, ideology, or sentimentality.

There's one salient difference. Lovett was devoid of any partisanship. When Truman made a political remark to him once, he responded, "Remember, Mr. President, I'm a Republican." Truman replied, "Damn it, I keep forgetting." That's not a line likely to be uttered about Baker.

Nor would it have been said about Clark Clifford, who began his public career as Truman's counsel and campaign strategist. He was as smooth a Democratic operator as Baker has been a Republican one. Like Baker, Clifford had a velvet manner and the ability to touch his fingertips together in a way that could seem either sagacious or scheming. When Lyndon Johnson fired his controversial defense secretary Robert McNamara, Clifford was called from semiretirement to replace him and help think through strategies for the Vietnam quagmire. But as hard as he tried to appear like a wise and revered statesman, he continued to be dogged by the aura of being a political fix-it man and corporate operative whose hands seemed faintly soiled by partisan maneuvers and Arab money.

It is, unfortunately, easy to understand why Baker—and Lee Hamilton, Vernon Jordan, Sandra Day O'Connor, and the other estimables in his study group—have a difficult time achieving Lovett-like status in this day and age. The foremost reason is that foreign policy, like just about everything else in the age of blogs and cable TV and Florida recounts, is far more partisan. In addition, today's more aggressive gotcha game played by politicians and the press means that even a saintly gent like Lovett would have found himself on the defensive about the wartime dealings of his partners and clients at Brown Brothers Harriman, the Union Pacific, and Pan American Airlines.

Yet there is a fundamental and important way in which Baker and his study group members resemble the wise elders of earlier eras. It is not in their nature to be transformationalists or radical visionaries, the way that the neoconservatives and democracy crusaders have been. When establishment venerables congregate to stroke their chins and reach consensus, not a whole lot of crockery is in danger of being broken. Instead, they will inevitably tend to be cautious, pragmatic, and—yes—wise.

This is partly institutional: Blue-ribbon consensus seekers tend not to embrace radical or bold visions. It is also personal, especially in the case of the pragmatic realist Baker. He was the secretary of state who urged the elder Bush not to try to occupy Baghdad during Gulf War One, and he cautioned against Gulf War Two before it was launched. Having been slammed for these stances by the neocons, he had a difficult time in his latest volume of memoirs suppressing his smugness that they produced what may be the worst foreign policy disaster in American history.

If Baker and his posse can come up with a plan that salvages some threads of our national interest from the debacle of Iraq, and if he stays around to help implement it, that would be such an awesome magic trick that those of us who dabble with the first drafts of history should reward him by carving a niche in the pantheon for him somewhere between Lovett and Dean Acheson. It's easy to disparage stability and containment as foreign policy goals and to make fun of blue-ribbon chin-strokers. But an aspiration to be statesmanlike, even if mainly motivated by the desire to polish up a legacy, is a welcome trait these days. So, too, is having the courage to be cautious and the self-confidence to be humble when it comes to foreign policy.

In our search for contemporary Wise Men, there is one irony that the builders of the original Pantheon would have noted. The closest person we have to a true Wise Man is someone who should be the easiest for the president to tap but, for reasons that only Sophocles or Shakespeare (or perhaps Freud) could explain, is actually the hardest: President Bush the Elder. In lieu of him, his consigliere James Baker will have to serve proxy, and fortunately, he is eager to don the mantle.

Madeleine's War

What do secretaries of state actually do every day? We read a lot about their vision and influence. But I have sometimes wondered how, when traveling the world, they actually conduct the nuts and bolts of statecraft. When I was editor of Time, *I made a point of getting out and writing a couple of stories a year. For this one, a 1999 cover story, I convinced Madeleine Albright to let me stay by her side for one busy week and figure out what diplomats do to earn their paychecks.*

"What's at stake here is the principle that aggression doesn't pay, that ethnic cleansing cannot be permitted." The troops gathered in a hangar at an air base in Germany cheer. Madeleine Albright is explaining the war in Kosovo to them. It is, to her, a defining mission for America in the post–cold war world. It is also, for someone who had to flee Hitler and then Stalin as a child, a very personal mission. As President Clinton proclaims when she is finished, "Secretary Albright, thank you for being able to redeem the lessons of your life story by standing up for the freedom of the people in the Balkans."

The Kosovo conflict is often referred to, by both her fans and foes, as Madeleine's War. To her, a stable Europe is central to our interests. Opposing ethnic cleansing is central to our values. And because of the worldview seared into her heart growing up, she believes that America's interests cannot be easily separated from its values. "We are reaffirming NATO's core purpose as a defender of democracy, stability, and human decency on European soil," she says.

Her critics argue that this has never been NATO's core purpose. For fifty years, it has been a defensive alliance, one that never before waged war against another European nation, no matter how lacking in democracy, stability, or human decency. They see Madeleine's War as the latest example of a foreign policy driven by moral impulses and mushy senti-

ments, one that hectors and scolds other nations to obey our sanctimo-
nious dictates and ineffectively bombs or sanctions them if they don't.

It was early in Clinton's first term, back when she was UN ambassador during the first showdown with Serbia over Bosnia, that Albright
showed her assertiveness. At a 1993 meeting with Joint Chiefs chairman
Colin Powell—who gave his name to the doctrine that the military
should be used only after a clear political goal has been set, and then only
with decisive force—she challenged the general: "What's the point of
having this superb military that you're always talking about if we can't
use it?" As Powell later recalled, "I thought I would have an aneurysm."

Thus arose the Albright Doctrine: a tough-talking interventionism
that believes in using force—including limited force such as calibrated
air power, if nothing heartier is possible—to back up a mix of strategic
and moral objectives. In an administration that grew up gun-shy by reading and misreading the lessons of Vietnam, she's the one who grew up
appeasement-shy by learning, in painfully personal ways, the lessons of
Munich.

Ever since February 1998, when Slobodan Milosevic began his grue-
some campaign against ethnic Albanians in his province of Kosovo,
Albright has been resolute about not allowing the West to dither as it did
in Bosnia. "History is watching us," she told a meeting of foreign ministers last year, in the same London conference room where Bosnia had
been debated. "In this very room our predecessors delayed as Bosnia
burned, and history will not be kind to us if we do the same." She was in
no mood to compromise. When the Italian and French ministers proposed a softening in the language they would use to threaten the Serbs,
Albright's close aide Jamie Rubin whispered to her that she could probably accept it. She snapped back, "Where do you think we are, Munich?"

More than a year later, seven weeks into a messy bombing campaign,
Albright still sees herself as a hard-liner whose job it is to restrain
assorted freelance Peace Prize seekers who are eager to cut a compromise. Last week, she met with Russian diplomats in Washington and
Europe, traveled with Clinton to NATO headquarters in Brussels and
military bases in Germany, and convened a meeting of foreign ministers
in Bonn. There were many issues she dealt with, but one serves as a good

example of last week's diplomatic maneuvering: the effort to get Russia to support the deployment of an international peacekeeping force in Kosovo.

Albright had been working with Russian foreign minister Igor Ivanov on this issue since January, when she flew to Moscow to tell him—during an intermission of *La Traviata* at the Bolshoi Theater— that NATO was issuing a bombing threat. Four weeks ago, they met at the Oslo airport, where Ivanov pulled from his breast pocket a paper with ten "principles" for a solution. Albright noticed some coincided with NATO's. She proposed that they get out pencils and mark the ones they could agree on. After three hours, Ivanov still had not accepted Washington's core demand for a NATO-led peacekeeping force. But there were enough points of agreement for Albright and Ivanov to emerge with a joint statement.

The process resumed last Monday, with the arrival in Washington of Viktor Chernomyrdin, the former Russian premier tapped by Boris Yeltsin to help mediate Kosovo. He made it clear that Russia was willing to accept, at least privately, the idea of an international security force, though not necessarily a NATO-led one. The discussions continued throughout the evening at Gore's official residence, while Albright attended a state dinner.

When he appeared for breakfast on Tuesday, Chernomyrdin spent a few minutes chatting with Albright in Russian, one of six languages she understands, about her days in Belgrade as a child when her father was the Czechoslovak ambassador. She described meeting Tito, giving him flowers. Chernomyrdin argued that the Russians would not publicly support anything the Serbs opposed. That was absurd, she told him bluntly. The Russian role should be to push the Serbs, not merely convey their positions. The U.S. insistence on a NATO-led force was a matter not of theology but of practicality: Everyone agreed the Kosovars should return home, but they wouldn't do so without a robust force guaranteeing their safety. When the meeting was over, Albright called Ivanov in Moscow to make sure both Russians got the same message.

That evening she left on an overnight flight to Europe with the president. After their meetings with the troops, Albright went off to work her cell phone. She talked to the Ukrainian foreign minister about Russia's evolving position, then the French and British foreign ministers about the statement she hoped to get at the G-8 meeting.

Most important were two calls to UN secretary-general Kofi Annan. A potential problem was brewing: Annan, who had remained on the sidelines, was suggesting that he appoint a group of negotiators to deal with Belgrade. Annan had been reliable from the outset in supporting the NATO position, which Albright appreciated. But the last thing she wanted was a pod of UN-anointed diplomats pushing compromises. "Kofi, we don't need negotiators running all over the place," she said.

On Thursday morning, Albright and her entourage broke away from the president's tour and took their own air force jet up to Bonn for the G-8 meeting of European and Russian foreign ministers. With a red folder marked INTEL on her lap, she conducted her regular morning staff meeting on the short flight. "Slobo's feeling the heat," she said, a twinkle in her eye, as she glanced up from a memo on how Milosevic was putting some former top military men under house arrest.

She was sardonic, sometimes amused, occasionally impatient, always crisp. "We've got to talk to Kofi again to make sure he doesn't have negotiators proliferating." But she knew how to use the initiative to her advantage. "When I see Ivanov, I'll stress the UN component to him."

Business done, she switched from CEO mode to professor. It's important to keep in mind Russia's complex history with Serbia, she lectured, leaning back in her seat and propping her glasses atop her head. There are long-standing cultural and religious ties, but Tito broke with Stalin and even supported the liberals in Czechoslovakia during the Prague Spring of 1968. Our fight with Serbia had dangerously alienated Russians, she noted, and it would be useful to allow them to be the ones to help solve it.

As soon as she arrived at the Petersberg conference center, a castle overlooking Bonn, Albright held a private meeting with Russia's Ivanov. It was planned with three aides for each side, but they decided to do it one-on-one, without even interpreters (each understands the other's language). They wrestled over the wording he would accept in the proposed statement, which would be Russia's first public endorsement of an international force for Kosovo. Albright suggested calling it a "military force." Ivanov replied that he would agree only to calling it a "presence."

"You have to agree to the word 'security,'" Albright said. "Igor, will you make me happy and just say yes to that?"

"Yes," he answered, with the hint of a smile, "but when will you make me happy? I keep waiting for my turn."

Ivanov took a piece of paper and sketched out the possible composition of a security arrangement, using circles to represent the role various forces would play. Albright used her pen to show how NATO had to be involved, but Ivanov didn't agree. "This isn't for the two of us to do," she finally said. "We ought to leave it to our experts to start work on this."

In the grand solarium of the Petersberg center, the formal meeting of the G-8 foreign ministers went as planned. Over fish and fruit, British foreign secretary Robin Cook and Albright teamed up on Ivanov for one last attempt to push him to accept something stronger than "security presence." Albright persuaded him to accept the added adjective "effective." Cook suggested adding the phrase "including a military force" in parentheses. Ivanov wouldn't go that far. "I'm sorry," he said. "This is all I can do today."

For Albright, it was enough, the culmination of a month of nudging the Russians to call publicly for an international force as part of any solution. Russia's concurrence opened the way for a resolution in the United Nations Security Council endorsing such a force.

Late Thursday evening, Albright and her crew reunited with the president, who had been visiting refugees in Germany, for the flight home on Air Force One. Relaxing in a Shetland sweater in his airborne office, Clinton described Kosovo as an example of a policy in which America's values and its interests are intertwined. "It's to our advantage to have a Europe that is peaceful and prosperous. And there is the compelling humanitarian case: If the U.S. walks away from an atrocity like this where we can have an impact, then these types of situations will spread. The world is full of ethnic struggles, from Ireland to the Middle East to the Balkans. If we can convince people to bridge these tensions, we've served our interests as well as our values."

Although Clinton appreciates Albright, they have not become close pals. She still resents that he allowed her to go before cameras early in the Lewinsky scandal and proclaim his innocence. Asked if he owes her a public apology, if he has anything to say about that, the president stares coldly for a few seconds and his face hardens. "No." Long pause. "No. I have nothing to say on that." He is more expansive on the personal qualities she brings to her role. "She not only learned the lessons of Munich, but also of Czechoslovakia under communism."

Indeed, Kosovo has illustrated how much Albright's outlook and style are rooted in her personal history. Her father, the wartime Czechoslovak diplomat Josef Korbel, was witty and gregarious, just like she is, with a knack for survival. Madeleine, who as a child spent two lonely years in Belgrade when he was ambassador there, developed an instinctive antipathy toward thugs. As *Time*'s Ann Blackman explains in her Albright biography, *Seasons of Her Life,* she mirrors him: She has a deep reservoir of intelligence and wit, but sometimes seems to wear blinders to protect her from things that clash with her self-image. For example, for years she almost willfully hid from herself, as her father had hidden from her, evidence that her family was Jewish, and that many of them perished in the Holocaust.

People generally come out of such experiences in one of two ways. Some, like Albright, develop an aggressive moralism and idealism, pledging "never again" to let the world turn a blind eye to atrocities. Others— Henry Kissinger, another refugee from the Nazis, is an example—become hardened realists with a fingertip feel for the nuances of power, a vision of how interests clash on the world stage, and a disdain for what they view as sentimental impulses and ideological fervor.

Albright does not have Kissinger's ability (or desire) to conceptualize overarching strategic frameworks and analyze how an action in one corner can ripple around the world as through a spiderweb. Nor does she excel at the cautious contingency planning that marked, and sometimes paralyzed, many of the corporate lawyers—Cyrus Vance, James Baker, Warren Christopher—who once held her job. Consequently, she urged intervention in Kosovo without worrying too much about either the geostrategic ramifications (how it would affect Russia, China, Macedonia, Greece, et al.) or about game-planning all the contingencies (how to cope with a horrific tide of refugees and be ready to use ground troops if Milosevic was defiant).

On the way back from Europe on Thursday night, Albright sits in a swivel chair in the small situation room next to the president's office on Air Force One. Do Kosovo and other morally inspired interventions, I ask her, represent a new view of American interests after the cold war? "I think threats to our national interest come from a variety of problems, [including] the creation of chaos and instability that come about as a result of ethnic cleansing." How do we pick and choose such fights? Why Kosovo and not Rwanda? "I don't think you can make a very simple matrix. You have to look at the immensity of what is happening. I happen to believe, and argued so at the time, we should have done more in Rwanda. We get involved where the crime is huge, where it's in a region that affects our stability—the stability of Europe is something that has been essential to the U.S. for the last two hundred years—and where there is an organization capable of dealing with it. Just because you can't act everywhere doesn't mean you don't act anywhere. We're evolving these rules. There's not a doctrine that really sets this forth in an organized way yet."

Colin Powell,
the Good Soldier

Honor is a difficult virtue. It requires a person to display both loyalty and honesty, which can conflict at times. It is also appreciated more in the abstract than in practice. When Colin Powell was ushered out as secretary of state by President Bush, he was criticized from both sides of the political spectrum, and he was denigrated by Bush and his inner circle. I thought all this unfair. During the run-up to the Iraq war, Powell believed flawed intelligence, but I think it was an honest mistake. He also turned out to be more right than others in the administration. And he acted honorably. So, I wrote this op-ed in the New York Times *in November 2004 defending him.*

One of Colin Powell's heroes is General George Marshall. He works under a portrait of, and at the desk once used by, the wise World War II army chief who served as Harry Truman's secretary of state.

Powell occasionally recounts the tale of the day in 1948 when Truman was considering whether the United States should recognize the newly declared State of Israel. Marshall advised against it, but Truman decided to go ahead. Powell describes how some of Marshall's aides gathered around "this desk" to say that he must now resign. Marshall responded by asking them who had made him the president? Truman was president, Marshall pointed out, and he got to make the decisions. The secretary of state's role was to give his best advice and then offer support.

When Powell tells the tale, in the wake of the Iraq invasion, it's clear that he's discussing himself as well as General Marshall. But it's worth noting that the main difference between the two men in these instances is that Powell turned out to be right about most of the advice he gave on Iraq, while Marshall was wrong on Israel. Despite this fact—or maybe because of it—neither today's commentators nor tomorrow's historians are likely to treat Powell with the veneration accorded Marshall. Nor, for that matter, has the White House.

Powell's problem is that both the Bush administration's loyalists and its critics are disappointed in him, the former because he was not fully supportive of the strategy and tactics that led to the occupation of Iraq, and the latter because he did not publicly throw himself in front of that train. He is deemed a failure because he lost the war of ideas to Dick Cheney, Donald Rumsfeld, and their neoconservative outriders.

Nevertheless, there should be an honored place in history's pages for statesmen whose ideas and instincts turned out to be right. Let's leave aside for a moment whether he could have done more to prevail and to prevent, and instead let's decide what lessons from his tenure ought to be written in ink.

Powell is an honorable man and we should take him at his word that, like most Americans of both parties, he thought that Saddam Hussein was acquiring weapons of mass destruction and should be removed from power. So he was not being disingenuous nor lending legitimacy to policies he opposed.

He did, however, offer cautions and reservations. The doctrine that has long been associated with his name is that any military intervention should have a well-defined mission, use enough force that it can be accomplished cleanly, and include a clear strategy for success and exit. He argued, before the invasion, for more time to line up a broader coalition of allies and for more serious planning for postwar security and occupation.

To varying degrees he lost out to the Pentagon civilians on each and every one of these points. And in almost every case, he turned out to be prescient. The lesson we should remember about him is not that he failed to prevail—but that he should have prevailed.

Powell entered office as perhaps the most respected man in America, a heroic soldier and wise statesman with rock star appeal. But his tenure as secretary was eventually marred by the unforeseen consequences of his one major bureaucratic success: persuading the president to go to the United Nations for a resolution of support on Iraq. His reward was the photograph that will dim his legacy, that of him at the United Nations with CIA Director George Tenet presenting the intelligence evidence, convincing except in hindsight, that Iraq was busily developing weapons of mass destruction.

The defining divide within the foreign policy establishment has long been between idealists, such as the neoconservatives who hope that the United States can help democratize the Middle East, and realists, who believe in a bit more caution and focus on America's cold strategic interests. One of the latter, Brent Scowcroft, a mentor to Powell and the steward of the enormously successful foreign policy of the first President Bush, calls it a struggle between transformationalists and traditionalists. Each approach is a necessary component of a sustainable foreign policy, and from the Monroe Doctrine to the Marshall Plan they have been woven together when American diplomacy is at its best.

During his forty years of national service, Colin Powell has been an exemplar of the balance that must be struck between these two approaches. His role in the Bush administration was to push for a little bit more realism—some more care and planning and humility—to be part of the current balance. It was a worthy role, one that ought not be discarded with him.

George Tenet and
the Instinct to Please

In my biographies, I have tried to explore two contrasting traits: those who are good at building a consensus, such as Franklin, and those who defy authority and conventional thinking, such as Einstein. Both types are useful to society. The danger is when either instinct goes too far: when a consensus builder becomes a collaborationist who kowtows to authority figures (as the secret White House tapes reveal that Kissinger sometimes did to Nixon), or when a dissenter becomes a counterproductive or self-righteous crank. In the previous piece, I explored how Colin Powell tried to sail those shoals, and in this one, written for the Huffington Post in April 2007, I look at former CIA director George Tenet.

As I was reading the excerpts of George Tenet's new book, *At the Center of the Storm,* I was reminded of a dinner I went to recently where I got to listen to Václav Havel, the playwright, former Czech president, prisoner, and human rights activist. He said that there were two types of people he had dealt with over the years: those with the soul of a collaborationist and those who were comfortable defying authority. He was obviously in the latter category, and he was speaking disparagingly about a European archbishop who had collaborated with the Communists.

George Tenet's woes, it seems to me, come from the very natural instinct to please rather than to tell uncomfortable truths to those in authority. Watching Bill Moyers's show on how the media failed to question the march to the war in Iraq, I reflected on how I, likewise, when I was at CNN, was too willing to accept what those in authority were telling me. And reading Bob Dallek's new book on Nixon and Kissinger, I was reminded how Kissinger, someone I once wrote about, was too willing to cater to and collaborate with the darker impulses of Nixon.

It's not always possible nor even a good thing to be defiant of authority, as I sometimes try to explain to my daughter. Yet Havel's distinction seems, each day, to become more relevant to me as I watch folks such as George Tenet try to explain themselves. I think, in contrast, of Brent Scowcroft, who repeatedly had the intellectual honesty to say publicly and privately when he disagreed with his former protégés in the Bush administration, even at the cost of being excluded from the inner circle.

A rebellious willingness to defy authority is what I think most characterized Albert Einstein, my most recent biography subject. You see it in his politics, when he becomes the sole dissenter among the academic elite in Berlin to oppose German militarism during World War I and later to oppose the Nazis, Communists, and then McCarthyites when he moved to America. In all cases, his dissent was impelled by his belief that people should not be compelled to cater to authority. Likewise in his personal life; even as a young kid, he gets asked to leave school because his attitude is undermining authority, and as a young patent examiner he learned to question every premise in front of him. And in his science, Einstein's triumphs came from questioning the received wisdom about space and time and gravity that was handed down from Newton.

Not everyone is an Einstein, and many people who repeatedly defy authority are cranks rather than heroes. On the other hand, Havel is right to draw an interesting distinction between people like Einstein and people whose laudable respect for authority spills over into an overeagerness to cater to power.

3. REAGAN
AND GORBACHEV

We Meet Again

Ronald Reagan was often regarded, by both critics and supporters, as a person with fixed ideological beliefs and an unyielding antipathy toward the Russians. When I covered his 1980 presidential race, I was struck by another side of his temperament: a sunny optimism and faith in human nature. On his campaign plane one day, he gestured out the window at a view of homes and swimming pools and told me that he felt he could convert any Communist leader if he could take him on a long helicopter ride over American suburbs and then bring him into the grocery stores and malls. These different sides of his personality— the fervent anti-Communist and the genial optimist—tugged at one another when he began to deal with Mikhail Gorbachev. I found the relationship fascinating. As they prepared for their third summit meeting in 1987, I wrote the following opening essay for the cover package we did at Time.

Harry Truman once compared "Uncle Joe" Stalin to Tom Pendergast, the Kansas City political boss: Both were wily machine politicians you could bargain with. Every president since then has been tempted to personalize America's unwieldy struggle with the Soviet Union. Even Ronald Reagan. Before dealing with Mikhail Gorbachev in Geneva, the former president of the Screen Actors Guild said he was reminded of his days dealing with the old studio moguls. Last week, awaiting the arrival of the world's most unlikely new superstar, Reagan came up with an even more fitting personal analogy. "I don't resent his popularity," the president told students in Jacksonville. "Good Lord, I costarred with Errol Flynn once."

So that's what video-age diplomacy has become: summits between costars in the global village. This week Reagan and Gorbachev will share the screen for the third time, matching the pace set by Nixon and Brezhnev during the heyday of détente and working toward a Moscow meeting next year that would set a new world record for summitry. Who would have thought it of these two very, very different men?

The geopolitical astrology has produced one of those rare conjunctions when two very different orbits are in alignment: the waning days of Reagan's tenure and the consolidation of Gorbachev's. Each leader faces political problems at home—a Politburo can be as cranky as a Congress—and sees a chance to solidify power by summit successes. Each confronts economic problems, from the perils of perestroika to the pratfalls of the Dow.

Summits embody a noble human conceit, one that seems particularly American: that the world's conflicts are caused by misunderstandings. If we sit down and talk, we can clear things up. Like most noble conceits, there is some truth to it. Summitry serves to lower the world's blood pressure. The two most powerful leaders on the planet smile at each other; somehow it seems that the rumbling forces of history, filled with clashing values and national interests, might thus be tamed. And like most conceits, there is some danger: Neither the president nor the public should be lulled into thinking that a personal rapport between leaders can smile away underlying conflicts that for forty years have divided East from West.

Television feeds this tendency to personalize great issues, and it permits everyone, not just presidents, to play: Gorbachev came into America's living rooms for a chat last week, followed by a televised debate between twelve candidates for the U.S. presidency and then the old master, Reagan. The whole nation got a chance to size everyone up personally. Smiling Mikhail, exuding the commanding presence that Americans yearn for in their own leaders, treated NBC's Tom Brokaw like a sharp schoolboy. When the candidates' turn came on Tuesday, Brokaw made them look like schoolboys. There was an unnerving upshot of turning everyone into a TV personality: Gorbachev, the leader of America's most dangerous global adversary, ended the week with a 2–1 approval ratio in most polls, a standing that lumps him alongside the top tier of presidential candidates and by some measures ahead of Reagan.

As often happens in a televised age, the image Gorbachev projected was divorced from the reality of what he actually said: that the Berlin wall was built by East Germany to protect itself from outside interference; that Moscow restricts emigration in order to thwart Western attempts to create a brain drain; that Soviet troops are in Afghanistan because of repeated requests from that country for protection from foreign subversion; that the USSR is pursuing its own Star Wars research.

The fundamental disputes between the two nations scarcely lend themselves to bargaining. Human rights, regional conflicts, and other such matters are often on summit agendas but rarely lead to solid deals. Arms control has thus become the coin of the realm for superpower diplomacy. Nuclear missiles, unsuitable for use as actual weapons of war, are deployed and manipulated as symbols of power, retaining only a vague connection to any possibility that their implied threat might ever be carried out. As such they can be traded easily, or at least more easily than other aspects of superpower conduct.

The president's conservative critics decry his current impulses as creeping nancyism, a desire driven by his protective wife to play to history. If every young senator sees a future president in the mirror each morning, every president sees a potential peacemaker. But there is certainly nothing wrong with that; playing to history beats playing to cramped political constituencies.

The disillusioned Right makes the same mistake that liberals have made for years: believing that Reagan does not really mean what he says. He came into office preaching that previous arms negotiations were "fatally flawed" because they sought to limit rather than reduce nuclear weapons. Even as he pursued his military buildup, he clung to the notion that its purpose was to force the Soviets to negotiate "real reductions." Perhaps he believed it from the outset, or perhaps (as is often the case with Reagan's verities) he said it so much that he convinced himself. Either way, he has now discombobulated everyone, from former nuclear freeze advocates to the hard-liners who once served with him on the Committee on the Present Danger, with his readiness to turn his rhetoric into reality.

Reagan clearly seems fascinated by the prospect of becoming the great disarmer, which is what gives conservatives the willies. All last week the president sought to soothe their nerves by waving his anti-Communist credentials. Speaking to the Heritage Foundation, he lashed out at the Kremlin's repression and reiterated his support for anti-Soviet freedom fighters around the globe. In his interview with network anchors, Reagan claimed that "I haven't changed from the time when I made a speech about an 'Evil Empire.'"

And yet the most striking note in his TV performance came when he chastised conservative critics of his arms control treaty. "Some of the people who are objecting the most," he said, "basically down in their deepest thoughts have accepted that war is inevitable." Not Reagan. If he could only get Gorbachev to join him on a helicopter ride over the pool-flecked neighborhoods of America, he believes, the Marxist leader might see things the same way he does.

The Gorbachev Challenge

One of my joys at Time *was working with Strobe Talbott, the Russia expert who was our longtime diplomatic correspondent and Washington bureau chief and later the deputy secretary of state. (He was also Bill Clinton's housemate at Oxford, and I suspect he may have helped him a bit on the paper about democracy in Russia that I mentioned in the introduction to this book.) Strobe and I went to Russia together in July 1987, and we came back convinced that Gorbachev's reforms would fundamentally alter Russia's relations with the West. We wrote a cover story that we had entitled "Is the Cold War Over?" Our top editor, Henry Grunwald, a hard-nosed foreign policy realist, was skeptical. He made us change the cover line to the far weaker "Is the Cold War Fading?" In the piece, we included a slight tweak at Grunwald, who had once edited a famous cover story for* Time *about God: "Even to ask whether the cold war is over is a bit like asking, 'Is God dead?'" By 1988, it was clear that the cold war was, in fact, not only fading but heading to the ash heap of history. I wrote this essay in December of that year, just after George H. W. Bush was elected president. Gorbachev had traveled to New York for a speech to the United Nations and a symbolic meeting with the outgoing Reagan and incoming Bush.*

Much of the first half of the twentieth century was dominated by the death spasms of an international system based on shifting European alliances. The subsequent forty years have been shaped by a struggle between two rival superpowers for military and ideological supremacy in all corners of a decolonized globe. Now comes Mikhail Gorbachev with a sweeping vision of a "new world order" for the twenty-first century. In a dramatic speech to the United Nations, the Soviet president painted an alluring ghost of Christmas future in which the threat of military force would no longer be an instrument of foreign policy, and ideology would cease to play a dominant role in relations among nations.

His vision, both compelling and audacious, was suffused with the romantic dream of a swords-into-plowshares "transition from the economy of armaments to an economy of disarmament." Included were enticing initiatives on Afghanistan, human rights, and arms control. Topping it off was a unilateral decision to cut Soviet armed forces 10 percent, withdraw fifty thousand troops from Eastern Europe, and reduce by half the number of Soviet tanks there. If George Bush can build on it, this surprise announcement could reinvigorate conventional arms-control talks, which in turn could alleviate strains within NATO over how to share the burden of maintaining a sturdy defense.

Yet Gorbachev's gambit is also fraught with potential dangers for the United States. The announced cuts are substantive enough to lure the West toward complacency, yet they are too small to dent significantly the advantages in men, matériel, and geography that the Soviet bloc has over NATO. In addition, by once more dazzling the world with cleverly packaged proposals, the self-assured Soviet leader displayed the seductive charms that could woo Western Europe into a neutered neutralism.

But perhaps the greater danger was that the United States would again find itself unable to produce an imaginative response. Gorbachev's UN speech was the most resonant enunciation yet of his "new thinking" in foreign policy, which has the potential to produce the most dramatic historic shift since George Marshall and Harry Truman helped build the Western Alliance as a bulwark of democracy. But as the Soviets play the politics of *da*—saying yes to issue after issue raised by the Reagan administration—the United States seems in peril of letting its wary "not yet" begin to sound like *nyet*.

Gorbachev's timing was adroit. He has proved to be a virtuoso at playing on Reagan's romantic notions about peace and disarmament. But now he is faced with an incoming president far more cautious than Reagan. So Gorbachev cleverly finagled a meeting at which his own vision of the future would go unchallenged. Bush could not properly respond until he takes office next month, and Reagan seemed barely relevant as he bubbled his favorite Russian phrase, "Trust but verify," at a press conference following Gorbachev's departure.

The Soviet leader also showed that with the magnetism of his personality and the crackle of his ideas, he remains the most commanding presence on the world stage. He is the one performer who can steal a scene from Ronald Reagan, and he did; as they viewed the Statue of Liberty, the visiting Communist played the self-confident superstar while Reagan ambled about like an amiable sidekick and Bush lapsed into the prenomination gawkiness that used to plague him whenever he stumbled across Reagan's shadow. Afterward, Mikhail and Raisa's foray into Manhattan provoked more excitement than any other visit since Pope John Paul II's in 1979.

What is destined to be remembered about Gorbachev's speech is not just his specific proposals—many of them had been made before—but also the way they fit together to transcend the ideological dogmas that have driven Soviet foreign policy for seventy years. With his metal-rimmed glasses glinting in the lights of the General Assembly's green marble dais, Gorbachev praised the "tremendous impetus to mankind's progress" that came from the French and Russian revolutions. "But," he added—and a listener should always lean forward when Gorbachev begins a sentence with that conjunction—"today we face a different world, for which we must seek a different road to the future." Marat might have been amused, but Lenin most likely froze in mid-scowl.

Again bordering on apostasy, Gorbachev addressed the cold war: "Let historians argue who is more and who is less to blame for it." In fact, understanding the reasons for the long twilight struggle is crucial to answering the most important question raised by Moscow's new thinking: Should the United States eagerly accept Gorbachev's tempting invitation to declare the cold war over? Significantly, he addressed, with words and proposed actions, each of the core causes of the cold war:

- The most concrete reason for the West's forty-year rivalry with the Soviet Union is the thrusting, threatening nature of that empire. Historic Russian expansionism, the Marxist-Leninist ideology of global class conflict, and a Kremlin mind-set that security can come only through the insecurity of adversaries have combined to create a nation whose defensive instincts can be frighteningly offensive. In his speech, Gorbachev proposed to preclude any "outward-oriented use of force," a phrase that nicely captures the essence of Soviet military policy since World War II. More important were his promised troop cuts. The West has long insisted that any conventional-forces agreement requires the Soviets to reconfigure their troops into a defensive posture. Gorbachev pledged to move in that direction by withdrawing assault units, river-crossing equipment, and tanks that threaten a blitzkrieg through central Europe. Deterring such an attack has been the core reason for NATO's existence.

- These troops have also served as the Soviet jackboot on the throat of Eastern European nations, whose subjugation is another cause of the cold war. Gorbachev's cuts will not necessarily raise the iron curtain, but his UN speech did pledge that "freedom of choice is a universal principle that should allow for no exceptions." In other words, Eastern European nations should be freed from Soviet control.

- Gorbachev's goal of shifting resources from military to domestic needs goes to the heart of a related source of East-West tensions, the militarization of Soviet society. Since Gorbachev took power, U.S. experts estimate that the money spent on defense has continued to increase. But in his speech, Gorbachev announced that Moscow would make public its plan for converting a few military plants to civilian use. If it does so, that will be a complement to his arms-control proposals, which are based on the new and vaguely defined doctrine of "reasonable sufficiency." The doctrine holds that Soviet capabilities need not have the potential for a preemptive strike but must merely be adequate to respond to an attack on the Soviet Union and its allies.

- The most profound quarrel many Westerners have with the Soviets is that their totalitarian system represses the individual. But Gorbachev stressed the Soviet goal of creating a "world community of states based on the rule of law." Sounding more like Jefferson than Lenin, he spoke of "ensuring the rights of the individual," guaranteeing "freedom of conscience," and forbidding persecution based on "political or religious beliefs."

- On the issue of emigration, Gorbachev pledged to remove the whole issue of refuseniks from the agenda by revising the laws that prevent many Soviet citizens from leaving the USSR. After a set period of time, he pledged, any person who wants to emigrate or travel will have the legal option to do so. More broadly, he spoke of the futility of maintaining restrictions designed to seal off the Soviet Union from the world. "Today, the preservation of any kind of 'closed' society is hardly possible," he said. Just before his arrival, the jamming of Radio Liberty ended.

- Another component of the cold war has been distrust, including a Western belief that the Soviets reserved the right to "lie and cheat," as Reagan put it eight years ago, if it served their interests. Gorbachev, who has reversed long-standing Kremlin policy by agreeing to on-site inspections of military installations, attempted in his UN speech to remove a major issue of compliance with the Antiballistic Missile Treaty: the Krasnoyarsk radar station. He said Moscow would accept the "dismantling and refitting" of certain components, and place the facility under UN control. At his lunch with Reagan and Bush just after the speech, one American asked, "Did we hear that word *dismantle* right?" Replied Gorbachev: "Yes, that was the word I used."

When Gorbachev's speech ended, Secretary of State George Shultz, who had not twitched his Buddha-like face throughout, walked over to Raisa for a chat. "A very good and important speech," he said. As Shultz knows as well as anyone, that will depend on whether Soviet realities come to match Gorbachev's rhetoric. If they do, the ramifications are enormous. Should Gorbachev succeed in reducing the expansionist threat that Moscow poses to the West, loosening its domination over Eastern Europe and changing its repressive relationship with its citizens, then indeed the fundamental reasons for the great global struggle between East and West—and the rationale for the containment policy that has shaped America's approach to the world for forty years—would evaporate.

Skepticism, of course, is probably warranted and certainly prudent. Gorbachev's vision has a boldness born of necessity: He was able to gift wrap his clamorous need to shift Soviet investment toward consumer needs and present it as a package of breathtaking diplomacy. Like the politician that he is, Gorbachev seeks to protect his power by producing triumphs on the world stage and the payoffs of perestroika at home. Offering a modest troop cut that would trim unnecessary flab from the armed forces neatly serves both goals.

Gorbachev's refrain of glasnost and perestroika also raises the specter of another Russian word, *peredyshka,* the old Leninist notion of seeking a "breathing space" by making temporary accommodations so that the revolution can eventually roar forward with renewed zeal.

Of greater danger, however, is the possibility that a wary and grudging attitude could cause the United States to be sidelined as the forces of history are rearranged. Those who sniff at Gorbachev's recent moves were proposing last year that many of these same steps—on emigration, troop configurations, individual rights, loosening controls in Eastern Europe—be used as litmus tests of Soviet intentions. They seem paralyzed by their disappointment in getting yes for an answer. With every Gorbachev move, the evidence mounts that he is seeking not just a breathing space but a fundamental change in the Soviet system.

By springing his ideas when the United States is in a transition between two presidents, Gorbachev guaranteed that he will retain the initiative that has made him the most popular world leader in much of Western Europe. Bush will thus start off in a position that has faced no other president: Until Gorbachev's time, it was the United States that did most of the initiating and the Soviets that snorted and stalled and finally gave grudging responses. Now the choreography is reversed.

Bush has never been one for "the vision thing," and incoming secretary of state James Baker has not yet shown that he can be a conceptualizer of strategic goals. But Gorbachev's initiatives create a grand opportunity for the new team: to redefine America's role in the world with a boldness that could quickly bring Bush out of the shadows of both Gorbachev and Reagan.

To counter Gorbachev's talk about Europe being a "common home" for Russia and the other European nations, Bush could emphasize the "common ideals"—free markets, free trade, and free people—that have been the positive basis for the American partnership with Western Europe that was born with the Marshall Plan. An alliance once based on necessity would become one based on shared values.

Bush could also lay out a vision of Western goals that transcend the cold war struggle. The necessity to contain Soviet influence often led U.S. policymakers to suppress America's natural idealism and support regimes whose only redeeming grace was their anticommunism. To the extent that Gorbachev's new thinking makes that less necessary, it frees the United States and the West to pursue more positive goals. Among them: attacking environmental problems that cannot be solved on a national basis; shaping aggressive new methods for containing the spread of nuclear, chemical, and biological weapons; reducing world famine and poverty; resolving regional conflicts.

Gorbachev has already seized the initiative on many of these issues and seeks to assert his leadership role. Each represents an opportunity for East and West to work together. But just as important, each offers Bush the chance to assert the vision and values that the United States and its allies offer the world. In the age of Gorbachev, "new thinking" has become a Soviet monopoly. If Bush hopes to define an age of his own, he must start by reminding the world that new thinking happens to be an American specialty.

Yes, He's for Real

In the summer of 1989, it became clear that a transformation was happening in Eastern Europe the likes of which had not been seen since the onset of the cold war more than forty years earlier. Even though I was Time's *national editor, I decided I had to get out of the office and spend time there. It was an astonishing confluence of journalism and history, and it produced many unforgettable moments, such as being at the Gdansk shipyards with Lech Wałęsa and at the Berlin wall with restive students. But the most memorable of all was being in Prague on the day that Václav Havel was released from prison. The* Time *stringer there was Havel's friend, so he took me to his apartment overlooking the Charles. I sat with him on the couch in awe. To me, he was the greatest Czech hero of our time—with one possible exception, a person whom I had revered since I first began following world affairs during the tumults of 1968. Then there was a knock on the door. I got up to open it, and as soon as I did I blurted out the name: Dubček. The hero of 1968, Alexander Dubček, had been living quietly in Bratislava, and he did not know Havel. But when he heard of Havel's release from prison, he took the train to Prague to pay his respects. I do not keep pictures of myself with politicians, but I have always treasured the snapshots of that day I got to be with Havel and Dubček as history was being made. This piece, reflecting on Gorbachev's role in those transformations, was written as part of a* Time *cover that November.*

For the Russians, tempered by centuries of land invasions, national security has long been defined as the control of territory and the subjugation of neighbors. Moscow's desire for a protective buffer, combined with a thousand-year legacy of expansionism and a twentieth-century overlay of missionary Marxism, was what prompted Stalin to leave his army in Eastern Europe after World War II and impose puppet regimes.

This Soviet quest for security necessarily meant insecurity for others. It also, as it turned out, meant the same for the Soviets. "One irony of history is that the security zone in Eastern Europe that Stalin created turned out to be one of the greatest imaginable sources of insecurity," says Princeton professor Stephen Cohen. It provoked an armed competition with the West and saddled the Soviets with a string of costly and cranky vassals.

Thus it was understandable, perhaps even inevitable, that Soviet control over Eastern Europe would erode. Nevertheless, when the breathtaking events of 1989 are assessed years hence, hindsight is unlikely to dilute the amazement of the moment. For suddenly, amid a barrage of headlines that a year ago would have seemed unimaginable, the architecture of Europe is being redrawn and the structure of international relations transformed by Mikhail Gorbachev's redefinition of Soviet security.

Historical timelines will someday boldface 1989 as the year that Eastern Europe as we have known it for four decades ended. The concept was always an artificial one: a handful of diverse nations suddenly iron-curtained off from their neighbors and force-fed an unwanted ideology. Soviet dominion over the region may someday be regarded as a parenthetical pause (1945–89) that left economic scars but had little permanent impact on the culture and history of central Europe.

In Budapest last week, acting president Mátyás Szűrös stood on a balcony overlooking a rally in Parliament Square and said that the 1956 uprising, which the Soviets suppressed with tanks and the hangman's rope, was actually a "national independence movement." He declared the People's Republic of Hungary, so named in 1949, dead. Now it is the Republic of Hungary, an independent state with plans to hold multiparty elections. When speakers mentioned the United States, the crowd cheered; for the Soviet Union, there were jeers. But along with shouts of "Russians, go home!" there were chants for the man who made the scene possible: "Gorby! Gorby! Gorby!"

When Gorbachev first spoke of "new thinking" in foreign policy, many in the West—especially in the United States—doubted his sincerity. The real test was whether Gorbachev would end the policy at the heart of the cold war: the subjugation of Eastern Europe. At the end of last year, in a speech at the United Nations, Gorbachev declared that he would. "Freedom of choice is a universal principle," he said. Yet the doubts lingered. They always seemed to come down to the question: Is Gorbachev for real?

There can be only one answer now: yes. Earlier this year, after Poland's Communists lost the most open elections since World War II but tried nevertheless to thwart Solidarity's effort to form a government, Gorbachev spoke by phone to the Communist Party leader, who subsequently backed down. Gorbachev has also provided public approval to the Hungarian reformers. In summing up a Warsaw Pact meeting in Bucharest last July, he pronounced, "Each people determines the future of its own country and chooses its own form of society." What it all adds up to is that Gorbachev has done what Western leaders have been demanding for twenty-one years: repealed the "Brezhnev Doctrine," under which the Soviets claimed the right to provide "military aid to a fraternal country" (translation: invade it) whenever there was "a threat to the common interests of the camp of socialism" (translation: a threat to Soviet dominance).

Gorbachev is clearly motivated by his nation's desperate internal situation. Perestroika, which aims to radically restructure the Soviet economy, has so far succeeded only in disrupting the clanky old centralized-state system that at least belched forth a few second-rate consumer goods for the store shelves. Now those shelves are barer than they have been for twenty years, there are fears of food riots this winter, and Gorbachev is not the hero at home that he is abroad.

For the first six months of the Bush administration, agnosticism about Gorbachev was an article of faith. White House spokesman Marlin Fitzwater went so far as to call him "a drugstore cowboy." Moreover, it was virtually taboo to use any form of the verb "to help" in the same sentence with Gorbachev. Senate Democratic leader George Mitchell accused the Bush administration of "status quo thinking" and exhibiting an "almost passive stance." Bush's attitude began to change when he visited Poland and Hungary in July. His hosts impressed on him that their survival, not to mention their success, depended on Gorbachev's. Bush commented afterward that he had understood the connection intellectually but now he understood it "in my gut."

Bush's conversion has not ended the deep schism within his administration. National Security Adviser Brent Scowcroft remains cautious about Gorbachev's ultimate aims, and his deputy Robert Gates is acidly skeptical about the Soviet leader's ability to prevail. In an unusual move, Baker last week forbade Gates to deliver a speech that was too pessimistic about Gorbachev's economic program. Vice President Dan Quayle directly challenged Baker in a Los Angeles speech by stressing "the darker side of Soviet foreign policy" and saying that instead of helping, the United States ought to "let them reform themselves."

The success of perestroika will depend on the Soviets, but Washington can help Gorbachev by reaching agreements to cut conventional arms and strategic nuclear arsenals. In addition, Soviet foreign minister Eduard Shevardnadze in his speech last week spoke of Moscow's desire to join such Western economic institutions as the World Bank, the International Monetary Fund, and GATT (the General Agreement on Tariffs and Trade). Like Hungary, the Soviet Union could benefit from most-favored-nation trade status.

Yet given the sweeping transformations under way, these measures seem limp. Such a step-by-step approach would be, at best, yet another example of the—dare one say timid?—incrementalism on arms control and trade that has marked Soviet-American relations for four decades. As Bush himself says, the opportunity is historic. The idea that the Warsaw Pact would launch a land invasion of Western Europe, which is what most of NATO expenditures are designed to prevent, has become nearly inconceivable. "It may be time to abandon incrementalism for a leapfrog approach, to see if we can really make a basic change in our relationship," says former assistant secretary of state Richard Holbrooke.

Dean Acheson compared the task of his fellow statesmen at the end of World War II to the one described in the first chapter of the Bible. "That was to create a world out of chaos; ours, to create half a world, a free half, out of the same material." The genesis that is now at hand may be just as formidable, because it involves transcending not chaos but a rigid order.

The postwar era was launched with a speech by Harry Truman outlining a vision of containment. Similarly, Bush could launch a postcontainment era by propounding a bold swords-into-plowshares scheme for a fundamental change in East-West relations. Such a clarion call for a radical new Bush Doctrine could command the bipartisan support that accompanied the Truman Doctrine. It could also, at the very least, regain for the United States the initiative on the world stage. And, who knows? Gorbachev might go along. More surprising things have happened this year.

Figuring Out Ronnie

Ronald Reagan was among the most amiable men I have ever met, but he was one of the most difficult for outsiders to know. He was a good storyteller, especially about his days at Warner Bros., and he was articulate in explaining what he believed. But rarely did you see his mind engage or his thought process kick into action. I am not sure any biographer will ever provide a fully rounded portrait. The best we have so far are a lot of angles on him. This New York Times *book review from 2004 looks at two of these angles.*

One of the great challenges facing historians a century hence will be assessing Ronald Reagan. There are so many basic questions that even his friends cannot quite figure out, such as (to start with the most basic one): Was he smart?

From the brilliant-versus-clueless question flows even more complex ones. Was he a visionary who clung to a few verities, or an amiable dunce who floated obliviously above facts and nuances? Was he a stubborn ideological coot or a clever negotiator able to change course when dealing with Congress and the Soviets and movie moguls? Was he a historic figure who stemmed the tide of government expansion and stared down Moscow, or an out-of-touch actor who bloated the deficit and deserves less credit than Gorbachev for ending the cold war?

The most solidly reported biography of Reagan so far—indeed, the only solidly reported biography—is by the scrupulously fair newspaperman Lou Cannon, who has covered him since the 1960s. Edmund Morris, who with great literary flair captured the life of Theodore Roosevelt, was given the access to write an authorized biography, but he became flummoxed by the topic; he took an erratic swing by producing *Dutch*, a semifictionalized ruminative bio-memoir, thus fouling off his precious opportunity. Both Garry Wills in his elegant 1987 sociobiography,

Reagan's America, and Dinesh D'Souza in his 1997 delicate drypoint, *Ronald Reagan,* do a good job of analyzing why he was able to make such a successful connection with the American people.

Despite these offerings, one of the greatest books yet to be written is the sweeping biography of Ronald Reagan, one that captures fully his genial magic and essential solitariness, answers convincingly what was behind his warm smile and slightly colder eyes, and assesses fairly his place in history's pantheon.

That will require, first and foremost, figuring out how his mind worked. And the best way to begin addressing that issue, I suspect, will be to explore the ambitions and calculations and ideals that propelled him along his unlikely path to power before he became president. Two new books will be useful as fodder for historians undertaking this task.

The first, *Ronnie and Nancy,* is from a somewhat unlikely source: Bob Colacello, a celebrity chronicler for *Vanity Fair* and former sidekick to Andy Warhol, who befriended Nancy Reagan in 1981 and has interwoven a joint biography showing how she and her husband worked together during his "long climb" toward the presidency. Respectful without being fawning, Colacello succeeds in that seldom-achieved alchemy of spinning social stories into personality insights.

As might be expected, the book suffers (or some may think benefits) from an excess of boldfaced name-dropping: Ann Miller and Mickey Rooney, Alfred and Betsy Bloomingdale, Gardner and Jan Cowles, Jerry Zipkin, Claudette Colbert, and Etti Plesch, "an Austrian-born dowager from Monte Carlo known for her prizewinning racehorses and her six rich husbands." And that's just in the book's first two paragraphs. Yet Colacello makes the case that paying attention to "the social side of life" can offer more serious insights into people's hearts and minds. "What seems superficial often reveals deeper truths," he writes. "And if any subject was about the confluence of the serious and the frivolous, the social and the political, it was the Reagans and the era they came to represent."

Colacello's approach serves to highlight the role of Mrs. Reagan, who was both less Machiavellian and more influential than commonly thought. She had a simple motive for her backstage actions and a simple motivation for her public performances: She genuinely adored her husband, and the feeling was mutual. "Please don't make me sound like some kind of master backstage manipulator," she tells Colacello. "Everything I did, I did for Ronnie."

The details of the Reagans' respective childhoods are not new, but Colacello weaves them together in a spirited and insightful way. He describes, for example, Reagan's work as a lifeguard as being "a job he loved—perhaps because it allowed him to be narcissistic and altruistic at the same time."

Colacello is particularly convincing in explaining Reagan's abandonment of his liberal Democratic roots, which occurred when he was trying to keep alive his sputtering movie career and serving as president of the Screen Actors Guild. Reagan cooperated with the congressional investigators hunting down Hollywood Communists during the Red scare, and the approbation aimed at him from the more saintly sorts, who refused to name names, drove him ever rightward.

The book's frequent digressions about various Hollywood social strutters and fretters, which read like unedited *Vanity Fair* articles, can be frightfully tiresome, and you may find yourself knowing so much about folks like the Wassermans or the Bloomingdales that you'll want to take a shower. Nevertheless, these indulgences do end up providing a good analysis of the enormous role played by the Reagans' social group and his influential kitchen cabinet.

So what do we learn of Reagan's mind? Colacello shows him at the Screen Actors Guild perfecting the art of conciliation, negotiation, and compromise. And despite the unbending bluntness of his public rhetoric, we then see him use precisely these skills as governor of California when he compromises on such things as a state welfare bill, a liberal abortion act, and the state's largest tax increase. "Reagan always prided himself on his ability to compromise," his aide Michael Deaver tells the author. "He would tell you stories about what he learned in his work with the unions and the studios and the Screen Actors Guild. That's where he really learned how to compromise."

Colacello also shows that Reagan wrote his own political scripts, figuratively and literally. On the first day of his first speaking tour for General Electric in 1954, he was invited to give a speech on education to a group of teachers who were meeting in the town he was visiting. His handler said there was no time to write a speech, but Reagan accepted anyway and quickly wrote it himself. "He got a good ten-minute standing applause afterward," the handler recalled. "This is when I finally began to realize the breadth and depth of his knowledgeability . . . everything that went into his mind stayed there."

For better or worse, that ability to spin yarns out of everything that ever went into his mind is on display in *Reagan's Path to Victory,* the third in a series of collected speeches, letters, and radio scripts that have been published over the past four years. This one is a chronological compilation of the syndicated radio talks he delivered from 1975 to 1979.

For those of us who enjoyed the first two such volumes—*Reagan, In His Own Hand* and *Reagan: A Life in Letters*—this one is a bit disappointing. Many of the short little commentaries are infected by the lazy trick of pundits of all persuasions, which is to pluck a tidbit of outrage from a news item—a welfare queen who cheats the system, the federal agency that spent $64,000 on remodeled washrooms—and use it as a basis for policymaking or as a whipping boy for the idiocy of government. However valid each rant may be, after a while it starts to feel like shooting snail darters in a barrel.

Reagan, in fact, does shoot at the snail darter, that beleaguered little fish whose protection came to symbolize environmental excess, as well as at other easy targets that permit him to ridicule the bureaucracy. Typical are his columns about Kidco, a little company started by four kids who sell horse manure as fertilizer for a golf course and private homes. When the state tries to get them to pay sales tax, Reagan scores a justifiable if cheap chortle. But Reagan cannot let go and is soon on his high horse about how the state is hampering the kids' new "profitable sideline business" of poisoning gophers. Reagan rails at how the bureaucrats were initially insisting, until they backed down, that the kids get a pest control license and reveal what poisons they are using. "It would seem to me that their mother would have satisfied herself as to its safety," he says. Call me a gooey liberal, but I am not sure I want a posse of prepubescent boys running a rodent-poisoning business without following any regulations on what chemicals they are using. But even if you think that's a cool idea, I suspect you might find Reagan's bureaucrat-bashing a bit overdone by this point. Of course, that, too, is an insight into how his mind worked.

4. THE CLINTONS

Fighting Words

When Hillary Clinton and her consigliere Sidney Blumenthal came out with memoirs in 2003, the New Yorker *asked if I would review them and also put them into the context of the evolution of White House memoirs. It was an interesting idea, and it allowed me to explore how that genre has changed.*

There are two abiding mysteries about Bill Clinton: Why do some people hate him so passionately? And why do some people adore him so loyally? The recent memoirs by his wife, Hillary Rodham Clinton, and by his intense outrider Sidney Blumenthal focus on the former issue while providing textbook studies of the latter.

Both authors were famous for propounding the theory that the Clinton scandals were the result of what Hillary Clinton called "a vast right-wing conspiracy," dedicated to destroying the progressive agenda. In *Living History,* she repeats the charge, conceding only that the coordinated crusade was so brazen that it might not have qualified as a conspiracy. In *The Clinton Wars,* Blumenthal, whose ornate conspiracy theories earned him the nickname Grassy Knoll, launches into a game of Trivial Pursuit that is filled with half-forgotten bit players (remember David Bossie and George Conway III?) linked to a web of rabid Clinton-haters stretching back to Arkansas's hardscrabble racists. Together, the authors amply prove the old maxim that even paranoids have enemies.

Although the books are scored in different keys—Clinton's generally attempts to be gauzy and warm, Blumenthal's is edgy and cold—their underlying refrain is the same. Both repeatedly delve into what Hillary Clinton calls "the mechanics of what was essentially a sting operation to entrap the President" and what Blumenthal declares was the work of "fiercely partisan Republicans who had embarked on a sexual fishing expedition." Like any fishing expedition, which indeed it was, it could be sustained only if there were a lot of fishy things below the surface, which indeed there were. But where most memoirists adopt an air of mellowed self-examination, these authors are not in the mood to make concessions. Instead, they go on the attack. Their aggressiveness marks an evolution, befitting our times, in the tone and style of memoirs by people who have worked in the White House.

The venerable tradition of the White House memoir goes back to President James Madison's extraordinary young slave Paul Jennings. Jennings's memoir, which he wrote after Daniel Webster bought his freedom, contained most of what we have come to expect from such books, including thumbnail sketches of important players:

> Mr. Robert Smith was then Secretary of State, but as he and Mr. Madison could not agree, he was removed, and Colonel Monroe appointed to his place. Dr. Eustis was Secretary of War—rather a rough, blustering man; Mr. Gallatin, a tip-top man, was Secretary of the Treasury; and Mr. Hamilton of South Carolina, a pleasant gentleman, who thought Mr. Madison could do nothing wrong, and who always concurred in every thing he said, was Secretary of the Navy.

Jennings also provided accounts of the policy battles over the War of 1812 ("Colonel Monroe was always fierce for it") and tried to debunk a few myths. "It has often been stated in print that when Mrs. Madison escaped from the White House, she cut out from the frame the large portrait of Washington . . . and carried it off," Jennings wrote. "This is totally false. She had no time for doing it. It would have required a ladder to get it down." (The Gilbert Stuart painting was actually saved by a doorkeeper and a gardener, he said.) Most important, Jennings's memoir set the genre's standard for presidential praise. "Mr. Madison, I think, was one of the best men that ever lived," he wrote. "I never saw him in a passion, and never knew him to strike a slave."

The modern era of such memoirs began with a gusher from the administration of Franklin Delano Roosevelt, whose insistence that his aides display a "passion for anonymity" had only a temporary restraining effect. The first of the Roosevelt books, *After Seven Years,* by the brain-truster Raymond Moley, established the tone: praise for the patron that subtly shades into self-praise, inside accounts of policy struggles in which the author turns out to have been right, a dollop of historical commentary, some gossip that gently settles old scores, and a good index for colleagues who may not want to read the whole thing. Moley was sometimes deft enough to work many of these themes into a single sentence: "I was able to achieve almost the impossible—the maintenance of friendly relations with both Louis Howe and Sam Rosenman—and the rivalry of these two men was the single factor that might have disrupted the logical course of events." Although most such memoirs ended up in the ash bin, a few helped elevate the genre. Roosevelt's best speechwriter, Robert E. Sherwood, who had won three Pulitzer Prizes as a playwright, won another for a memoir cast as a character study: *Roosevelt and Hopkins.* In 1965, two of John Kennedy's speechwriters produced similarly stately tomes. Theodore Sorensen's *Kennedy* is notable for being unflinching, at least in parts. Its assessment of the failed Bay of Pigs invasion, for instance, begins by saying of Kennedy, "His own mistakes were many and serious," and then proceeds to catalogue them. The eminent historian Arthur Schlesinger Jr. has sometimes been labeled a hagiographer for the Camelot chords he struck, but *A Thousand Days* is an intricate and serious narrative biography with sweeping historical themes and incisive dry-point character sketches. His depiction of Secretary of State Dean Rusk is typical: "As he would talk on and on in his even, low voice, a Georgia drawl sounding distantly under the professional tones of a foundation executive, the world itself seemed to lose reality and dissolve into a montage of platitudes."

The Watergate scandal posed a new challenge to White House memoirists: how to deal with the character flaws that unraveled a presidency. William Safire, a Nixon speechwriter, set out to produce a book that would be "sympathetic but not sycophantic," and the result, *Before the Fall,* succeeds by peeling back the multiple layers of Nixon's tortured personality and offering up candid (and amusing) portraits of Henry Kissinger and other members of the court. Safire defended much of

Nixon's record, but recognized that Nixon might be "the only genuinely tragic hero in our history, his ruination caused by the flaws in his own character." In *White House Years,* Kissinger, too, was willing to explore the loneliness, paranoia, insecurity, and lack of generosity that infected Nixon and unsettled his tenure. He notices the little things about Nixon— "his pant legs as always a trifle short, his look of defiance mixed with uncertainty"—and concludes by ruminating about "what extraordinary vehicles destiny selects to accomplish its design."

It subsequently became part of the tradition for aides to try to establish their credibility and integrity, and make some headlines, by including a few denigrating revelations about their former patrons. James Fallows, a Carter speechwriter, wrote a magazine memoir before Carter even had a chance to run for reelection, in which he described Carter as "passionless" and revealed that the president micromanaged the sign-up schedule for the White House tennis court. Even more damaging was Donald T. Regan's revelation about "the most closely guarded domestic secret" of Ronald and Nancy Reagan: "Virtually every major move and decision the Reagans made during my time as White House Chief of Staff was cleared in advance with a woman in San Francisco who drew up horoscopes to make certain that the planets were in a favorable alignment." The current administration has already produced such a memoir, by a former speechwriter, David Frum, in *The Right Man,* which is generally as flattering as the title implies but contains a few discomforting little revelations about the tenor of the White House—Frum, who is Jewish, opens the book with the line "Missed you at Bible study" spoken by one aide to another—and about Bush's own shortcomings: "He is impatient and quick to anger; sometimes glib, even dogmatic; often uncurious and as a result ill-informed; more conventional in his thinking than a leader probably should be."

Minor score-settling aside, though, previous White House memoirs tried to appear reflective, above the fray, and candid about mistakes that were made. This was true, certainly, of the only other best-selling memoir so far from a Clinton aide, George Stephanopoulos's *All Too Human.* Stephanopoulos dealt with the scandals in an admirably honest manner, and revealed his own conflicting emotions in an anguished portrayal of the period. "I didn't think I was a hypocrite, because my defense of Clinton against past bimbo eruptions had been predicated on my belief that he wouldn't create new ones, but maybe I *was* complicit because when I worked for Clinton I had been willing to suspend my disbelief about some of his more suspect denials," he writes. "For several years, I had served as his character witness. Now I felt like a dupe."

Sidney Blumenthal—who spent years covering Washington politics for the *New Republic* and then for the *New Yorker*, before becoming an assistant to President Clinton—has no time for such self-examination. He unabashedly rises to the president's defense in each and every (and every and every) particular, embedding a controlled, seemingly dispassionate, and at times persuasive pro-Clinton polemic within the pages of a high-minded history. In doing so, he has helped to create something like a new genre—the attack memoir.

The result reads like two very different books shuffled together, jostling one another uncomfortably as they alternate turns over nearly eight hundred pages. The first book consists of Blumenthal aspiring to emulate Schlesinger. From the opening scene, in which the new president visits the Franklin D. Roosevelt Library, in Hyde Park, the author unblushingly places himself at the center of momentous historical forces. "I could hear my own footsteps as I walked past black-and-white photographs of FDR grandly gesturing to roaring crowds," he writes. When Bill Clinton arrives, "the dust started to be shaken; the pinned exhibits almost seemed to want to move; the past was no longer at rest." And then, in a metaphorical gesture, the president beckons Blumenthal over: "He wanted me to accompany him as he toured FDR's library."

Blumenthal's assessment of Clinton occasionally transcends hagiography and approaches deification. His black students in Arkansas, we are informed, "called him Wonder Boy for his utter absence of racial distinction," and a member of the National Symphony "told me he was the only guest conductor they'd ever had who knew what he was doing." By the end of the book, Clinton has been carved into the progressive pantheon with both Roosevelts. "Just as the presidents of the late twentieth century operated in the shadow of FDR," Blumenthal declares, "those of the first part of the twenty-first century will stand in the shadow of Clinton."

But it would be unfair, albeit easy, to make fun of Blumenthal as a human incarnation of Buddy the dog, tirelessly chasing errant balls and panting with pure affection. When stripped of some of the excesses, his character sketches and his digressions into the roots of great historical themes can be fascinating. He is especially enlightening about the Third Way movement, through which Clinton and British prime minister Tony Blair shed the paralyzing dogmas of the old Left in order to take up policies of forceful engagement abroad along with fiscal responsibility at home. By this approach, Blumenthal argues, Clinton showed how strong executive leadership could be brought to the cause of progressive social policies. The result was "the greatest prosperity" in America's history, "the greatest reduction in poverty" since Lyndon Johnson's Great Society, "the greatest public health insurance coverage of children, and the greatest budget surplus ever." Despite Blumenthal's efforts, few will be convinced that the Clinton administration's haphazard policymaking was responsible for all these successes, but he does make the best possible case that it deserves a lot of the credit.

Time and again, unfortunately, Blumenthal's revealing anecdotes and sweeping policy analysis get elbowed aside by his parallel book, the one in which he dives into the murky depth of each successive scandal. Suddenly the tone turns conspiratorial. A legion of enemies small and large, from Arkansas lowlifes to the independent counsel Kenneth Starr, are woven into a tangled web of buffoons who share the same sinister motives and tactics. And many in the press are portrayed either as willing dupes or as craven coconspirators. (At one point, Blumenthal accuses *Time* of purposely positioning a photograph of Hillary Clinton on the cover so that the "M" in the logo would look like devil horns. As the editor of the magazine then, I can attest that the "M" was in the same place it had been for eighty years, ever since Henry Luce decided against calling his magazine *The Synthetic Review*, and that we had no diabolical designs.) Blumenthal's valid points about the tactics of the probers are thus lost to his lack of subtlety and his unwillingness to reflect on the Clintonian behavior that created the morass in the first place. Once again, it's necessary to strip away Blumenthal's excesses in order to uncover his insights.

The most compelling of these insights flow from his recounting of how he secretly befriended David Brock, an apostate conservative journalist who first published the sex allegations made against Clinton by Arkansas state troopers. On the day that the Monica Lewinsky story broke, Blumenthal called Brock, who had already been expiating his guilt by leaking to Blumenthal the maneuvers of the most ardent Clinton-haters. Brock proceeded to detail the collusion of Kenneth Starr's office, journalists at *Newsweek,* Lewinsky's turncoat confessor, Linda Tripp, the merry mischief-maker Lucianne Goldberg, the Internet gossip Matt Drudge, and a motley if not vast right-wing conspiracy that included a collection of freelance investigators and legal "elves" funded by the conservative millionaire Richard Mellon Scaife.

The machinations of members of this anti-Clinton cabal are interesting enough and, indeed (as many of them will proudly admit), true enough, but Blumenthal and Hillary Clinton were notably unsuccessful at focusing press attention on them rather than on the president's own misdeeds. One reason is that there was an even more interesting personal question, both then and now: Could these two aggressive defenders truly have believed the president's slippery denials? Blumenthal's answer is that, on the day the story appeared, he discussed the situation with the president and reached a tacit willingness to suspend disbelief. Both the president and his wife "wanted me to believe the story as he told it," Blumenthal writes, "because he wanted her to believe it and she wanted to believe him."

In Hillary's version, she did believe her husband, right up to the day, seven months later, when he was forced to confess in his deposition. Their lawyer, Bob Barnett, tried to warn her the night before that maybe "there's more to this than you know," but even then, she writes, she stuck with her credulity. " 'Look, Bob,' I said. 'My husband may have his faults, but he has never lied to me.'" When she learns the following morning that he had indeed lied, she writes, "I was dumbfounded, heartbroken and outraged that I'd believed him at all."

Like Blumenthal's, Clinton's book melds together disparate forms. One is a traditionally treacly first lady memoir, similar to the ghosted

efforts that were produced for most of her predecessors, which duti-
fully describes the pleasures of meeting so many fascinating people in so
many far-flung places, all with touching tales and meaningful lessons. In
other sections, she has produced a typical campaign biography, the sort
designed to lay the ground for a future candidacy, which chronicles the
formative events in her life, her evolving philosophy, and the ideals that
motivate her.

Not all of it is formulaic. There are passages that read as if she grabbed
the keyboard away from her ghostwriters in order to shake free from the
perception of phoniness that dogs her. She is particularly affecting when
she describes her protective feelings toward her daughter, Chelsea, and
even somewhat wry about the empty-nest syndrome that descended
when Chelsea left for Stanford. "Sometimes I'd catch Bill just sitting in
Chelsea's bedroom, looking around wistfully," she writes. "I had to admit
that my husband and I were caught up in a generational cliché, a milestone in life that only members of our self-conscious age group would
define as a syndrome."

On policy issues as well, she is often revealing. She provides, for example, a detailed description of her role in the debates over the president's
welfare-reform proposals, and says, "I told him and his top staff that I
would speak out against any bill" if it did not contain certain liberal safe-
guards. Unlike previous first ladies, she is not shy about crediting herself
as a full policy partner: "By the time Bill and I left the White House,
welfare rolls had dropped 60 percent." She tells how she pushed her husband to barrel ahead with her doomed plan for national health-care coverage, and in a small deviation from the account by Blumenthal, who is
not even mentioned until page 422 of her book, she takes a good deal of
the credit for organizing the Third Way discussions with Prime Minister
Blair.

What's most striking, however, is the way she has interspersed her
campaign biography and first lady memoir with sections in which, like
Blumenthal, she wages a Manichaean struggle against the Vast Conspiracy. Despite the drama of the four pages describing her fury at her husband's betrayal, most of her anger in the 530 other pages is directed at

the enemies she claims sought to destroy his presidency. This is what motivated her, she says, to reconcile with her husband. "If men like Starr and his allies could ignore the Constitution and abuse power for ideological and malicious ends to topple a President, I feared for my country," she explains. "Bill's Presidency, the institutional Presidency and the integrity of the Constitution hung in the balance. I knew what I did and said in the next days and weeks would influence not just Bill's future and mine, but also America's."

She is no less assertive than Blumenthal in her depiction of the enemies they were battling:

> I do believe there was, and still is, an interlocking network of groups and individuals who want to turn the clock back on many of the advances our country has made, from civil rights and women's rights to consumer and environmental regulation, and they use all the tools at their disposal—money, power, influence, media and politics—to achieve their ends. In recent years, they have also mastered the politics of personal destruction. Fueled by extremists who have been fighting progressive politicians and ideas for decades, they are funded by corporations, foundations and individuals like Richard Mellon Scaife.

Although she does not descend to the "politics of personal destruction"—there are no dark intimations of murder or sex scandals—she is not averse to firing a bit of buckshot. When Newt Gingrich's mother let slip that her son, the new House Speaker, often referred to Hillary as a "bitch," she invited them both, along with his "then wife," to the White House. What ensues is a scene in which Gingrich's wife belittles him for babbling about things he does not understand, and his mother retorts, "Newty *always* knows what he's talking about." Similarly, she ridicules Chief Justice William Rehnquist for presiding over her husband's Senate trial wearing a robe he had designed with chevrons of gold braid. "He said he got the idea from the costumes in a production of Gilbert & Sullivan's comic opera *Iolanthe,*" she writes. "How fitting that he should wear a theatrical costume to preside over a political farce."

Both Blumenthal and Clinton, with their wrenching lurches from policy discourses to scandal dissections, are able to re-create the vertigo of the era, during which missile attacks on al Qaeda came in the wake of squirmy testimony about inappropriate behavior, and stories about Moscow summits vied with those about distinguishing genital characteristics. They also present a largely persuasive case that prosecutors and the press (though not the American public) became overly, even weirdly, obsessed with the Whitewater story. Combined with their excesses of loyalty and their unwillingness to reflect on the president's pathological indiscipline, the result is yet another type of vertigo: that which comes from rolling your eyes and nodding your head at the same time.

These books, of course, will not for a moment sway any of the Clintons' ardent adversaries, nor does that seem to be their intention. Like much of the discourse from the period, they appear to be meant to stoke old partisan arguments rather than to quell them. In this they exemplify the very trend—the shrilling of political discourse—that they decry.

Raucous, partisan debate can be healthy, up to a point, and liberals will point out that conservatives have heretofore dominated the bestseller lists, as well as cable television, and have been notably more aggressive in tearing down their opponents. Partly that is because liberals are less cohesive and angry, more timid and easily cowed. Even when liberals have strong beliefs, they act as if they were not quite sure they actually agree with them. They are congenitally more comfortable humming the theme of *All Things Considered* than the theme of *Crossfire*.

Until now, the most successful authors on the provocative Left have been those who cloaked their jabs with humor, such as Michael Moore, Molly Ivins, and Al Franken. This may be changing. All three will be publishing more pugnacious books this year, and so will the liberal columnists Paul Krugman and Joe Conason. Eventually they may even be joined by Bill Clinton, if he decides to emulate his wife and his old Knight Templar by producing a memoir that ravages as well as ruminates.

All this best-selling bellicosity is likely to continue the trend away from the old recollected-in-tranquillity manner of White House memoirs. At the very least, it will make for more interesting reading. And we are unlikely to miss, at least for a while, the quaint platitudes of a Raymond Moley, who concluded his memoir by calling for a future politics based on "fine thinking and generous impulse."

I'm Okay, You're Okay

The publication of Bill Clinton's highly anticipated memoirs in 2004 set off a frenzy. There was tight security around the release of the book, but Michiko Kakutani of the New York Times *managed to get an early copy and review it a few days before it was released. The* Washington Post *wanted to keep up. I am not as fast a reader nor as sure a reviewer as Michi, but I was able to find a bookstore in Colorado that was willing to slip me an early copy, so I was only a few days behind her with this review.*

If each era gets the leaders it deserves, then it is also true that each gets the memoirs it deserves. Not surprisingly, Bill Clinton, avatar of the 1990s and of the aging baby boom, has written one suited for the Age of Oprah.

Like a boomer's version of *Pilgrim's Progress,* it has a hero who wanders through the wilderness of the Vietnam-to-9/11 world filled with earnest idealism jostling with unabashed ambition, while confronting trials that produce a conflicting mix of self-righteousness and self-awareness. Faith in psychotherapy joins with religious faith in a quest for sensitive personal insights suitable for sharing. As a result, Clinton's 957-page *My Life* captures and conveys, in ways that are sometimes brilliant and at other times unintentional, the essence of his personality and presidency: fascinating, undisciplined, deeply intelligent, self-indulgent, and filled with great promise alternately grasped and squandered.

It is those qualities, too, that make his book a reflection of his day and generation. The Indulgent Nineties, between the fall of the Berlin wall and the fall of the Twin Towers, were disciplined neither by a cold war nor a war on terrorism. It was a time of optimism unleavened by sacrifice. Digitally driven exuberance produced an economic boom and a psychological bubble. Although Clinton portrays this period as one filled with

Herculean struggles by progressive forces to beat back the regressive Right, which was occasionally the case, more often the fights were so bitter because the stakes were so small.

Clinton's psychological introspection, rendered in lingo from personal therapy and couples' counseling, is another reason his memoir reads like a period piece. In that regard, it contrasts with the most underrated modern presidential memoir, Richard Nixon's *RN*, the product of a more emotionally inhibited generation. Nixon's crisp opening sentence—"I was born in a house my father built"—stands starkly without further reflection. Clinton's opening sentence likewise describes his birth, but it's clogged with fact-filled clauses and followed by pages of analysis about how both his father and stepfather helped to instill his drives and demons.

Perhaps the best presidential autobiography, or so we were informed repeatedly in the walk-up to the Clinton launch, is Ulysses S. Grant's *Personal Memoirs*, which wins this month's Alexis de Tocqueville award for being the book most often cited by people who have not actually read it. Its opening sentence is likewise revealing of the tenor of its times: "My family is American, and has been for generations, in all its branches, direct and collateral." The critic Edmund Wilson called it "a unique expression of the national character." It was helped by having a great editor—Mark Twain—who relentlessly pushed Grant to write it, then edited it into shape and promoted it brilliantly. In a blurb that would have dazzled even today's promotion-savvy publishers, Twain called the memoir "the best of any general's since Caesar's."

Which brings up one additional way, alas, that Clinton's tome reflects our times. It is the product of an age of hypermarketed blockbusters that are rushed into print and hurled into promotional orbit. Clinton was inexplicably pushed by the normally stately House of Knopf to meet an arbitrary deadline, and guessing whether he would meet it became a public pastime. The result is as messy as certain months of his presidency. His beguiling recollection of his childhood is stapled together with a hastily disgorged data dump on the day-by-day chronology of his presidency that features stretches of unrelated paragraphs beginning with such phrases as "Also that week . . ."

Despite all of this, Clinton's finished product evokes another quote from Twain: Like Wagner's music, it's not as bad as it sounds. His life is too fascinating, his mind too brilliant, his desire to charm too strong to permit him to produce a boring book. The combination of analytic and emotional intelligence that made him a great politician now makes him a compelling raconteur.

Clinton's ruminations on his complex childhood are even more richly layered than Jimmy Carter's delightful childhood memoir, *An Hour Before Daylight*. Particularly striking is how revealing Clinton is about his insecurities. Back in high school, he recalls, he wrote an essay that still rings eerily accurate:

"I am a living paradox—deeply religious, yet not as convinced of my exact beliefs as I ought to be; wanting responsibility yet shirking it; loving the truth but often giving way to falsity. . . . I detest selfishness, but see it in the mirror every day."

His teacher gave him a 100 on the essay and said it was a "beautiful and honest attempt" to fulfill the classical injunction to "know thyself." Indeed, what makes Clinton's book so engaging, sometimes in a rubbernecking sort of way, is his fealty to Socrates' maxim that the unexamined life is not worth living. He examines with gusto every aspect of his life. It is, quite obviously, a subject that interests him.

His great insight is how, during his childhood, he developed the character traits that led him to cause, but then also survive, the scandals that dogged his presidency. His stepfather—"a handsome, hell-raising, twice-divorced man from Hot Springs"—was a mean drunk who abused Clinton's beloved mother. Clinton recalls one fight when his stepfather shot off a gun, and another when Clinton stood up to him as he was "beating on her" by brandishing a golf club. "Something more poisonous than alcohol drove him to that level of debasement," Clinton writes. "It would be a long time before I could understand such forces in others or in myself."

As a result, Clinton learned how to have a public life in conflict with his hidden private one, how to revel in the world of secrets. "We all have them and I think we're entitled to them," he declares. In a revealing passage, he describes the spiritual crisis this caused when he was thirteen:

I now know this struggle is at least partly the result of growing up in an alcoholic home and the mechanisms I developed to cope with it. It took me a long time just to figure that out. It was even harder to learn which secrets to keep, which to let go of, which to avoid in the first place. I am still not sure I understand that completely. It looks as if it's going to be a lifetime project.

One cannot quite imagine Nixon or Reagan, and certainly not Ulysses S. Grant, making such a confession.

Clinton's intense devotion to his spunky mother is the other main theme of his childhood. She told him how her father cried one Easter because he could not afford the dollar to buy her a new dress, so every Easter she dressed little Bill in a new outfit. "I remember one Easter in the 1950s, when I was fat and self-conscious," he recalls. "I went to church in a light-colored short-sleeved shirt, white linen pants, pink and black Hush Puppies, and a matching pink suede belt."

In her own sassy memoir, *Leading with My Heart,* Clinton's mother wrote about her son's promiscuous appetite for affection. If he walked into a room of a hundred people, she said, and ninety-nine of them liked him, he would head for the lone holdout and try to charm him. (This trait is evident in his book, where he treats folks such as his prodigal pollster Dick Morris and his political doppelgänger Newt Gingrich with notable gentility.) She was the opposite, Clinton recalls. "Unlike me, she actually enjoyed making some of these people mad. I tended to make enemies effortlessly, just by being me, or, after I got into politics, because of the positions I took and the changes I tried to make."

The imprints from his childhood both helped and hounded him throughout his life. After giving a detailed and somewhat tortured explanation about how he did not really, truly, or maybe at least not intentionally, wiggle disingenuously out of the draft in 1968, he goes into another riff on his inner life. "My struggles with the draft rekindled my long-standing doubts about whether I was, or could become, a really good person," he writes. "I think this problem arises from leading parallel lives, an external life that takes its natural course and an internal life where the secrets are hidden."

Not surprisingly, these strands all come together, either neatly or messily depending on your disposition, as an explanation—but not, he takes care to insist, an excuse—for his less than Scout-like honesty and discipline in Gennifer-Paula-Monica matters. But he makes a forceful case that Kenneth Starr and his other pursuers far exceeded the bounds of legality and propriety. Their tactics, he says, helped him win back Hillary and escape his banishment to the couch.

Somehow or another (the logic doesn't fully track) the whole mess ends up being redemptive with the help of Jesus' famous maxim in John 8:7 so beloved by saved sinners:

> I had had a lot of stones cast at me, and through my own self-inflicted wounds I had been exposed to the whole world. In some ways it was liberating; I had nothing more to hide. And as I tried to understand why I had made my own mistakes, I also attempted to figure out why my adversaries were so consumed with hatred, and so willing to say and do things inconsistent with their professed moral convictions. . . . My sense of my own mortality and human frailty and the unconditional love I'd had as a child had spared me the compulsion to judge and condemn others. And I believed my personal flaws, no matter how deep, were far less threatening to our democratic government than the power lust of my accusers.

Clinton juxtaposes his personal turmoil with a grander theme, the political turmoil that also grew up in the '60s. The year 1968, he says, "broke open the nation and shattered the Democratic Party" by causing conservative populism to replace progressive populism. "The middle-class backlash would shape and distort American politics for the rest of the century." Clinton saw his mission as preserving the advances that came out of the '60s while preventing Republicans from convincing the public that "Democrats were weak on family, work, welfare, crime, and defense" and unable to "draw distinctions between right and wrong."

Both through his policies and his defeat of the "right-wing coup" attempt, Clinton argues, he was able to hold back the forces of reaction. And by triangulating between the old Democratic Left and the

Republican Right to find "common ground" on such issues as affirmative action, school prayer, and welfare reform, he helped to save the Democratic Party.

There is a lot to be said in Clinton's favor on these issues, and though nobody is likely to criticize his book for being too short, he actually could have said more about them. But in his rush to meet his publication deadline, Clinton seems to have sacrificed a more thoughtful historical analysis in favor of pouring every meeting, meal, and travelogue into print.

Those of us who may someday struggle to put Clinton's presidency in perspective, indeed those who will struggle to do so a century from now, are likely to be as flummoxed, and as divided, as we are today about the place he deserves in history's pantheon. His book will help if only by reminding us how messy and mesmerizing he and his era were.

But if historians are lucky, Clinton will do what he sometimes does on the golf course and take a mulligan or do-over on the second half of his book. Five or ten years from now, when passions have cooled and some perspective is possible, he might write a more studied and reflective account of his presidency, not rushing against a deadline. That book would have the potential of being truly enlightening, rather than merely a fascinating reflection of the tenor of our times.

5. ALBERT EINSTEIN

———◦•◦———

Einstein's God

When my biography of Einstein was published in 2007, Time *decided to do an excerpt. They chose a section that explored Einstein's religious beliefs. Both atheists and people of faith try to claim Einstein. As he showed us is the case with all things in the universe, the reality is more complex.*

He was slow in learning how to talk. "My parents were so worried," he later recalled, "that they consulted a doctor." Even after he had begun using words, sometime after the age of two, he developed a quirk that prompted the family maid to dub him *der Depperte* (the dopey one). Whenever he had something to say, he would try it out on himself, whispering it softly until it sounded good enough to pronounce aloud. "Every sentence he uttered," his worshipful younger sister recalled, "no matter how routine, he repeated to himself softly, moving his lips." It was all very worrying, she said. "He had such difficulty with language that those around him feared he would never learn."

His slow development was combined with a cheeky rebelliousness toward authority, which led one schoolmaster to send him packing and another to amuse history by declaring that he would never amount to much. These traits made Albert Einstein the patron saint of distracted schoolkids everywhere. But they also helped to make him, or so he later surmised, the most creative scientific genius of modern times.

His cocky contempt for authority led him to question received wisdom in ways that well-trained acolytes in the academy never contemplated. And as for his slow verbal development, he thought that it allowed him to observe with wonder the everyday phenomena that others took for granted. Instead of puzzling over *mysterious* things, he puzzled over *commonplace* things. "The ordinary adult never bothers his head about the problems of space and time," he once explained. "These are things he has thought of as a child. But I developed so slowly that I began to won-der about space and time only when I was already grown up. Conse-quently, I probed more deeply into the problem than an ordinary child would have."

Einstein's awe regarding the laws of nature and his rebellious attitude toward authority also shaped his religious outlook. It initially led him to rebel against his parents' secularism. Then it caused him to reject the con-cepts of religious ritual and of a personal God who intercedes in the daily workings of the world. And then, finally, he was able to settle comfort-ably into a spiritual and religious deism, one based on what he called the "spirit manifest in the laws of the Universe" and a sincere belief in a "God who reveals Himself in the lawful harmony of all that exists."

Einstein was descended, on both parents' sides, from Jewish trades-men and peddlers who had, for at least two centuries, made modest liv-ings in the rural villages of Swabia in southwestern Germany. With each generation they had become, or at least so they thought, increasingly assimilated into the German culture that they loved. Although Jewish by cultural designation and kindred instinct, they displayed scant interest in religion or its rituals.

In his later years, Einstein would tell an old joke about an agnostic uncle, who was the only member of his family who went to synagogue. When asked why he did so, the uncle would respond, "Ah, but you never know." Einstein's parents, on the other hand, were "entirely irreligious" and felt no compulsion to hedge their bets. They did not keep kosher or attend synagogue, and his father, Hermann, referred to Jewish rituals as "ancient superstitions," according to a relative.

Consequently, when Albert turned six and had to go to school, his parents did not care that there was no Jewish one near their home. Instead he went to the large Catholic school in their neighborhood. As the only Jew among the seventy students in his class, Einstein took the standard course in Catholic religion and ended up enjoying it immensely. Indeed, he did so well in his Catholic study that he helped his classmates with it.

Despite his parents' secularism, or perhaps because of it, Einstein rather suddenly developed a passionate zeal for Judaism. "He was so fervent in his feelings that, on his own, he observed Jewish religious strictures in every detail," his sister recalled. He ate no pork, kept kosher dietary laws, and obeyed the strictures of the Sabbath, all rather difficult to do when the rest of his family had a lack of interest bordering on disdain for such displays. He even composed his own hymns for the glorification of God, which he sang to himself as he walked home from school.

Einstein's greatest intellectual stimulation came from a poor medical student who used to dine with his family once a week. It was an old Jewish custom to take in a needy religious scholar to share the Sabbath meal; the Einsteins modified the tradition by hosting instead a medical student on Thursdays. His name was Max Talmud, and he began his weekly visits when he was twenty-one and Einstein was ten.

Talmud brought him science books, including a popular illustrated series called People's Books on Natural Science, "a work which I read with breathless attention," said Einstein. The twenty-one little volumes were written by Aaron Bernstein, who stressed the interrelations between biology and physics, and he reported in great detail the scientific experiments being done at the time, especially in Germany.

Talmud also helped Einstein explore the wonders of mathematics by giving him a textbook on geometry two years before he was scheduled to learn that subject in school. When Talmud arrived each Thursday, Einstein delighted in showing him the problems he had solved that week. Initially, Talmud was able to help him, but he was soon surpassed by his pupil. "After a short time, a few months, he had worked through the whole book," Talmud recalled. "Soon the flight of his mathematical genius was so high that I could no longer follow."

Einstein's exposure to science and math produced a sudden transformation at age twelve, just as he would have been readying for a bar mitzvah. He suddenly rejected religious dogma and gave up following Jewish rituals.

Bernstein, in his popular science volumes, had reconciled science with religious inclination. As he put it, "The religious inclination lies in the dim consciousness that dwells in humans that all nature, including the humans in it, is in no way an accidental game, but a work of lawfulness, that there is a fundamental cause of all existence."

Einstein would later come close to these sentiments. But at the time, his leap away from faith was a radical one. "Through the reading of popular scientific books, I soon reached the conviction that much in the stories of the Bible could not be true. The consequence was a positively fanatic orgy of freethinking coupled with the impression that youth is intentionally being deceived by the state through lies; it was a crushing impression."

Einstein's rebellion against religious dogma had a profound effect on his general outlook toward received wisdom. It inculcated an allergic reaction against all forms of dogma and authority, which was to affect both his politics and his science. "Suspicion against every kind of authority grew out of this experience, a skeptical attitude towards the convictions that were alive in any specific social environment—an attitude which has never again left me," he later said. Indeed, it was this comfort with being a nonconformist that would define both his science and his social thinking for the rest of his life.

Einstein did, however, retain from his childhood religious phase a profound faith in, and reverence for, the harmony and beauty of what he called the mind of God as it was expressed in the creation of the universe and its laws. For much of his early career, he tended not to pronounce much on the topic. But around the time he turned fifty, he began to articulate more clearly—in various essays, interviews, and letters—his deepening appreciation of his belief in God, albeit a rather impersonal, deistic concept of God.

There were probably many reasons for this, in addition to the natural propensity toward reflections about the eternal that can occur at age fifty. But mainly, his beliefs seemed to arise from the sense of awe about the divine order that he discovered through his scientific work.

Both when embracing the beauty of his gravitational field equations or rejecting the uncertainty in quantum mechanics, he displayed a profound faith in the orderliness of the universe. This served as a basis for his scientific outlook—and also his religious outlook. "The highest satisfaction of a scientific person," he wrote shortly after turning fifty in 1929, is to come to the realization "that God himself could not have arranged these connections any other way than that which does exist, any more than it would have been in his power to make four a prime number."

One evening in Berlin that year, Einstein and his wife were at a dinner party when a guest expressed a belief in astrology. Einstein ridiculed the notion as pure superstition. Another guest stepped in and similarly disparaged religion. Belief in God, he insisted, was likewise a superstition.

At this point the host tried to silence him by invoking the fact that even Einstein harbored religious beliefs.

"It isn't possible!" the skeptical guest said, turning to Einstein to ask if he was, in fact, religious.

"Yes, you can call it that," Einstein replied calmly. "Try and penetrate with our limited means the secrets of nature and you will find that, behind all the discernible laws and connections, there remains something subtle, intangible and inexplicable. Veneration for this force beyond anything that we can comprehend is my religion. To that extent I am, in fact, religious."

For Einstein, as for most people, a belief in something larger than himself became a defining sentiment. It produced in him an admixture of confidence and humility that was leavened by a sweet simplicity. Given his proclivity toward being self-centered, these were welcome graces. Along with his humor, they helped him to avoid the pretense and pomposity that could have afflicted the most famous mind in the world.

His religious feelings of awe and humility also informed his sense of social justice. It impelled him to cringe at trappings of hierarchy or class distinction, to eschew excess consumption or materialism, and to dedicate himself to efforts on behalf of refugees and the oppressed.

Shortly after his fiftieth birthday, Einstein gave a remarkable interview in which he was more revealing than he had ever been about his religious thinking. It was with a pompous but ingratiating poet and propagandist named George Sylvester Viereck, who had been born in Germany, moved to America as a child, and then spent his life writing gaudily erotic poetry, interviewing great men, and expressing his complex love for his fatherland. For reasons not quite clear, Einstein assumed Viereck was Jewish. In fact, Viereck proudly traced his lineage to the family of the Kaiser, and he would later become a Nazi sympathizer who was jailed in America during World War II for being a German propagandist.

Viereck began by asking Einstein whether he considered himself a German or a Jew. "It's possible to be both," replied Einstein. "Nationalism is an infantile disease, the measles of mankind."

Should Jews try to assimilate? "We Jews have been too eager to sacrifice our idiosyncrasies in order to conform."

To what extent are you influenced by Christianity? "As a child I received instruction both in the Bible and in the Talmud. I am a Jew, but I am enthralled by the luminous figure of the Nazarene."

You accept the historical existence of Jesus? "Unquestionably! No one can read the Gospels without feeling the actual presence of Jesus. His personality pulsates in every word. No myth is filled with such life."

Do you believe in God? "I'm not an atheist. I don't think I can call myself a pantheist. The problem involved is too vast for our limited minds. We are in the position of a little child entering a huge library filled with books in many languages. The child knows someone must have written those books. It does not know how. It does not understand the languages in which they are written. The child dimly suspects a mysterious order in the arrangement of the books but doesn't know what it is. That, it seems to me, is the attitude of even the most intelligent human being toward God. We see the universe marvelously arranged and obeying certain laws but only dimly understand these laws."

Is this a Jewish concept of God? "I am a determinist. I do not believe in free will. Jews believe in free will. They believe that man shapes his own life. I reject that doctrine. In that respect I am not a Jew."

Is this Spinoza's God? "I am fascinated by Spinoza's pantheism, but I admire even more his contribution to modern thought because he is the first philosopher to deal with the soul and body as one, and not two separate things."

Do you believe in immortality? "No. And one life is enough for me."

Einstein tried to express these feelings clearly, both for himself and all of those who wanted a simple answer from him about his faith. So in the summer of 1930, amid his sailing and ruminations in Caputh, a village near Potsdam where he had a summer house, he composed a credo, "What I Believe," that he recorded for a human rights group and later published. It concluded with an explanation of what he meant when he called himself religious:

> The most beautiful emotion we can experience is the mysterious. It is the fundamental emotion that stands at the cradle of all true art and science. He to whom this emotion is a stranger, who can no longer wonder and stand rapt in awe, is as good as dead, a snuffed-out candle. To sense that behind anything that can be experienced there is something that our minds cannot grasp, whose beauty and sublimity reaches us only indirectly: this is religiousness. In this sense, and in this sense only, I am a devoutly religious man.

People found it evocative, even inspiring, and it was reprinted repeatedly in a variety of translations. But not surprisingly, it did not satisfy those who wanted a simple, direct answer to the question of whether or not he believed in God. As a result, getting Einstein to answer that question concisely replaced the earlier frenzy of trying to get him to give a one-sentence explanation of relativity.

A Colorado banker wrote that he had already gotten responses from twenty-four Nobel Prize winners to the question of whether they believed in God, and he asked Einstein to reply as well. "I cannot conceive of a personal God who would directly influence the actions of individuals or would sit in judgment on creatures of his own creation," Einstein scribbled on the letter.

> I cannot do this in spite of the fact that mechanistic causality has, to a certain extent, been placed in doubt by modern science. My religiosity consists of a humble admiration of the infinitely superior spirit that reveals itself in the little that we can comprehend about the knowable world. That deeply emotional conviction of the

presence of a superior reasoning power, which is revealed in the incomprehensible universe, forms my idea of God.

A little girl in the sixth grade of a Sunday school in New York posed the question in a slightly different form. "Do scientists pray?" she asked. Einstein took her seriously. "Scientific research is based on the idea that everything that takes place is determined by laws of nature, and this holds for the actions of people," he explained. "For this reason, a scientist will hardly be inclined to believe that events could be influenced by a prayer, i.e., by a wish addressed to a supernatural Being."

That did not mean, however, there was no Almighty, no spirit larger than ourselves. As he went on to explain to the young girl:

Everyone who is seriously involved in the pursuit of science becomes convinced that a spirit is manifest in the laws of the Universe—a spirit vastly superior to that of man, and one in the face of which we with our modest powers must feel humble. In this way the pursuit of science leads to a religious feeling of a special sort, which is indeed quite different from the religiosity of someone more naïve.

For some, only a clear belief in a personal God who controlled our daily lives qualified as a satisfactory answer, and Einstein's ideas about an impersonal cosmic spirit, as well as his theories of relativity, deserved to be labeled for what they were. "I very seriously doubt that Einstein himself really knows what he is driving at," Boston's Cardinal William Henry O'Connell said. But one thing seemed clear. It was godless. "The outcome of this doubt and befogged speculation about time and space is a cloak beneath which hides the ghastly apparition of atheism."

This public blast from a cardinal prompted the noted Orthodox Jewish leader in New York Rabbi Herbert S. Goldstein to send a very direct telegram: DO YOU BELIEVE IN GOD? STOP. ANSWER PAID. 50 WORDS. Einstein used only about half his allotted number of words. It became the most famous version of an answer he gave often: I BELIEVE IN SPINOZA'S

GOD, WHO REVEALS HIMSELF IN THE LAWFUL HARMONY OF ALL THAT
EXISTS, BUT NOT IN A GOD WHO CONCERNS HIMSELF WITH THE FATE
AND THE DOINGS OF MANKIND.

Einstein's response was not comforting to everyone. Some religious
Jews, for example, noted that Spinoza had been excommunicated from
the Jewish community of Amsterdam for holding these beliefs, and he
had also been condemned by the Catholic Church for good measure.
"Cardinal O'Connell would have done well had he not attacked the Einstein theory," said one Bronx rabbi. "Einstein would have done better had
he not proclaimed his nonbelief in a God who is concerned with fates
and actions of individuals. Both have handed down dicta outside their
jurisdiction."

Nevertheless, most people were satisfied, whether they fully agreed or
not, because they could appreciate what he was saying. The idea of an
impersonal God, whose hand is reflected in the glory of creation but who
does not meddle in daily existence, is part of a respectable tradition in
both Europe and America. It is to be found in some of Einstein's favorite
philosophers, and it generally accords with the religious beliefs of many
of America's founders, such as Jefferson and Franklin.

Some religious believers dismiss Einstein's frequent invocations of
God as a mere figure of speech. So do some nonbelievers. There were
many phrases he used, some of them playful, ranging from *der Herrgott*
(the Lord God) to *der Alte* (the Old One). But it was not Einstein's style
to speak disingenuously in order to appear to conform. In fact, just the
opposite. So we should do him the honor of taking him at his word when
he insists, repeatedly, that these oft-used phrases were not merely a
semantic way of disguising that he was actually an atheist.

Throughout his life, Einstein was consistent in deflecting the charge
that he was an atheist. "There are people who say there is no God," he
told a friend. "But what makes me really angry is that they quote me for
support of such views."

Unlike Sigmund Freud or Bertrand Russell or George Bernard Shaw,
Einstein never felt the urge to denigrate those who believed in God;
instead, he tended to denigrate atheists. "What separates me from most

so-called atheists is a feeling of utter humility toward the unattainable secrets of the harmony of the cosmos," he explained.

In fact, Einstein tended to be more critical of the debunkers, who seemed to lack humility or a sense of awe, than of the faithful. "The fanatical atheists," he wrote in a letter, "are like slaves who are still feeling the weight of their chains which they have thrown off after hard struggle. They are creatures who—in their grudge against traditional religion as the 'opium of the masses'—cannot hear the music of the spheres."

Einstein would later engage in an exchange on this topic with a U.S. Navy ensign he had never met. Was it true, the sailor asked, that Einstein had been converted by a Jesuit priest into believing in God? That was absurd, Einstein replied. He went on to say that he considered the belief in a God who was a fatherlike figure to be the result of "childish analogies." Would Einstein permit him, the sailor asked, to quote his reply in his debates against his more religious shipmates? Einstein warned him not to oversimplify. "You may call me an agnostic, but I do not share the crusading spirit of the professional atheist whose fervor is mostly due to a painful act of liberation from the fetters of religious indoctrination received in youth," he explained. "I prefer the attitude of humility corresponding to the weakness of our intellectual understanding of nature and of our own being."

How did this religious instinct relate to his science? For Einstein, the beauty of his faith was that it informed and inspired, rather than conflicted with, his scientific work. "The cosmic religious feeling," he said, "is the strongest and noblest motive for scientific research."

Einstein later explained his view of the relationship between science and religion at a conference on that topic at the Union Theological Seminary in New York. The realm of science, he said, was to ascertain what was the case, but not evaluate human thoughts and actions about what *should* be the case. Religion had the reverse mandate. Yet the endeavors worked together at times. "Science can be created only by those who are thoroughly imbued with the aspiration toward truth and understanding," he said. "This source of feeling, however, springs from the sphere of religion."

The talk got front-page news coverage, and his pithy conclusion became famous. "The situation may be expressed by an image: science without religion is lame, religion without science is blind."

But there was one religious concept, Einstein went on to say, that science could not accept: a deity who could meddle at whim in the events of his creation or in the lives of his creatures. "The main source of the present-day conflicts between the spheres of religion and of science lies in this concept of a personal God," he argued. Scientists aim to uncover the immutable laws that govern reality, and in doing so they must reject the notion that divine will, or for that matter human will, plays a role that would violate this cosmic causality.

This belief in causal determinism, which was inherent in Einstein's scientific outlook, conflicted not only with the concept of a personal God. It was also, at least in Einstein's mind, incompatible with human free will. Although he was a deeply moral man, his belief in strict determinism made it difficult for him to accept the idea of moral choice and individual responsibility that is at the heart of most ethical systems.

Jewish as well as Christian theologians have generally believed that people have this free will and are responsible for their actions. They are even free to choose, as happens in the Bible, to disobey God's commandments, despite the fact that this seems to conflict with a belief that God is all-knowing and all-powerful.

Einstein, on the other hand, believed—as did Spinoza—that a person's actions were just as determined as that of a billiard ball, planet, or star. "Human beings in their thinking, feeling and acting are not free but are as causally bound as the stars in their motions," Einstein declared in a statement to a Spinoza Society in 1932.

Human actions are determined, beyond their control, by both physical and psychological laws, he believed. It was a concept he drew also from his reading of Schopenhauer, to whom he attributed, in his 1930 "What I Believe" credo, a maxim along those lines:

> I do not at all believe in free will in the philosophical sense. Everybody acts not only under external compulsion but also in accordance with inner necessity. Schopenhauer's saying, "A man can do as he wills, but not will as he wills," has been a real inspiration to

me since my youth; it has been a continual consolation in the face of life's hardships, my own and others', and an unfailing wellspring of tolerance.

Do you believe, Einstein was once asked, that humans are free agents? "No, I am a determinist," he replied. "Everything is determined, the beginning as well as the end, by forces over which we have no control. It is determined for the insect as well as for the star. Human beings, vegetables, or cosmic dust, we all dance to a mysterious tune, intoned in the distance by an invisible player."

This attitude appalled some friends such as Max Born, who thought it completely undermined the foundations of human morality. "I cannot understand how you can combine an entirely mechanistic universe with the freedom of the ethical individual," he wrote Einstein. "To me a deterministic world is quite abhorrent. Maybe you are right, and the world is that way, as you say. But at the moment it does not really look like it in physics—and even less so in the rest of the world."

For Born, quantum uncertainty provided an escape from this dilemma. Like some philosophers of the time, he latched on to the indeterminacy that was inherent in quantum mechanics to resolve "the discrepancy between ethical freedom and strict natural laws."

Born explained the issue to his high-strung wife, Hedwig, who was always eager to debate Einstein. She told Einstein that, like him, she was "unable to believe in a 'dice-playing' God." In other words, unlike her husband, she rejected quantum mechanics' view that the universe was based on uncertainties and probabilities. But, she added, "nor am I able to imagine that you believe—as Max has told me—that your 'complete rule of law' means that everything is predetermined, for example whether I am going to have my child inoculated." It would mean, she pointed out, the end of all ethics.

In Einstein's philosophy, the way to resolve this issue was to look upon free will as something that was useful, indeed necessary, for a civilized society, because it caused people to take responsibility for their own actions. Acting *as if* people were responsible for their actions would, psychologically and practically, prompt them to act in a more responsible manner. "I am compelled to act as if free will existed," he explained, "because if I wish to live in a civilized society I must act responsibly." He could even hold people responsible for their good or evil, since that was both a pragmatic and sensible approach to life, while still believing intellectually that everyone's actions were predetermined. "I know that philosophically a murderer is not responsible for his crime," he said, "but I prefer not to take tea with him."

In defense of Einstein, it should be noted that philosophers through the ages have struggled, sometimes awkwardly and not very successfully, to reconcile free will with determinism and an all-knowing God. Whether Einstein was more or less adept than others at grappling with this knot, there is one salient fact about him that should be noted: He was able to develop, and to practice, a strong personal morality, at least toward humanity in general if not always toward members of his family, that was not hampered by all these irresolvable philosophical speculations. "The most important human endeavor is the striving for morality in our actions," he wrote a Brooklyn minister. "Our inner balance and even our existence depend on it. Only morality in our actions can give beauty and dignity to life."

The foundation of that morality, he believed, was rising above the "merely personal" to live in a way that benefited humanity. There were times when he could be callous to those closest to him, which shows that, like the rest of us humans, he had flaws. Yet more than most people, he dedicated himself honestly and sometimes courageously to actions that he felt transcended selfish desires in order to help human progress and the preservation of individual freedoms.

For some people, miracles serve as evidence of God's existence. For Einstein it was the absence of miracles that reflected divine providence. The fact that the world was comprehensible, that it followed laws, was worthy of awe.

Einstein considered this feeling of reverence, this cosmic religion, to be the wellspring of all true art and science. It was what guided him. "When I am judging a theory," he said, "I ask myself whether, if I were God, I would have arranged the world in such a way." It is also what graced him with his beautiful mix of confidence and awe. He was a rebel who was suffused with reverence, and that was how an imaginative, impertinent patent clerk became the mind reader of the Creator of the cosmos.

Creative Thinker

Wired magazine wanted an essay on Einstein when my book came out in 2007. I used the opportunity to explore the relationship of Einstein's rebelliousness to his creativity. A key to his success was his willingness to question authority and think in unconventional ways. There is a caveat, which I stress to people, young and old, who tell me that they are like Einstein in that they question authority and think out of the box. Einstein knew what was in the box before he started thinking outside it. It's important to understand fully what you are rebelling against before you take too much pride in being a rebel.

Albert Einstein, as every kid knows, was a smart guy. But as we discover when we get older, smart gets you only so far. It's worth remembering, especially now, that what made Einstein special was his impertinence, his nonconformity, and his distaste for dogma.

At a time when the United States, worried about competition from China, is again emphasizing math and science education, Einstein's genius reminds us that a society's competitive advantage comes not from teaching the multiplication or periodic tables but from nurturing rebels. Grinds have their place, but unruly geeks change the world. And, as recent research into Einstein's personal papers shows, there's no better glimpse into his offbeat creativity than the way he puzzled out the special theory of relativity.

As a child, Einstein was slow to speak. This, combined with his cheeky defiance of authority and his distaste for rote learning, led one schoolmaster to send him packing and another to dismiss him as a lazy dog.

Einstein alienated so many professors that he was unable to earn a doctorate, much less land an academic job. At the age of twenty-six, he was working as a third-class examiner at the Swiss patent office in Bern. As it happens, the patent office provided a better launchpad than any university. On his way to work, Einstein would see trains rolling past the city's twelfth-century clock tower, which by then had been synchronized with clocks in the nearby train station, and many of the patent applications he was reviewing proposed using signals traveling at the speed of light to sync up even more distant clocks.

By May 1905, Einstein was convinced of two postulates: First, that the laws of physics, including Maxwell's equations for electromagnetic waves, were the same for all frames of reference in constant-velocity motion relative to one another, so there was no way to know whether one observer was at rest and the other in motion. Second, that the speed of light was always the same, regardless of the motion of the source.

Yet the two ideas were "seemingly incompatible." He visualized a light beam racing down a railway track. The postulates, taken together, would mean that a man standing next to the track would see the light beam race by him at the same speed that a woman sitting in a railway car would see it—whether she was zooming toward the beam's source or away from it.

Then something delightful happened. Einstein went to visit his best friend, Michele Besso, a brilliant but unfocused engineer he had recruited to come work at the patent office. Einstein told Besso about the dilemma. "I'm going to give it up," he said. But as they walked to work, Einstein took one of the most elegant imaginative leaps in the history of physics. "I suddenly understood the key to the problem," he later recalled. "Time cannot be absolutely defined."

Imagine lightning striking at both ends of a long, fast-moving train. If the light from each strike reaches a person standing on the embankment at the midpoint of the train at the same moment, he would say the strikes happened at the same time. But a person riding inside the train at its midpoint would be a bit closer to the front lightning strike by the time the light arrived; she would say that the light from the front strike reached her first, so the strikes were not simultaneous.

From that sprang Einstein's special theory of relativity. Two events that are simultaneous in one reference frame may not be simultaneous for someone moving relative to that reference frame. Therefore, time is relative depending on your state of motion. Try to catch up with a light beam and, though the speed of light remains constant, time slows down.

Other scientists had come close to his insight, but they were too confined by the dogmas of the day. Einstein alone was impertinent enough
to discard the notion of absolute time, one of the sacred tenets of classical physics since Newton. "Imagination is more important than knowledge," Einstein later said. Indeed, if we are ever going to unravel the
further mysteries of dark matter, come up with a unified theory, or discover the true nature of energy, we should carve that proclamation above
all of our blackboards.

A New Way to View Science

I wanted to use the publication of my Einstein book in 2007 as an opportunity to encourage ordinary folks, usually intimidated by science, to try to appreciate its magic and beauty. We want our kids to be taught science, but some folks allow themselves to be intimidated at the prospect of learning it themselves. I used an essay in USA Today to make my case.

Sometimes when I tell people I've written a biography of Albert Einstein, they snap their heads as if to say they've never understood science. They may feel that the Founding Fathers are easily comprehensible, and even so is Shakespeare (which he isn't), but that Einstein is completely intimidating.

Einstein has come to personify the perception that modern physics is something ordinary folks can't try to appreciate. Indeed, scientific illiteracy is sometimes worn as a badge of pride. Most educated people would be ashamed to admit they don't know the difference between Hamlet and King Lear, but they might jovially brag that they don't know a gene from a chromosome or relativity theory from the uncertainty principle. When people tell me that they think science is too difficult but that they love *Hamlet,* I sometimes ask them: But does Hamlet love Ophelia? They pause and say that's very complicated. I agree. Both Shakespeare and Einstein can both be complicated at times, but we should enjoy wrestling with their complexities as well as admiring the beauty and creativity of their work.

We are now engaged in one of our periodic spasms of trying to make sure that our kids learn science and math. Congress this year is expected to reauthorize the No Child Left Behind law, and fear that we will lose our ability to compete globally has prompted something called the America Competes Act, which would fund proposals including a science policy summit, new research projects, summer internships and prize programs for high school students, and teacher-training programs.

None of these education endeavors, however, will truly change things unless we revise the way that we grownups view science. Many nonscientists, and I daresay most of our politicians, balk at understanding and celebrating science themselves. To the extent that we allow ourselves to be intimidated by math and science, we are less likely to convey to our kids that it can be a creative and imaginative pursuit, no less so than poetry and music.

Einstein was a wonderfully creative and imaginative thinker. He visualized vivid mental pictures that make his theories come alive. Time varies depending on your motion? The fabric of space is warped by massive objects? Gravity can bend light? Light is both a wave and a stream of particles? His theories contain a wondrous mix of Huh? and Wow! that can capture the public imagination.

He devised most of them by using thought experiments—that's what you and I would call daydreaming, but if you're Einstein you get to call it a thought experiment. The pictures he visualized can be used, with no math necessary, to give a glimpse of the creativity at the heart of true genius.

As a sixteen-year-old, for example, Einstein looked at James Maxwell's equations describing electromagnetic waves and tried to imagine what they'd look like to a boy riding alongside a light beam. If he caught up, the waves should appear stationary relative to him, but Maxwell's equations didn't allow for that. Einstein wandered around with sweating palms, anxious about this for months, he recalled, not the sort of thing that was causing most of us sweaty palms at sixteen.

Ten years later, he solved the problem with another thought experiment, which can be described by imagining lightning striking both ends of a fast-moving train. To a person watching from an embankment nearby, the strikes might seem simultaneous. But to a person in the train at the midpoint, the strike in front would seem to come first because he had moved in that direction a bit by the time the light from the strikes reached him. So people in different states of motion will have different views of simultaneity, and thus of time. For a boy trying to catch up with a light beam, Maxwell's equations would still hold true, but time would slow down. Okay, it's not obvious, but at least it's something we can visualize.

Likewise, when he was trying to turn this special theory of relativity into a general theory that included accelerated motion, he used a thought experiment about being in an enclosed elevator. If it was in free fall, you'd feel weightless. If it was accelerating upward in deep space where there was no gravity, your feet would be pressed to the floor and a coin pulled from your pocket would drop in a way that was indistinguishable from the effects of gravity.

From this he came up with a description of gravity that applied the theory of relativity to accelerated motion.

A popular feel for science should, if possible, be restored, given the needs of the twenty-first century. We should teach it as a creative endeavor, involving visual and imaginative thinking, rather than as the crunching of numbers and the memorization of laws. More broadly, we should embrace as a society an appreciation for the beauty and creativity of science. What science teaches us, very importantly, is the correlation between factual evidence and general theories, something well illustrated in Einstein's life.

Science also helps us remain in touch with that childlike capacity for wonder, about such ordinary things as falling apples and elevators, which characterizes Einstein and other great theorists.

Einstein and the Bomb

There are two popular conceptions about Einstein and the atomic bomb. The first is that he wrote the recipe for it, E=mc², and helped to design it. The other is that he had almost nothing to do with it, as he once insisted to an interviewer, other than signing a letter to President Franklin Roosevelt. Neither of these views is true. In my research, I was able to find the letter drafts and notes leading up to the writing of the Roosevelt letter, and Einstein's involvement was substantial. But for reasons that seem today ironic, he was not directly a part of the Manhattan Project. I described this in an essay for Discover *magazine in 2008.*

In the popular imagination, Albert Einstein is associated with the making of the atomic bomb. We recall that he was the one who sent a letter to President Franklin Roosevelt warning that a controlled atomic chain reaction could lead to the construction of weapons, and we dimly discern his equation relating energy to mass when we picture the resulting mushroom cloud. A few months after the weapon was used against Japan in August of 1945, *Time* magazine put him on its cover with an explosion mushrooming behind him that had $E=mc^2$ emblazoned on it. In a story that was overseen by an editor named Whittaker Chambers, the magazine noted with its typical prose flair from the period:

> There will be dimly discernible, to those who are interested in cause & effect in history, the features of a shy, almost saintly, child-like little man with the soft brown eyes, the drooping facial lines of a world-weary hound, and hair like an aurora borealis . . . Albert Einstein did not work directly on the atom bomb. But Einstein was the father of the bomb in two important ways: 1) it was his

initiative which started U.S. bomb research; 2) it was his equation $(E = mc^2)$ which made the atomic bomb theoretically possible.

Newsweek, likewise, did a cover on him, with the headline "The Man Who Started It All." It was a perception that was fostered by the U.S. government. It released an official history of the atomic bomb project, which Princeton physics professor Henry DeWolf Smyth had been secretly compiling for months, that assigned great weight to the letter Einstein had written to Roosevelt.

All of this troubled Einstein. "Had I known that the Germans would not succeed in producing an atomic bomb," he told *Newsweek,* "I never would have lifted a finger." And he pointed out, correctly, that he had never actually worked on the bomb project. As he claimed to a Japanese newspaper, "My participation in the production of the atom bomb consisted in a single act: I signed a letter to President Roosevelt." In fact, as the archives show, Einstein did not merely sign the letter. He was deeply involved in writing it, revising it, and deciding how to get it to Roosevelt.

The tale begins with Leó Szilárd, a charming and slightly eccentric Hungarian physicist, who was an old friend of Einstein's. While living in Berlin in the 1920s, they had collaborated on the development of a new type of refrigerator, which they patented but were unable to market successfully. After Szilárd fled the Nazis, he made his way to England and then New York, where he worked at Columbia University on ways to create a nuclear chain reaction, an idea he had conceived while waiting at a stoplight in London a few years earlier. When he heard of the discovery of fission using uranium, Szilárd realized that element might be used to produce this phenomenon.

Szilárd discussed this possibility with his friend Eugene Wigner, another refugee physicist from Budapest, and they began to worry that the Germans might try to buy up the uranium supplies of the Congo, which was then a colony of Belgium. But how, they asked themselves, could two Hungarian refugees in America find a way to warn the Belgians? Then Szilárd recalled that Einstein happened to be friends with that country's queen mother.

"We knew that Einstein was somewhere on Long Island but we didn't know precisely where," Szilárd recalled. So he phoned Einstein's Princeton office and was told he was renting the house of a man named Dr. Moore in the village of Peconic. On Sunday, July 16, 1939, they embarked on their mission with Wigner at the wheel (Szilárd, like Einstein, did not drive).

But when they arrived, they couldn't find the house, and nobody seemed to know who Dr. Moore was. Just as they were ready to give up, Szilárd saw a young boy standing by the curb. "Do you, by any chance, know where Professor Einstein lives?" Like most people in town, even those who had no idea who Dr. Moore was, the boy did, and he led them up to a cottage near the end of Old Grove Road, where they found Einstein lost in thought.

Sitting around a bare wooden table on the porch of the sparsely furnished cottage, Szilárd explained the process of how an explosive chain reaction could be produced in uranium layered with graphite by the neutrons released from nuclear fission. "I never thought of that!" Einstein interjected. He asked a few questions, went over the process for fifteen minutes, and then quickly grasped the implications. Instead of writing the queen mother, Einstein suggested, perhaps they should write a Belgian minister he knew.

Wigner, showing some sensible propriety, suggested that perhaps three refugees should not be writing a foreign government about secret security matters without consulting with the State Department. In which case, they decided, perhaps the proper channel was a letter from Einstein (who was the only one of them famous enough to be heeded) to the Belgian ambassador, with a cover letter to the State Department. With that tentative plan in mind, Einstein dictated a draft in German. After he returned home, Wigner translated it, gave it to his secretary to be typed, and then sent it to Szilárd.

A few days later, a friend arranged for Szilárd to talk to Alexander Sachs, an economist at Lehman Brothers and a friend of President Roosevelt's. Showing a bit more savvy than the three theoretical physicists, Sachs insisted that the letter should go right to the White House, and he offered to hand deliver it.

It was the first time Szilárd had met Sachs, but his bold plan was appealing. "It could not do any harm to try this way," he wrote Einstein. Einstein wrote back asking Szilárd to come back out to Peconic so they could revise the letter. By that point Wigner had gone to California for a visit. So Szilárd enlisted, as driver and scientific sidekick, Edward Teller, another friend from the amazing group of Hungarian refugees who were theoretical physicists.

Szilárd brought with him the original draft from two weeks earlier, but Einstein realized that they were now planning a letter that was far more momentous than one asking Belgian ministers to be careful about Congolese uranium exports. The world's most famous scientist was about to tell the president of the United States that he should begin contemplating a weapon of almost unimaginable impact. "Einstein dictated a letter in German," Szilárd recalled, "which Teller took down, and I used this German text as a guide in preparing two drafts of a letter to the President."

According to Teller's notes, Einstein's dictated draft raised not only the question of Congo's uranium, it also explained the possibility of chain reactions, suggested that a new type of bomb could result, and urged the president to set up formal contact with physicists working on this topic. Szilárd then prepared and sent back to Einstein a forty-five-line version and a twenty-five-line one—both dated August 2, 1939—"and left it up to Einstein to choose which he liked best." Einstein signed them both in a small scrawl.

The longer version, which is the one that eventually reached Roosevelt, read in part:

> *Sir:*
>
> *Some recent work by E. Fermi and L. Szilárd, which has been communicated to me in a manuscript, leads me to expect that the element uranium may be turned into a new and important source of energy in the immediate future. Certain aspects of this situation which has arisen seem to call for watchfulness and, if necessary, quick action on the part of the Administration. I believe therefore that it is my duty to bring to your attention the following facts and recommendations:*

*It may become possible to set up a nuclear chain reaction in a large
mass of uranium, by which vast amounts of power and large quantities
of new radium-like elements would be generated. Now it appears almost
certain that this could be achieved in the immediate future.*

*This new phenomenon would also lead to the construction of bombs,
and it is conceivable—though much less certain—that extremely
powerful bombs of a new type may thus be constructed.*

Once the letter had been written and signed, they still had to figure
out who could best get it into the hands of President Roosevelt. Einstein was unsure about Sachs. They considered, instead, financier Bernard
Baruch and MIT president Karl Compton.

More amazingly, when Szilárd sent back the typed version of the letter, he suggested that they use as their intermediary Charles Lindbergh,
whose solo transatlantic flight twelve years earlier had made him a celebrity. All three of the refugee Jews were apparently unaware that the avia-
tor had been spending time in Germany, was decorated the year before
by the Nazi Hermann Göring with that nation's medal of honor, and was
becoming an isolationist and a Roosevelt antagonist.

Einstein had briefly met Lindbergh a few years earlier in New York,
so he wrote a note of introduction, which he included when he returned
the signed letters to Szilárd. "I would like to ask you to do me a favor of
receiving my friend Dr. Szilárd and think very carefully about what he
will tell you," Einstein wrote to Lindbergh. "To one who is outside of
science the matter he will bring up may seem fantastic. However, you will
certainly become convinced that a possibility is presented here which has
to be very carefully watched in the public interest."

Lindbergh did not respond, so Szilárd wrote him a reminder letter on
September 13, again asking for a meeting. Two days later, they realized
how clueless they had been when Lindbergh gave a nationwide radio
address. It was a clarion call for isolationism. "The destiny of this country
does not call for our involvement in European wars," Lindbergh began.
Interwoven were hints of Lindbergh's pro-German sympathies and even
some anti-Semitic implications about Jewish ownership of the media.
"We must ask who owns and influences the newspaper, the news picture,

and the radio station," he said. "If our people know the truth, our country is not likely to enter the war."

Szilárd's next letter to Einstein stated the obvious. "Lindbergh is not our man," he wrote.

Their other hope was Alexander Sachs, who had been given the formal letter to Roosevelt that Einstein signed. Even though it was obviously of enormous importance, Sachs was not able to find the opportunity to deliver it for almost two months.

By then, events had turned what was an important letter into an urgent one. At the end of August 1939, the Nazis and Soviets stunned the world by signing their war-alliance pact and proceeded to carve up Poland. That prompted Britain and France to declare war.

Szilárd went to see Sachs in late September and was horrified to discover that he still had not been able to schedule an appointment with Roosevelt. "There is a distinct possibility Sachs will be of no use to us," Szilárd wrote Einstein. "Wigner and I have decided to accord him ten days grace." Sachs barely made the deadline. On the afternoon of Wednesday, October 11, he was ushered into the Oval Office carrying Einstein's letter, Szilárd's memo, and an eight-hundred-word summary he had written on his own.

The president greeted him jovially. "Alex, what are you up to?"

Sachs worried that if he simply left Einstein's letter and the other papers with Roosevelt, they might be glanced at and then pushed aside. The only reliable way to deliver them, he decided, was to read them aloud. Standing in front of the president's desk, he read his summation of Einstein's letter and parts of Szilárd's memo.

"Alex, what you are after is to see that the Nazis don't blow us up," the president said.

"Precisely," Sachs replied.

Roosevelt called in his personal assistant. "This requires action," he declared.

The following week, Einstein received a polite and formal thank-you letter from the president. "I have convened a board," Roosevelt wrote, "to thoroughly investigate the possibilities of your suggestion regarding the element of uranium."

Einstein never worked directly on the bomb project. J. Edgar Hoover, who was the director of the FBI even back then, wrote a letter to General Sherman Miles, who initially organized the efforts, that described Einstein's pacifist activities and suggested that he was a security risk. Einstein did play a smaller role. He was asked by Vannevar Bush, one of the scientific overseers, to help on a specific problem involving the separation of isotopes that shared chemical traits. Einstein was happy to comply. Drawing on his old expertise in osmosis and diffusion, he worked on a process of gaseous diffusion in which uranium was converted into a gas and forced through filters.

The scientists who received Einstein's report were impressed, and they discussed it with Vannevar Bush. But in order for him to be more useful, they said, he should be given more information about how the isotope separation fit in with other parts of the bomb-making challenge.

Bush refused. He knew that Einstein didn't have and couldn't get the necessary security clearance. "I wish very much that I could place the whole thing before him and take him fully into confidence," Bush wrote, "but this is utterly impossible in view of the attitude of people here in Washington who have studied his whole history."

Thus it was that the scientist who had explained the need for a bomb-making project was considered too risky to be told about it.

Einstein's Final Quest

Charlotte Hays, who edits a magazine for the Templeton Foundation, is an old friend from New Orleans. When she wanted me to contribute to an issue they were doing in 2009 celebrating the virtue of grit and perseverance, I agreed to write about an aspect of Einstein's career rarely covered: his dogged but futile quest for a unified field theory tying together all the forces of nature.

In the later years of his life, after he had fled Nazi Germany in 1933 at age fifty-four and moved to Princeton, New Jersey, Albert Einstein focused his scientific energies on what would turn out to be a futile quest: the search for a unified field theory that would tie together the forces of gravity and electromagnetism with the subatomic forces described by quantum theory. He had befriended a fellow refugee physicist, Leopold Infeld, who occasionally tried to help in that effort. Most of Einstein's colleagues were mildly bemused by his stubbornness, but Infeld admired what he saw as yet another example of the determination that, over the decades, had made Einstein so great. "His tenacity in sticking to a problem for years, in returning to the problem again and again—this is the characteristic feature of Einstein's genius," he said.

Was Infeld right? Was tenacity—grit—one of the characteristic features of Einstein's genius? Yes. Ever since he was a young boy, he had been blessed with that trait. When he was six, his father had given him a compass. Einstein spent days and nights twisting and turning it, marveling at how the needle would twitch and point north even though nothing seemed to be physically touching it. Most of us remember getting a compass when we were kids and being fascinated by it for a while, at least for a few minutes until we found something else intriguing—oh, look, a dead bird!—and promptly quit puzzling about the compass. Unlike most of us, Einstein remained fascinated by the mystery and magic of force fields, and how to relate electromagnetic fields to gravitational fields, for the rest of his life. Even on his deathbed, he was scribbling field equations that he hoped would lead to a unified theory.

This tenacity was most notably on display during his long quest, which culminated in 1915, to come up with a general theory of relativity. Perhaps the most elegant theory in the history of science, it was the product of a decade of solitary persistence during which Einstein wove together the laws of space, time, and motion based on a simple yet amazing insight that gravity and acceleration produced equivalent effects.

In his quest for a unified field theory, Einstein was not aided by a physical insight such as the equivalence of gravity and acceleration. Instead, he was driven by his discomfort at how quantum theory, which primarily focuses on activities in the subatomic realm, had evolved into a new view of mechanics in which things can happen by chance, in which probabilities govern events, and in which there is an inherent uncertainty in nature—rather than a fixed reality—that makes it impossible to know the position and momentum of a particle at the same instant.

To Einstein, this simply did not smell true. The ultimate goal of physics, he repeatedly said, was to discover the laws that strictly determined causes and effects. He could not believe that things happened by chance, by probability, like some cosmic game of dice. This led to one of Einstein's most famous quotes. "Quantum mechanics is certainly imposing," he said. "But an inner voice tells me that it is not yet the real thing. The theory says a lot, but it does not really bring us any closer to the secrets of the Old One. I, at any rate, am convinced that He does not play dice." He repeated this declaration that "God would not play dice with the universe" so often that at one conference his colleague Niels Bohr was moved to exclaim, with mock exasperation, "Einstein, please quit telling God what to do!"

Einstein hoped that a unified field theory would unite the various forces of nature in a way that would explain away what seemed like the uncertainties and probabilities of quantum mechanics. Even though the vast majority of the physics priesthood considered this quest to be quixotic, there were usually one or two younger physicists in Princeton willing to assist him. One of them, Ernst Straus, remembers working on an approach that Einstein pursued with astonishing grit and determination for almost two years. Then one evening, Straus found that their equations led to some conclusions that clearly could not be true. The next day, he and Einstein explored the issue from all angles, but they could not avoid the disappointing result. So they went home early. Straus was dejected, and he assumed that Einstein would be even more so. To his surprise, Einstein was as eager and excited as ever the next day, and he proposed yet another approach they could take. "This was the start of an entirely new theory, also relegated to the trash heap after a half year's work and mourned no longer than its predecessor," Straus recalls.

Einstein's quest was driven by his belief that mathematical simplicity was a feature of nature's handiwork. Every now and then, when a particularly elegant formulation cropped up, he would exult to Straus, "This is so simple God could not have passed it up."

Enthusiastic letters to friends poured forth from Princeton about the progress of his crusade against the quantum theorists who seemed wedded to probabilities and averse to believing in an underlying reality. "I am working with my young people on an extremely interesting theory with which I hope to defeat modern proponents of mysticism and probability and their aversion to the notion of reality in the domain of physics," he wrote a longtime colleague in 1938.

Occasionally Einstein's pursuit made headlines. "Soaring over a hitherto unscaled mathematical mountain-top, Dr. Albert Einstein, climber of cosmic Alps, reports having sighted a new pattern in the structure of space and matter," the distinguished *New York Times* science reporter William Laurence reported in a page-one article in 1935. And again, the same writer and the same paper reported on page one in 1939:

Albert Einstein revealed today that after twenty years of unremitting search for a law that would explain the mechanism of the cosmos in its entirety, reaching out from the stars and galaxies in the vastness of infinite space down to the mysteries within the heart of the infinitesimal atom, he has at last arrived within sight of what he hopes may be the "Promised Land of Knowledge," holding what may be the master key to the riddle of creation.

The triumphs in Einstein's salad days had come partly from having an instinct that could sniff out underlying physical realities. He could intuitively sense the implications of the relativity of all motion, or the constancy of the speed of light, or the equivalence of gravitational and inertial mass. Now, in his quest for a unified theory, there seemed to be a lot of mathematical equations but very few fundamental physical insights guiding him. "In his earlier search for the general theory, Einstein had been guided by his principle of equivalence linking gravitation with acceleration," said Banesh Hoffmann, a Princeton collaborator. "Where were the comparable guiding principles that could lead to the construction of a unified field theory? No one knew. Not even Einstein. Thus the search was not so much a search as a groping in the gloom of a mathematical jungle inadequately lit by physical intuition."

After a while, the optimistic headlines and letters stopped emanating from Princeton, and Einstein publicly admitted that he was, at least for the time being, stymied. "I am not as optimistic," he told the *New York Times*. For years the paper had regularly headlined each of Einstein's purported breakthroughs toward a unified theory, but now its headline read "Einstein Baffled by Cosmos Riddle."

So why did he persevere? Deep inside, the disjunctures and dualities that other physicists had learned to accept—different field theories for gravity and electromagnetism, distinctions between particles and fields—deeply discomforted him. Simplicity and unity, he intuitively believed, were hallmarks of the Old One's handiwork. He simply could not "accept the view that events in nature are analogous to a game of chance."

And so he continued his quest. Even if he failed to find a unified theory, he felt that the effort would be meaningful. "It is open to every man to choose the direction of his striving," he explained, "and every man may take comfort from the fine saying that the search for truth is more precious than its possession."

He continued throughout the 1940s to try one mathematical approach after another, stubbornly plowing ahead with new formulas every time an old one had to be discarded. Like modern string theorists are doing today, he conjured up the possibility of a universe that had five, six, or even more dimensions. Another strategy involved "bivector fields," which led him to abandon temporarily the idea that particles existed in only one location in space and time. A third strategy, which he pursued for an entire decade until his death, involved a tensor calculus that produced a metric with sixteen quantities that he hoped—to no avail—might supply what was needed to describe both gravity and electromagnetism in one field theory.

Einstein sent early versions of this work to his longtime colleague Erwin Schrödinger, who appreciated his quest more than quantum theorists such as Wolfgang Pauli did. "I am sending them to nobody else, because you are the only person known to me who is not wearing blinders in regard to the fundamental questions in our science," Einstein wrote. "Pauli stuck his tongue out at me when I told him about it."

"You are after big game," Schrödinger replied. But Einstein soon began to realize that the gossamer theories he was spinning were mathematically elegant but never seemed to relate to anything physical. "Inwardly I am not so certain as I previously asserted," he confessed to Schrödinger a few months later. "We have squandered a lot of time on this, and the result looks like a gift from the devil's grandmother."

Yet still he soldiered on. When a new edition of his book *The Meaning of Relativity* was being prepared in 1949, he added the latest version of the paper he had shown Schrödinger, "Generalization of Gravitation Theory," as an appendix. The *New York Times* reprinted an entire page of complex equations from the manuscript along with a front-page story headlined "New Einstein Theory Gives a Master Key to Universe; Scientist, After 30 Years' Work, Evolves Concept That Promises to Bridge Gap Between the Star and the Atom."

Unfortunately, Einstein soon realized that it still wasn't right. During the six weeks between when he submitted the chapter and it went to the printer, he had second thoughts and revised it yet again. In fact, he continued to revise the theory repeatedly, year after year, remaining determined despite each setback.

On one level it is fair to say that his search was futile, that all of his grit and determination amounted to naught. And if it turns out a century from now that there is indeed no unified theory to be found, the quest will also look misconceived. But Einstein never regretted his dedication to it. When a colleague asked him one day why he was spending—perhaps squandering—his time in this lonely endeavor, he replied that even if the chance of finding a unified theory was small, the attempt was worthy. He had already made his name, he noted. His position was secure, and he could afford to take the risk and expend the time. A younger theorist, however, could not take such a risk, since he might thus sacrifice a promising career. So it was, Einstein said, his duty to do it.

Even during the final year of his life, Einstein continued to amble to his office in Princeton to wrestle with his equations and try to push them a little closer toward the receding horizon of a unified field theory. He would come in with his new ideas, often clutching equations on scraps of paper he had scribbled the night before, and go over them with his assistant that final year, Bruria Kaufman, a female physicist from Israel.

She would write the new equations on a blackboard and point out problems. Einstein would then try to counter them. Even when they were defeated by the obstacles to a new approach, as they invariably were, Einstein remained optimistic. "Well, we've learned something," he would say as the clock ticked down.

In writing to colleagues who questioned why he pursued so tenaciously what seemed to them like a hopeless quest, Einstein began to apologize for his stubbornness. Nevertheless, he proudly refused to abandon it. "I must seem like an ostrich who forever buries its head in the relativistic sand in order not to face the evil quanta," he wrote Louis de Broglie, another of his colleagues in the long struggle against the uncertainties found in quantum mechanics. He refused to let go of his underlying principle that there must be some unified theory that would dispel such uncertainties. He had discovered general relativity by trusting an underlying principle, and that made him a "fanatic believer" that comparable methods would eventually lead to a unified field theory. "This should explain the ostrich policy," he wryly told de Broglie.

This belief in the certainty of nature's laws became not just a principle but an article of faith as he grew older. And that faith was, for him, religious in nature. As he responded in a letter to a young girl who asked him whether he believed in God: "Everyone who is seriously involved in the pursuit of science becomes convinced that a spirit is manifest in the laws of the Universe—a spirit vastly superior to that of man, and one in the face of which we with our modest powers must feel humble. In this way the pursuit of science leads to a religious feeling of a special sort."

One day in April of 1955, when he was working at his office on yet another set of unified field equations, Einstein began to feel a great pain in his stomach. He had long been plagued by an aneurysm in his abdominal aorta, and it had started to rupture. A group of doctors convened at his home the next day, and they recommended a surgeon who might be able, though it was thought unlikely, to repair the aorta. Einstein refused. "It is tasteless to prolong life artificially," he told his assistant Helen Dukas. "I have done my share, it is time to go. I will do it elegantly."

He was taken to Princeton Hospital, where one of his final requests was for some notepaper and pencils so he could continue to work on his elusive unified field theory. He died shortly after 1 a.m. on April 18, 1955. By his bed were twelve pages of tightly written equations, littered with cross-outs and corrections. To the very end, he struggled to read the mind of the Creator of the cosmos. And the final thing he wrote, before he went to sleep for the last time, was one more line of symbols and numbers that he hoped might get him, and the rest of us, just a little step closer to the spirit manifest in the laws of the universe.

$$u_i{}^n_n\, u_q{}^q{}_k\left(-\frac{16}{9}+\frac{2}{9}-\frac{4}{9}+\frac{2}{9}+\frac{2}{9}+\frac{2}{9}\right)+u_k{}^n_n\,u_{qi}{}^q\left(\frac{4}{9}+\frac{2}{9}-\frac{1}{9}+\frac{2}{9}-\frac{1}{9}\mp\frac{1}{9}\right)$$

6. THE AGE OF TECHNOLOGY

In Search of the Real
Bill Gates

*The digital revolution has elevated, gloriously, the status of geeks—
people with great passions, mental processing agility, and a thirst for
data. Part of the stereotype, which often has some truth to it, is that
their analytic intelligence is not always accompanied by the trappings
of emotional intelligence, such as social skills, empathy, and the ability
to process interpersonal cues. Bill Clinton, for example, has a surplus of
emotional connectivity; I've seen him cast a spell of personal intimacy
with dozens of people in a room sequentially, men as well as women.
He can always (as if performing a parlor trick) remember something
you told him in a previous conversation and lead you to believe he had
been thinking about it ever since. Bill Gates, on the other hand, seemed
to me on the other end of the spectrum when I first got to know him. In
conversation, he loved to drill down analytically on any topic, but he
could seem emotionally distant.*

*In this piece, written in 1997, I set out in search of the real Bill
Gates and found him more personable than I had expected; I think he
has become even more so in the subsequent decade or so. I wrote this
when I was editor of* Time, *partly because I wanted to show, by trying to do one myself, the type of narrative, biographical, highly personal
stories that I thought should be a staple of the magazine. Looking back
on it, I am surprised by his comment near the end that he hoped to be
running Microsoft for another ten years, and then promised to focus as
intensely on giving his money away. He followed that plan precisely.
He has also continued to broaden his outlook and realize that analytic
intelligence is not the most important part of the human mind. As he
said back then, "I don't think that IQ is as fungible as I used to. To succeed, you also have to know how to make choices and how to think more
broadly." And in the ensuing years, he has shown his ability to do that.*

When Bill Gates was in the sixth grade, his parents decided he needed counseling. He was at war with his mother, Mary, an outgoing woman who harbored the belief that he should do what she told him. She would call him to dinner from his basement bedroom, which she had given up trying to make him clean, and he wouldn't respond. "What are you doing?" she once demanded over the intercom.

"I'm thinking," he shouted back.

"You're thinking?"

"Yes, Mom, I'm thinking," he said fiercely. "Have you ever tried thinking?"

The psychologist they sent him to "was a really cool guy," Gates recalls. "He gave me books to read after each session, Freud stuff, and I really got into psychology theory." After a year of sessions and a battery of tests, the counselor reached his conclusion. "You're going to lose," he told Mary. "You had better just adjust to it because there's no use trying to beat him." Mary was strong-willed and intelligent herself, her husband recalls, "but she came around to accepting that it was futile trying to compete with him."

A lot of computer companies have concluded the same. In the twenty-one years since he dropped out of Harvard to start Microsoft, William Henry Gates III, forty-one, has thrashed competitors in the world of desktop operating systems and application software. Now he is attempting the audacious feat of expanding Microsoft from a software company into a media and content company.

In the process he has amassed a fortune worth (as of last Friday) $23.9 billion. The 88 percent rise in Microsoft stock in 1996 meant he made on paper more than $10.9 billion, or about $30 million a day. That makes him the world's richest person, by far. But he's more than that. He has become the Edison and Ford of our age. A technologist turned entrepreneur, he embodies the digital era.

His success stems from his personality: an awesome and at times frightening blend of brilliance, drive, competitiveness, and personal intensity. So, too, does Microsoft's. "The personality of Bill Gates determines the culture of Microsoft," says his intellectual sidekick Nathan

Myhrvold. But though he has become the most famous business celebrity in the world, Gates remains personally elusive to all but a close circle of friends.

Part of what makes him so enigmatic is the nature of his intellect. Wander the Microsoft grounds, press the Bill button in conversation, and hear it described in computer terms: He has "incredible processing power" and "unlimited bandwidth," an agility at "parallel processing" and "multitasking." Watch him at his desk, and you see what they mean. He works on two computers, one with four frames that sequence data streaming in from the Internet, the other handling the hundreds of e-mail messages and memos that extend his mind into a network. He can be so rigorous as he processes data that one can imagine his mind may indeed be digital: no sloppy emotions or analog fuzziness, just trillions of binary impulses coolly converting input into correct answers.

"I don't think there's anything unique about human intelligence," Gates says over dinner one night at a nearly deserted Indian restaurant in a strip mall near his office. Even while eating, he seems to be multitasking; ambidextrous, he switches his fork back and forth throughout the meal and uses whichever hand is free to gesture or scribble notes. "All the neurons in the brain that make up perceptions and emotions operate in a binary fashion," he explains. "We can someday replicate that on a machine." Earthly life is carbon based, he notes, and computers are silicon based, but that is not a major distinction. "Eventually we'll be able to sequence the human genome and replicate how nature did intelligence in a carbon-based system." The notion, he admits, is a bit frightening, but he jokes that it would also be cheating. "It's like reverse-engineering someone else's product in order to solve a challenge."

Might there be some greater meaning to the universe? When engaged or amused, he is voluble, waving his hands and speaking loudly enough to fill the restaurant. "It's possible, you can never know, that the universe exists only for me." It's a mix of Descartes' metaphysics and Tom Stoppard's humor. "If so," he jokes, "it's sure going well for me, I must admit." He laughs; his eyes sparkle. Here's something machines can't do

(I don't think): giggle about their plight in the cosmos, crack themselves up, have fun.

Right? Isn't there something special, perhaps even divine, about the human soul? His face suddenly becomes expressionless, his squeaky voice turns toneless, and he folds his arms across his belly and vigorously rocks back and forth in a mannerism that has become so mimicked at Microsoft that a meeting there can resemble a round table of ecstatic rabbis. Finally, as if from an automaton, comes the answer: "I don't have any evidence on that." Rock, rock, rock. "I don't have any evidence on that."

The search for evidence about the soul that underlies Bill Gates's intellectual operating system is a task that even this boyish man might find a challenge.

"As a baby, he used to rock back and forth in his cradle himself," recalls Gates's father, a man as big and huggable as his son is small and tightly coiled. A retired lawyer, he still lives in the airy suburban Seattle house overlooking Lake Washington where Bill III—the boy he calls "Trey"—grew up. (The name comes from the card term for three, though the father is now resigned to being called Bill Sr.)

His mother, Mary, was "a remarkable woman," Bill Sr. says. A banker's daughter, she was adroit in both social and business settings, and served on numerous boards, including those of the University of Washington, the United Way, USWest, and First Interstate Bancorp. After her death in 1994, the city council named the avenue leading into their neighborhood after her.

"Trey didn't have a lot of confidence in social settings," says his father. "I remember him fretting for two weeks before asking a girl to the prom, then getting turned down. But Mary did. She was a star at social intercourse. She could walk into a room . . ." He has the same toothy smile as his son, the same smudgy glasses covering twinkling eyes. But now, for just a moment, he is starting to tear up. His mind does not seem like a computer. He folds his arms across his stomach and starts to rock, gently.

He gets up to show some more pictures of Mary and of her mother. Both loved cards, and they would organize bridge games, as well as Password and trivia contests, after the big family dinners they held every Sunday. "The play was quite serious," Bill Sr. recalls. "Winning mattered."

As he wanders through the house, he points out more framed pictures of his son: Trey, the towheaded Cub Scout; Trey with sister Kristi, a year older, who now has the joy of being his tax accountant; and with Libby, nine years younger, who lives a few blocks away raising her two kids; with Bill Sr. and his new wife, Mimi, the director of the Seattle Art Museum; and hugging his wife, Melinda, while listening to Willie Nelson play at their New Year's Day 1994 wedding in Hawaii.

"He's a busy guy," says Bill Sr., "so we don't see him a lot, but we spend holidays together." Thanksgiving was in Spokane, Washington, at Kristi's house, Christmas playing golf in Palm Springs, California, where Bill Sr. and Mimi have a place. They communicate mainly by e-mail. Just this morning he got one describing a photocopier Trey bought him for his birthday.

He lumbers over to a table where he has gathered some pictures of summer vacations they used to take with friends at a cluster of rental cabins known as Cheerio on the Hood Canal, about two hours away. There were nightly campfires, family skits, and the type of organized competitive games the Gates family loved. "On Saturdays there was a tennis tournament, and on Sundays our Olympics, which were a mixture of games and other activities," Bill Sr. recalls. "Trey was more into the individual sports, such as water-skiing, than the team ones."

In 1986, after Microsoft became successful, Gates built a four-house vacation compound dubbed Gateaway for his family. There his parents would help him replicate his summer activities on a grander scale for dozens of friends and coworkers in what became known as the Micro-games. "There were always a couple of mental games as well as performances and regular games," says Bill Sr. as he flips through a scrapbook. These were no ordinary picnics: One digital version of charades, for example, had teams competing to send numerical messages using smoke-signal machines, in which the winners devised their own four-bit binary code.

"We became concerned about him when he was ready for junior

high," says his father. "He was so small and shy, in need of protection, and his interests were so very different from the typical sixth grader's." His intellectual drive and curiosity would not be satisfied in a big public school. So they decided to send him to an elite private school across town.

Walking across the rolling quad of the Lakeside School, Bill Sr. points out the chapel where his son played the lead in Peter Shaffer's *Black Comedy*. "He was very enthusiastic about acting. But what really entranced him was in there," he says, pointing to a New England–style steepled classroom building. With the proceeds from a rummage sale, the Mothers' Club had funded a clunky Teletype computer terminal.

Learning BASIC language from a manual with his pal Paul Allen, Trey produced two programs in the eighth grade: one that converted a number in one mathematical base to a different base, and another (easier to explain) that played tic-tac-toe. Later, having read about Napoleon's military strategies, he devised a computer version of Risk, a board game he liked in which the goal is world domination.

Trey and Paul were soon spending their evenings at a local company that had bought a big computer and didn't have to pay for it until it was debugged. In exchange for computer time, the boys' job was to try (quite successfully) to find bugs that would crash it. "Trey got so into it," his father recalls, "that he would sneak out the basement door after we went to bed and spend most of the night there."

The combination of counseling and the computer helped transform him into a self-assured young businessman. By high school he and his friends had started a profitable company to analyze and graph traffic data for the city. "His confidence increased, and his sense of humor increased," his father says. "He became a great storyteller, who could mimic the voices of each person. And he made peace with his mother."

"In ninth grade," Gates recalls over dinner one night, "I came up with a new form of rebellion. I hadn't been getting good grades, but I decided to get all A's without taking a book home. I didn't go to math class, because I knew enough and had read ahead, and I placed within the top ten people in the nation on an aptitude exam. That established my independence and taught me I didn't need to rebel anymore." By tenth grade he was teaching computers and writing a program that handled class scheduling, which had a secret function that placed him in classes with the right girls.

His best friend was Kent Evans, son of a Unitarian minister. "We read *Fortune* together; we were going to conquer the world," says Gates. "I still remember his phone number." Together with Paul Allen, they formed the official-sounding Lakeside Programmers Group and got a job writing a payroll system for a local firm. A furious argument, the first of many, ensued when Allen tried to take over the work himself. But he soon realized he needed the tireless Gates back to do the coding. "Okay, but I'm in charge," Gates told him, "and I'll get used to being in charge, and it'll be hard to deal with me from now on unless I'm in charge." He was right.

To relieve the pressures of programming, Evans took up mountain climbing. One day Gates got a call from the headmaster: Evans had been killed in a fall. "I had never thought of people dying," Gates says. There is a flicker of emotion. "At the service, I was supposed to speak, but I couldn't get up. For two weeks I couldn't do anything at all."

After that he became even closer to Paul Allen. They learned an artificial-intelligence language together and found odd jobs as programmers. "We were true partners," Gates says. "We'd talk for hours every day." After Gates went off to Harvard, Allen drove his rattletrap Chrysler cross-country to continue their collaboration. He eventually persuaded Gates to become that university's most famous modern dropout in order to start a software company, which they initially dubbed Micro-Soft (after considering the name Allen & Gates Inc.), to write versions of BASIC for the first personal computers. It was an intense relationship: Gates the workaholic code writer and competitor, Allen the dreamy visionary.

Over the years they would have ferocious fights, and Allen would, after a Hodgkin's disease scare, quit the company and become estranged. But Gates worked hard to repair the relationship and eventually lured Allen, who is now one of the country's biggest high-tech venture-capital investors (and owner of the Portland Trail Blazers), back onto the Microsoft board. "We like to talk about how the fantasies we had as kids actually came true," Gates says. Now, facing their old classroom building at Lakeside is the modern brick Allen/Gates Science Center. (Gates lost the coin toss.)

Steve Ballmer, big and balding, is bouncing around a Microsoft conference room with the spirit of the Harvard football-team manager he once was. "Bill lived down the hall from me at Harvard sophomore year," he says. "He'd play poker until six in the morning, then I'd run into him at breakfast and discuss applied mathematics." They took graduate-level math and economics courses together, but Gates had an odd approach toward his classes: He would skip the lectures of those he was taking and audit the lectures of those he wasn't, then spend the period before each exam cramming. "He's the smartest guy I've ever met," says Ballmer, continuing the unbroken sequence of people who make that point early in an interview.

Ballmer nurtured the social side of Gates, getting him to join one of the college's eating clubs (at his initiation Gates gave a drunken disquisition on an artificial-intelligence machine), playing the video game Pong at hamburger joints, and later wandering with him to places like the old Studio 54 during visits to New York City. "He was eccentric but charismatic," says Ballmer.

When Microsoft began to grow in 1980, Gates needed a smart non-techie to help run things, and he lured Ballmer, who had worked for Procter & Gamble, to Seattle as an equity partner. Though he can be coldly impersonal in making business decisions, Gates has an emotional loyalty to a few old friends. "I always knew I would have close business associates like Ballmer and several of the other top people at Microsoft, and that we would stick together and grow together no matter what happened," he says. "I didn't know that because of some analysis. I just decided early on that was part of who I was."

As with Allen, the relationship was sometimes stormy. "Our first major row came when I insisted it was time to hire seventeen more people," Ballmer recalls. "He claimed I was trying to bankrupt him." Gates has a rule that Microsoft, rather than incurring debt, must always have enough money in the bank to run for a year even with no revenues. (It currently has $8 billion in cash and no long-term debt.) "I was living with him at the time, and I got so pissed off I moved out." The elder Gates smoothed things over, and soon the new employees were hired.

"Bill brings to the company the idea that conflict can be a good thing," says Ballmer. "The difference from P&G is striking. Politeness was at a premium there. Bill knows it's important to avoid that gentle civility that keeps you from getting to the heart of an issue quickly. He likes it when anyone, even a junior employee, challenges him, and you know he respects you when he starts shouting back." Around Microsoft, it's known as the math camp mentality: a lot of cocky geeks willing to wave their fingers and yell with the cute conviction that all problems have a right answer. Among Gates's favorite phrases is "That's the stupidest thing I've ever heard," and victims wear it as a badge of honor, bragging about it the way they do about getting a late-night e-mail from him.

The contentious atmosphere can promote flexibility. The Microsoft Network began as a proprietary online system like CompuServe or America Online. When the open standards of the Internet changed the game, Microsoft was initially caught flat-footed. Arguments ensued. Soon it became clear it was time to try a new strategy and raise the stakes. Gates turned his company around in just one year to disprove the maxim that a leader of one revolution will be left behind by the next.

During the bachelor years in the early '80s, the math camp mentality was accompanied by a frat-boy recreational style. Gates, Ballmer, and friends would eat out at Denny's, go to movies, and gather for intellectual games like advanced forms of trivia and Boggle. As friends started getting married, there were bachelor parties involving local strippers and skinny-dipping in Gates's pool. But eventually, after Gates wed, he took up more mature pursuits such as golf. "Bill got into golf in the same addictive way he gets into anything else," says Ballmer. "It gets his competitive juice flowing."

It's a rainy night, and Gates is bombing around in his dark blue Lexus. He loves fast cars. When Microsoft was based in Albuquerque, New Mexico, in its early years, he bought a Porsche 911 and used to race it in the desert; Paul Allen had to bail him out of jail after one midnight escapade. He got three speeding tickets—two from the same cop who was trailing him—just on the drive from Albuquerque the weekend he moved Microsoft to Seattle. Later he bought a Porsche 930 Turbo he called the "rocket," then a Mercedes, a Jaguar XJ6, a $60,000 Carrera Cabriolet 964, a $380,000 Porsche 959 that ended up impounded in a customs shed because it couldn't meet import emission standards, and a Ferrari 348 that became known as the "dune buggy" after he spun it into the sand.

Despite this record, Gates is not wearing a seat belt. (A dilemma: Is it too uncool to use mine?) He rarely looks at you when he talks, which is disconcerting, but he does so when he's driving, which is doubly disconcerting. (I buckle up. As his mother and others have learned, it's not always prudent to compete.) He turns into a dark drive with a chain-link fence that slides open as the Lexus approaches. It's nearing midnight, and the security guard looks a bit startled.

Gates's home of the future has been under construction for more than four years, and is not expected to be completed until this summer. Built into a bluff fronting Lake Washington, it has forty thousand square feet of space and will cost about $40 million. Looming against the night sky are three connected pavilions of glass and recycled Douglas fir beams, looking a bit like a corporate conference center masquerading as a resort.

Gates swings into a vaulted thirty-car garage carved into the hillside. In the corner, like a museum piece, sits his parents' red Mustang convertible, which he drove as a kid. "The first pavilion is mainly for public entertaining," he says as he picks his way past construction debris down four levels of stairs. Despite the hour, three technicians are working in the ground-floor reception hall, with its view of the Olympic Mountains across Lake Washington, adjusting two dozen forty-inch monitors that will form a flat-screen display covering an entire wall. "When you visit, you'll get an electronic pin encoded with your preferences," he explains. "As you wander toward any room, your favorite pictures will appear along with the music you like or a TV show or movie you're watching. The system will learn from your choices, and it will remember the music or pictures from your previous visits so you can choose to have them again or have similar but new ones. We'll have to have hierarchy guidelines, for when more than one person goes to a room." Like Gates himself, it's all very fascinating, fun, and a little intimidating.

Moving into the center pavilion, Gates shows off what will be the library. A mammoth carved wooden dome hangs just above the floor, waiting to be raised into the cupola. (I wonder: Does this grand chamber dispel my fear that he will relegate print to museum status? Or inadvertently confirm it?) He has hired a New York rare-books dealer to stock the library for him. His current reading is eclectic. "On a recent trip to Italy," he says, "I took the new Stalin biography, a book about Hewlett-Packard, *Seven Summits* [a mountaineering book by Dick Bass and the late Disney president Frank Wells], and a Wallace Stegner novel." He's also a fan of Philip Roth's, John Irving's, Ernest J. Gaines's, and David Halberstam's, but his all-time favorite novels are the schoolboy standards *The Catcher in the Rye, The Great Gatsby,* and *A Separate Peace.* A nearby room will be filled by an enormous trampoline; at the office he sometimes surprises colleagues by joyfully leaping to touch the ceiling, and he finds bouncing on a trampoline as conducive to concentration as rocking.

The only completed part of the house is the indoor pool under the family quarters. A sleek lap pool reflecting images from a wall snakes through glass into an outdoor Japanese bath area. The security guard reappears and warns, "Be careful of what you do in there, since the boats on the lake can see inside." As the door to the pool room closes, Gates doubles over in laughter. Does he come in here often at night? "Sometimes with Melinda," he says.

We wander out to the deck, and the wind slams the door shut. It's locked. Gates tries to call the guard, but he's disappeared to a distant part of the estate. So he leads the way past bulldozers into trenches that will someday become an estuary and a stocked trout stream. At the moment, however, it's a quagmire that proves impassable. Remarkably, Gates is able to avoid looking sheepish. After a few more minutes of shouting, he attracts the guard's attention.

Gates chose the austere and natural architectural style before he got married, but Melinda is now putting her own imprint on it. "The exposed concrete is going to have to go," he says, expressing some concern about how the architect might take this.

Gates met Melinda French ten years ago at a Microsoft press event in Manhattan. She was working for the company and later became one of the executives in charge of interactive content. Their daughter, Jennifer, was born last April. Melinda, thirty-two, is no longer at Microsoft, and she is active in charity work and on the board of Duke, where she studied computer science as an undergraduate and then got a graduate degree in business. Like Gates, she is smart and independent. Like his mother, she is also friendly and social, with an easy manner of organizing trips and activities. But she zealously guards her privacy and doesn't give interviews.

"I used to think I wouldn't be all that interested in the baby until she was two or so and could talk," says Gates as he shows off the more intimate family quarters. "But I'm totally into it now. She's just started to say 'ba-ba' and have a personality."

Melinda is Catholic, goes to church, and wants to raise Jennifer that way. "But she offered me a deal," Gates says. "If I start going to church— my family was Congregationalist— then Jennifer could be raised in whatever religion I choose." Gates admits that he is tempted, because he would prefer she have a religion that "has less theology and all" than Catholicism, but he has not yet taken up the offer. "Just in terms of allocation of time resources, religion is not very efficient," he explains. "There's a lot more I could be doing on a Sunday morning."

If Ballmer is Gates's social goad, his intellectual one is Nathan Myhrvold (pronounced Meer-voll), thirty-seven, who likes to joke that he's got more degrees than a thermometer, including a doctorate in physics from Princeton. With a fast and exuberant laugh, he has a passion for subjects ranging from technology (he heads Microsoft's advanced-research group) to dinosaurs (he's about to publish a paper on the aerodynamics of the apatosaurus tail) to cooking. He sometimes moonlights as a chef at Rover's, a French restaurant in Seattle.

When he arrives there for dinner, owner Thierry Rautureau comes out to hug him and pour champagne. There follows a procession of a dozen courses, from black truffles and pureed celery root in smoked game consommé to venison with obscure types of mushrooms, each with different vintage wines. (The bill for two comes to $390, and picking it up assuages my discomfort that Gates had insisted on putting the previous evening's $37 tab at the Indian restaurant on his MasterCard.)

"There are two types of tech companies," Myhrvold says in between pauses to inhale the aroma of the food. "Those where the guy in charge knows how to surf, and those where he depends on experts on the beach to guide him." The key point about Gates is that he knows—indeed loves—the intricacies of creating software. "Every decision he makes is based on his knowledge of the merits. He doesn't need to rely on personal politics. It sets the tone."

Myhrvold describes a typical private session with Gates. Pacing around a room, they will talk for hours about future technologies such as voice recognition (they call their team working on it the "wreck a nice beach" group, because that's what invariably appears on the screen when someone speaks the phrase "recognize speech" into the system), then wander onto topics ranging from quantum physics to genetic engineering. "Bill is not threatened by smart people," he says, "only stupid ones."

Microsoft has long hired based on IQ and "intellectual bandwidth." Gates is the undisputed ideal: Talking to most people is like sipping from a fountain, goes the saying at the company, but with Gates it's like drinking from a fire hose. Gates, Ballmer, and Myhrvold believe it's better to get a brilliant but untrained young brain—they're called "Bill clones"—than someone with too much experience. The interview process tests not what the applicants know but how well they can process tricky questions: If you wanted to figure out how many times on average you would have to flip the pages of the Manhattan phone book to find a specific name, how would you approach the problem?

Gates's intellect is marked by an ability, as he puts it, to "drill down." On a visit to Time Inc.'s new-media facility, he answered questions from a collection of magazine editors as if by rote, but on his way out he asked to see the Internet servers and spent forty-five minutes grilling the claque of awed techies there. Broad discussions bore him, he shows little curiosity about other people, and he becomes disengaged when people use small talk to try to establish a personal rapport. Even after spending a lot of time with him, you get the feeling that he knows much about your thinking but nothing about such things as where you live or if you have a family. Or that he cares.

In that regard he is the opposite of, say, Bill Clinton, who brackets the other end of the baby boom: Gates analytically rigorous and emotionally reserved, the president equally smart but intellectually undisciplined and readily intimate. They played golf on Martha's Vineyard once, and the president, as usual, worked hard at bonding emotionally and being personally charming and intimate. He expressed sorrow about the death of Gates's mother, shared the pain of the recent death of his own mother, and gave golfing tips to Melinda. But Gates noticed that Clinton never bored in or showed rigorous curiosity about technological issues. Though he vaguely considers himself a Democrat, Gates stayed neutral in the presidential election.

Warren Buffett, the Omaha, Nebraska, investor whom Gates demoted to being merely the second-richest American, seems an unlikely person to be among his closest pals. A jovial, outgoing sixty-six-year-old grandfather, Buffett only recently learned to use a computer. But as multibillionaires go, both are unpretentious, and they enjoy taking vacations together. Buffett's secretary apologetically explains that Buffett isn't giving interviews these days and at the moment is traveling, but she promises to pass along the request. Less than three hours later, Buffett calls to say he happens to be in the Time-Life Building with some free time between meetings in Manhattan, and he would be happy to come by to be interviewed. He likes to talk about Gates.

His favorite story is about the 1995 excursion to China that Bill and Melinda organized for seven couples. "For part of the trip we stayed on a ship in the Yangtze with five decks that normally accommodates hundreds of people," he says with the glee of a kid describing Walt Disney World. "Each evening Melinda arranged different activities." There was karaoke singing in the ship's ballroom, performances of quickie versions of Shakespeare plays, "and a trivia quiz on such things as how many meals we'd eaten, with prizes that Melinda and Bill handed out." When relaxed, Buffett says, Gates has a fun sense of humor. In the Forbidden City they were given a show of huge ancient scrolls that were silently rolled and unrolled by women trained for the task. "There's a two-dollar fine," Gates whispered, "if you return a scroll not rewound."

When Gates decided to propose to Melinda in 1993, he secretly diverted the chartered plane they were taking home from Palm Springs one Sunday night to land in Omaha. There Buffett met them, arranged to open a jewelry store that he owned, and helped them pick a ring. That year Gates made a movie for Buffett's birthday. It featured Gates pretending to wander the country in search of tales about Buffett and calling Melinda with them from pay phones. After each call, Gates is shown checking the coin slot for loose change. When she mentions that Buffett is only the country's second-richest man, he informs her that on the new Forbes list Buffett had (at least that one year) regained the top spot. The phone suddenly goes dead. "Melinda, Melinda," Gates sputters, "you still there? Hello?"

Last October, Gates brought Melinda and their new daughter to visit Buffett and his wife in San Francisco. They ended up playing bridge for nine hours straight. Another marathon session in Seattle started in the morning and lasted—with a break for Melinda to pick up lunch at Burger King—until guests started arriving for dinner. "He loves games that involve problem solving," Buffett says. "I showed him a set of four dice with numbers arranged in a complex way so that any one of them would on average beat one of the others. He was one of three people I ever showed them to who figured this out and saw the way to win was to make me choose first which one I'd roll." (For math buffs: The dice were nontransitive. One of the others who figured it out was the logician Saul Kripke.)

Their relationship is not financial. Buffett, who does not invest in technology stocks, bought a hundred shares of Microsoft just as a curiosity back when he met Gates ("I wish I'd bought more," he laughs), and Gates describes his investment with Buffett as "only" about $10 million ("I wish I'd invested more," he likewise jokes). But Gates shares Buffett's interest in the media world and even likes to joke that he has created a digital encyclopedia called Encarta that now outsells World Book, which is controlled by Buffett. So far Microsoft has mainly treated content as something that its software managers can create from scratch. But given the relative cheapness of some media stocks compared with that of Microsoft, Gates may someday look for some big acquisitions (he was in serious talks about taking a $2 billion stake in CNN before Time Warner merged with Turner Communications), and Buffett would be a useful partner.

Another of Gates's vacation companions is Ann Winblad, the software entrepreneur and venture capitalist he dated during the 1980s. They met in 1984 at a Ben Rosen–Esther Dyson computer conference and started going on "virtual dates" by driving to the same movie at the same time in different cities and discussing it on their cell phones. For a few years she even persuaded him to stop eating meat, an experiment he has since resolutely abandoned.

They were kindred minds as well as spirits. On a vacation to Brazil, he took James Watson's eleven-hundred-page textbook, *Molecular Biology of the Gene,* and they studied bioengineering together. On another vacation, to a Santa Barbara, California, ranch, she took tapes of Richard Feynman's lectures at Cornell, and they studied physics. And on a larger excursion with friends to central Africa, which ended at some beach cottages on an island off Zanzibar, among their companions was anthropologist Donald Johanson, known for his work on the human ancestor Lucy, who helped teach them about human evolution. In the evenings on each trip they would go to the beach with four or five other couples for bonfires, Hood Canal–style games, and a tradition they called the sing-down, where each team is given a word and has to come up with songs that feature it. Winblad remembers Gates disappearing on a dark beach after his group had been given the word *sea,* and then slowly emerging from the mist singing a high-pitched solo of "Puff, the Magic Dragon."

They broke up in 1987, partly because Winblad, five years older, was more ready for marriage. But they remain close friends. "When I was off on my own thinking about marrying Melinda," Gates says, "I called Ann and asked for her approval." She gave it. "I said she'd be a good match for him because she had intellectual stamina." Even now, Gates has an arrangement with his wife that he and Winblad can keep one vacation tradition alive. Every spring, as they have for more than a decade, Gates spends a long weekend with Winblad at her beach cottage on the Outer Banks of North Carolina, where they ride dune buggies, hang-glide, and walk on the beach. "We can play putt-putt while discussing biotechnology," Gates says. Winblad puts it more grandly. "We share our thoughts about the world and ourselves," she says. "And we marvel about how, as two young overachievers, we began a great adventure on the fringes of a little-known industry and it landed us at the center of an amazing universe."

After a recent whirl of travel that included a speech in Las Vegas and a meeting in Switzerland, Gates detoured to a secluded resort in New York's Adirondacks to spend a weekend with Melinda and Jennifer. There they played with thousand-piece jigsaw puzzles from a craftsman in Vermont who makes them for customers like Gates. Melinda has helped broaden her husband. Instead of studying biotechnology together, they find time to take singing lessons.

Gates is ambivalent about his celebrity. Although he believes that fame tends to be "very corrupting," he is comfortable as a public figure and as the personification of the company he built. Like Buffett, he remains unaffected, wandering Manhattan and Seattle without an entourage or driver. Nestled into a banquette one Sunday night at 44, a fashionable Manhattan restaurant, he is talking volubly when another diner approaches. Gates pulls inward, used to people who want his autograph or to share some notion about computers. But the diner doesn't recognize him and instead asks him to keep his voice down. Gates apologizes sheepishly. He seems pleased to be regarded as a boyish cutup rather than a celebrity.

The phone in Gates's office almost never rings. Nor do phones seem to ring much anywhere on the suburban Microsoft "campus," a cluster of thirty-five low-rise buildings, lawns, white pines, and courtyards that resemble those of a state polytechnic college. Gates runs his company mainly through three methods: He bats out a hundred or more e-mail messages a day (and night), often chuckling as he dispatches them; he meets every month or so with a top management group that is still informally known as the boop (Bill and the Office of the President); and most important, taking up 70 percent of his schedule by his own calculation, he holds two or three small review meetings a day with a procession of teams working on the company's various products.

There is a relaxed, nonhierarchical atmosphere as the seven young managers of the WebDVD group, all in the standard winter uniform of khakis and flannel shirts, gather in a windowless conference room near Gates's office. They have been working for almost a year on a digital videodisc intended to provide content along with Web browsing for television sets, and he wants to review their progress before leaving for Japan, where he will meet with such potential partners as Toshiba.

Craig Mundie, the veteran Microsoft exec who oversees all noncomputer consumer products, lets the younger team members lead the discussion. Gates quickly flips ahead through the deck of papers and within minutes has the gist of their report. He starts rocking, peppering them with questions that segue between the politics of their potential partners, the details of the technology, the potential competition, and the broad strategy. The answers are crisp, even as Gates drills down into arcane details. No one seems to be showing off or competing for attention, but neither do any hesitate to speak up or challenge Gates. To a man (and they all are), they rock when they think.

"Does this allow scripting in HTML?" he asks, referring to the authoring language used to create Web sites. They explain how. He challenges them about why it requires four megabytes of memory. They explain; he drills down more; they finally prevail. There is an intense discussion of layers, sectors, modes, error corrections, and MPEG-2 video-compression standards. "Our basic strategy must be processor agnostic," Gates decrees. Everyone nods. Then he shifts without missing a beat to corporate tactics. "Are we going to get Philips and other manufacturers and the moviemakers to agree on a standard?" We'll get to that in a minute, he's told. He wants to get to it now. There is a rapid discussion of the internal politics of Philips, Sony, Time Warner (the corporate parent of this magazine), Matsushita, and Toshiba, along with their respective Hollywood alliances.

Gates doesn't address anyone by name, hand out praise, or stroke any egos. But he listens intently, democratically. His famous temper is in check, even when he disagrees with someone's analysis of the DVD's capability to handle something called layering. "Educate me on that," he says in challenging the analysis, and after a minute or so cuts off the discussion by saying, "Send me the specs."

Gates does not hide his cutthroat instincts. "The competitive landscape here is strange, ranging from Navio to even WebTV," he says. He is particularly focused on Navio, a consumer-software consortium recently launched by Netscape and others designed to make sure that Windows and Windows CE (its consumer-electronics cousin) do not become the standard for interactive television and game machines. "I want to put something in our product that's hard for Navio to do. What are their plans?" The group admits that their intelligence on Navio is poor. Gates rocks harder. "You have to pick someone in your group," he tells Mundie, "whose task it is to track Navio full-time. They're the ones I worry about. Sega is an investor. They may be willing to feed us info." Then he moves on to other competitors. "What about the Planet TV guys?" Mundie explains that they are focusing on video games, "a platform we haven't prioritized." Gates counters, "We can work with them now, but they have other ambitions. So we'll be competitive with them down the line."

Though the videodisc is not at the core of Microsoft's business, this is a competition Gates plans to win. The group argues that the $10-per-unit royalty is too low. "Why charge more?" he asks. They explain that it will be hard to make a profit at $10, given what they are putting in. Gates turns stern. They are missing the big picture. "Our whole relationship with the consumer-electronic guys hangs in the balance," he declares. "We can get wiped." Only the paranoid survive. "The strategic goal here is getting Windows CE standards into every device we can. We don't have to make money over the next few years. We didn't make money on MS-DOS in its first release. If you can get into this market at ten dollars, take it." They nod.

His mother may have come to terms with this competitive intensity, but much of the computer world has not. There are Web sites dedicated to reviling him, law firms focused on foiling him, and former friends who sputter at the mention of his name. Companies such as Netscape, Oracle, and Sun Microsystems publicly make thwarting his "plan for world domination" into a holy crusade.

The criticism is not just that he is successful but that he has tried to leverage, unfairly and perhaps illegally, Microsoft's near monopoly in desktop operating systems in ways that would let him dominate everything from word processing and spreadsheets to Web browsers and content. The company is integrating its Internet Explorer browser and Microsoft Network content into its Windows operating system, a process that will culminate with the "Active Desktop" planned for Windows 97, due out in a few months. Critics see a pattern of Microsoft's playing hardball to make life difficult for competing operating systems and applications: Microsoft Word has been buggy on Macintosh operating systems, users have found it tricky to make Netscape their default browser when going back and forth from Windows to the Microsoft Network, and application developers have complained that they don't get the full specs for new releases of Windows as quickly as Microsoft's own developers do.

"They are trying to use an existing monopoly to retard introduction of new technology," says Gary Reback, the Silicon Valley antitrust lawyer representing Netscape and other Microsoft competitors. The stakes are much higher than whose Web browser wins. Netscape is enhancing its browser to serve as a platform to run applications. "In other words," says Reback, "if Netscape is successful, you won't need Windows or a Microsoft operating system anymore." On the other hand, if Microsoft is allowed to embed its Web browser into its operating system in a manner that maintains its monopoly, Reback warns, "where will it stop? They'll go on to bundle in content, their Microsoft Network, financial transactions, travel services, everything. They have a game plan to monopolize every market they touch."

Gates makes no apologies. "Any operating system without a browser is going to be f——ing out of business," he says. "Should we improve our product, or go out of business?" Later, on his trip to Japan, he returns to the subject in a two-page e-mail. "Customers are benefiting here in the same way they benefited from graphical interfaces, multitasking, compressions and dozens of other things," he writes. "If improving a product based on customer input is willful maintenance of trying to stay in business and not have Netscape turn their browser into the most popular operating system, then I think that is what we are supposed to do."

Though the stakes are clear, the law (which was developed in the era of railway barons) is not. After deadlocking, the Federal Trade Commission in 1993 surrendered jurisdiction over Microsoft to the Justice Department. FTC Commissioner Christine Varney, an expert in the field, says it's hard to apply antitrust law in a fluid situation. "My concern is with the law's ability to keep pace with market conditions in fields that change so rapidly," she says. "Once it's clear a practice is anticompetitive, the issue may already be moot."

Longtime competitors raise a more philosophical issue about Gates: His intensely competitive approach has poisoned the collaborative hacker ethos of the early days of personal computing. In his book *Startup*, Jerry Kaplan describes creating a handwriting-based system. Gates was initially friendly, he writes, and Kaplan trusted him with his plans, but he eventually felt betrayed when Gates announced a similar, competing product. Rob Glaser, a former Microsoft executive who now runs the company that makes RealAudio, an Internet sound system, is an admirer who compliments Gates on his vision. But, he adds, Gates is "pretty relentless. He's Darwinian. He doesn't look for win-win situations with others, but for ways to make others lose. Success is defined as flattening the competition, not creating excellence." When he was at Microsoft, for example, Glaser says the "atmosphere was like a Machiavellian poker game where you'd hide things even if it would blindside people you were supposed to be working with."

It comes down to the same traits that his psychologist noted when Gates was in sixth grade. "In Bill's eyes," says Glaser, "he's still a kid with a start-up who's afraid he'll go out of business if he lets anyone compete." Esther Dyson, whose newsletter and conferences make her one of the industry's fabled gurus, is another longtime friend and admirer who shares such qualms. "He never really grew up in terms of social responsibility and relationships with other people," she says. "He's brilliant but still childlike. He can be a fun companion, but he can lack human empathy."

"If we weren't so ruthless, we'd be making more creative software? We'd rather kill a competitor than grow the market?!?" Gates is pacing around his office, sarcastically repeating the charges against him. "Those are clear lies," he says coldly. "Who grew this market? We did. Who survived companies like IBM, ten times our size, taking us on?" He ticks off the names of his rivals at Oracle, Sun, Lotus, Netscape in an impersonal way. "They're every bit as competitive as I am."

"We win because we hire the smartest people. We improve our products based on feedback, until they're the best. We have retreats each year where we think about where the world is heading." He won't even cop a plea to the charge that Microsoft tends to react to competitors' ideas— the graphical interface of Apple, the Web browser of Netscape—more than it blazes new trails of its own. "Graphical interfaces were done first at Xerox, not Apple. We bet on them early on, which is why Microsoft Office applications became the best."

Gates is enjoying this. Intellectual challenges are fun. Games are fun. Puzzles are fun. Working with smart people is superfun. Others may see him as ruthless, cold, or brutal, but for him the competition is like a sport, a blood sport perhaps, but one played with the same relish as the summer games at Hood Canal. He sprawls on a couch, uncoils, and pops open a Fresca. Though rarely attempting the social warmth of his mother (he doesn't actually offer me a Fresca but acquiesces when I ask), Gates has an intensity and enthusiasm that can be engaging, even charming. He takes a piece of paper and draws the matrix of strategies he faced when creating applications to compete with WordPerfect and Lotus. See what an exciting puzzle it was? His language is boyish rather than belligerent. The right stuff is "really neat" and "supercool" and "hard-core," while bad strategies are "crummy" and "really dumb" and "random to the max."

His office is rather modest, sparsely decorated, and filled with standard-issue furniture. The biggest piece of art is a huge photo of a Pentium processor chip. There are smaller pictures of Einstein, Leonardo da Vinci, and Henry Ford, though he admits that he has little admiration for the latter. The few personal pictures include one of the original dozen Microsoft employees (most with scruffy beards, except him), one of Ann Winblad on a trip to Germany, and one with Melinda and nine friends on a 1995 vacation to Indonesia. There are no pictures of Jennifer displayed, but he pulls a snapshot out of his desk showing him proudly cradling her.

He hopes to be running Microsoft for another ten years, he says, then promises to focus as intensely on giving his money away. He says he plans to leave his children about $10 million each. "He will spend time, at some point, thinking about the impact his philanthropy can have," Buffett says. "He is too imaginative to just do conventional gifts." Already he's given $34 million to the University of Washington, partly to fund a chair for human genome–project researcher Leroy Hood; $15 million (along with $10 million from Ballmer) for a new computer center at Harvard; and $6 million to Stanford. An additional $200 million is in a foundation run by his father, and he has talked about taking over personally the funding of Microsoft's program to provide computers to inner-city libraries, to which he's donated $3 million in book royalties. "I've been pushing him gently to think more about philanthropy," his father says. "I think his charitable interests will run, as they do now, to schools and libraries."

Asked about his regrets, Gates talks about not getting a Microsoft e-mail application to the market quickly enough. "We were too busy, and at a retreat where I wrote our next priorities on a board, everyone said I had to take one off, so we took off e-mail."

It is hard to get him to delve more personally. But especially since Jennifer's birth, friends say, he has begun to reflect more on his life and what he might end up contributing. He speaks of the promise of computing, not just in business terms but in social ones. "Everyone starts out really capable," he says. "But as you grow and turn curious, either you get positive feedback by finding answers or you don't, and then this incredible potential you have is discouraged. I was lucky. I always had a family and resources to get more and more answers. Digital tools will allow a lot more people to keep going the next step rather than hitting a wall where people stop giving them information or tell them to stop asking questions."

He has also become less enamored with pure intelligence. "I don't think that IQ is as fungible as I used to," he says. "To succeed, you also have to know how to make choices and how to think more broadly."

So has family life dulled Gates's intensity? "Well, predictably, he's pumped and focused on Jennifer," says Ballmer. "He showed a picture of her at our last sales conference and joked that there was something other than Netscape keeping him awake at nights. He may be a bit less exhausting and a bit more civil. But he still pushes as hard, still keeps score." Gates likes repeating Michael Jordan's mantra—"They think I'm through, they think I'm through"—and the one Intel's CEO Andrew Grove used as a book title, "Only the paranoid survive." As Ballmer says, "He still feels he must run scared." Gates puts another spin on it: "I still feel this is superfun."

And what about his feeling that there is nothing unique about the human mind, that intelligence can someday be replicated in binary code? Has watching a daughter learn to smile at a father's face changed that at all? At our last meeting, I ask him these questions, but they don't seem to engage him. As I wander out of his office, he offers none of life's standard see-you-again-someday pleasantries, but he agrees that I should feel free to e-mail him. So in an e-mail a few days later, I pose these questions again, along with some more mundane technical ones. Answers to the tech issues come promptly. But he ignores the philosophical ones.

Finally, weeks later, an e-mail pops up unexpectedly in my mailbox from billg@microsoft.com.

Analytically, I would say nature has done a good job making child raising more pleasure than pain, since that is necessary for a species to survive. But the experience goes beyond analytic description. Evolution is many orders of magnitude ahead of mankind today in creating a complex system. I don't think it's irreconcilable to say we will understand the human mind someday and explain it in software-like terms, and also to say it is a creation that shouldn't be compared to software. Religion has come around to the view that even things that can be explained scientifically can have an underlying purpose that goes beyond the science. Even though I am not religious, the amazement and wonder I have about the human mind is closer to religious awe than dispassionate analysis.

The Passion of Andrew Grove

This piece was also written in 1997. It was the introduction to Time's *Man of the Year issue. I felt that the magazine, in focusing on politics and world affairs, sometimes missed the larger trends affecting our lives. For example, people who had invented such things as television, penicillin, the polio vaccine, or the model for DNA had never been men of the year and rarely had been on the cover. It seemed to me that the microchip, computers, and the networking of computers were transforming our time. That is why we decided to make Andrew Grove and Jeff Bezos persons of the year, and why we did a lot of covers on technologists such as Marc Andreessen, Bill Gates, and Steve Jobs. In this introduction, I did not try to profile Grove (that was done by Daniel Eisenberg and Joshua Cooper Ramo in an accompanying piece), but instead tried to put him and the microchip into a historical context on the fiftieth anniversary (which no one else seemed to celebrate) of the birth of the digital age.*

Fifty years ago this week—shortly after lunchtime on December 23, 1947—the digital revolution was born. It happened on a drizzly Tuesday in Murray Hill, New Jersey, when two Bell Labs scientists demonstrated a tiny contraption they had concocted from some strips of gold foil, a chip of semiconducting material, and a bent paper clip. As their colleagues watched with a mix of wonder and envy, they showed how their gizmo, which was dubbed a transistor, could take an electric current, amplify it, and switch it on and off.

That digital revolution is now transforming the end of this century the way the Industrial Revolution transformed the end of the last one. Today, millions of transistors, each costing far less than a staple, can be etched on wafers of silicon. On these microchips, all the world's information and entertainment can be stored in digital form, processed, and zapped to every nook of a networked planet. And in 1997, as the United States completed nearly seven years of growth, the microchip has become the dynamo of a new economy marked by low unemployment, negligible inflation, and a rationally exuberant stock market.

Andrew Grove, chairman and CEO of Intel, is the person most responsible for the amazing growth in the power and innovative potential of microchips. His character traits are emblematic of this amazing century: a paranoia bred from his having been a refugee from the Nazis and then the Communists; an entrepreneurial optimism instilled as an immigrant to a land brimming with freedom and opportunity; and a sharpness tinged with arrogance that comes from being a brilliant mind on the front line of a revolution.

Like his fellow wealth builders of the digital age, Grove's mission is his product, and he shuns the philosophical mantle and higher callings often adopted by titans of an earlier era. Ask him to ruminate on issues like the role of technology in our society, and his pixie face contorts into a frozen smile with impatient eyes. "Technology happens," he clips. "It's not good, it's not bad. Is steel good or bad?" The steel in his own character comes through at such moments. He has a courageous passion alloyed with an engineer's analytic coldness, whether it be in battling his prostate cancer or in guiding Intel's death-defying climb to dominate the market for the world's most important product.

These traits have allowed Grove to push with paranoiac obsession the bounds of innovation and to build Intel, which makes nearly 90 percent of the planet's PC microprocessors, into a company worth $115 billion (more than IBM), with $5.1 billion in annual profits (seventh most profitable in the world) and an annual return to investors of 44 percent during the past ten years. Other great entrepreneurs, most notably Bill Gates, have become richer and better known by creating the software that makes use of the microchip. But more than any other person, Andy Grove has made real the defining law of the digital age: the prediction by his friend and Intel cofounder Gordon Moore that microchips would double in power and halve in price every eighteen months or so. And to that law Grove has added his own: We will continually find new things for microchips to do that were scarcely imaginable a year or two earlier.

The result is one of the great statistical zingers of our age: Every month, four quadrillion transistors are produced, more than half a million for every human on the planet. Intel's space-suited workers etch more than seven million, in lines one four-hundredth the thickness of a human hair, on each of its thumbnail-size Pentium II chips, which sell for about $500 and can make 588 million calculations a second.

The dawn of a new millennium—which is the grandest measure we have of human time—permits us to think big about history. We can pause to notice what Grove calls, somewhat inelegantly, "strategic inflection points," those moments when new circumstances alter the way the world works, as if the current of history goes through a transistor and our oscilloscopes blip. It can happen because of an invention (Gutenberg's printing press in the fifteenth century), or an idea (individual liberty in the eighteenth century), or a technology (electricity in the nineteenth century), or a process (the assembly line early in this century).

The microchip has become—like the steam engine, electricity, and the assembly line—an advance that propels a new economy. Its impact on growth and productivity numbers is still a matter of dispute, but not its impact on the way we work and live. This new economy has several features:

- *It's global.* Money now respects no borders. With clicks of a keyboard, investors trade $1.5 trillion worth of foreign currencies and $15 trillion in stocks worldwide each day, putting errant or unlucky nations at the mercy of merciless speculators.
- *It's networked.* Handbags from Italy and designer shoes from Hong Kong are available to Web surfers throughout cyberspace; clerical work or software programming can be outsourced from anywhere to workers in Omaha or Bangalore; and the illness of a child in Bali can be diagnosed by a doctor in Bangor.
- *It's based on information.* In today's knowledge-based economy, intellectual capital drives the value of products.
- *It decentralizes power.* As the transistor was being invented, George Orwell, in his book *1984*, was making one of the worst predictions in a century filled with them: that technology would be a centralizing,

totalitarian influence. Instead, technology became a force for democracy and individual empowerment. The Internet allows anyone to be a publisher or pundit, e-mail subverts rigid hierarchies, and the tumult of digital innovation rewards wildcats who risk battle with monolithic companies. The symbol of the atomic age, which tended to centralize power, was a nucleus with electrons held in tight orbit; the symbol of the digital age is the Web, with countless centers of power all equally networked.

- *It rewards openness.* Information can no longer be easily controlled nor ideas repressed nor societies kept closed. A networked world facilitates free minds, free markets, and free trade.
- *It's specialized.* The old economy was geared to mass production, mass marketing, and mass media: cookie-cutter products spewed from assembly lines in central factories; entertainment and ideas were broadcast from big studios and publishers. Now products can be individualized. Need steel that's tailored for your needs? Some high-tech mini-mill will provide it. Prefer opinions different from those on this page? A thousand Webzines and personalized news products are waiting to connect with you.

No one believes the microchip has repealed the business cycle or deleted the threat of inflation. But it has, at the very least, ended the sway of decline theorists and the "limits to growth" crowd, ranging from the Club of Rome Cassandras to more recent doomsayers convinced that America's influence is destined to wane.

The United States now enjoys what in many respects is the healthiest economy in its history, and probably that of any nation ever. More than four hundred thousand new jobs were created last month, bringing unemployment down to 4.6 percent, the lowest level in almost twenty-five years. Labor-force participation has also improved: The proportion of working-age people with jobs is the highest ever recorded. Wage stagnation seems to be ending: Earnings have risen more than 4 percent in the past twelve months, which is the greatest gain in twenty years when adjusted for inflation. The Dow is at 7,756, more than doubling in three years, and corporate profits are at their highest level ever. Yet inflation is a negligible 2 percent, and even the dour Fed chairman Alan Greenspan seems confident enough in the new economy to keep interest rates low.

Driving all this is the microchip. The high-tech industry, which accounted for less than 10 percent of America's growth in 1990, accounts for 30 percent today. Every week a Silicon Valley company goes public. It's an industry that pays good wages and makes both skilled and unskilled workers more efficient. Its products cost less each year and help reduce the prices in other industries. That, along with the global competition that computers and networks facilitate, helps keep inflation down.

Economists point out that the digital revolution has not yet been reflected in productivity statistics. The annual growth of nonfarm productivity during the 1980s and 1990s has averaged about 1 percent, in contrast to almost 3 percent in the 1960s. But that may be changing. During the past year, productivity grew about 2.5 percent. And in the most recent quarter the rate was more than 4 percent.

In addition, the traditional statistics are increasingly likely to understate growth and productivity. The outputs of the old economy were simpler to measure: Steel and cars and widgets are easily totted up. But the new economy defies compartmentalized measurement. Corporate software purchases, for instance, are not counted as economic investment. What is the value of cell phones that keep getting cheaper, or of e-mail that can be free? By traditional measures banking is contracting, yet there has been explosive growth in automated banking and credit-card transactions.

Even the cautious Greenspan has become a wary believer in the new economy. When he decided not to raise interest rates this year despite the hot economy, he told Congress it was because of "the increasingly successful and pervasive application of recent technological advances, especially in telecommunications and computers, to enhance efficiencies in the production process." Translation: Productivity is increasing, inventories can now be managed more efficiently, and production capacity can more quickly respond to changes in demand. A fanatic for data, Greenspan has soaked up the evidence of surging corporate investment in technology and says managers presumably are doing so because they believe it will enhance productivity and profits. "The anecdotal evidence is ample," he says.

Anecdotal? Economists are supposed to eschew that. Yet the most powerful evidence of the way the digital revolution has created a new economy comes from the testimony of those embracing it. A manager at a service company in Kansas talks about not having to raise prices because he's reaping increased profits through technology. An executive of an engine company in Ohio tells of resolving an issue with colleagues on three continents in a one-day flurry of e-mail, a task that once would have taken weeks of memos and missed phone calls. At a Chrysler plant in Missouri, a shop steward describes labor-saving technology that his union members embraced because they see how their factory, which had been shut down in the late '80s, is now expanding. And the greatest collection of anecdotal insight, the stock market, has spent the year betting on ever-increasing profits.

Of course the microchip, like every new technology, brings viruses. Increased reliance on technology has led to the threat of growing inequality. Workers and students not properly trained will be left behind, opening the way for the social disruptions that accompanied the shift to the industrial age. At a time when they are most needed, schools have been allowed to deteriorate, and worker-training programs have fallen prey to budget austerity. For all the spending on computers and software ($800 billion in the United States during the past five years), the most obvious investment has not been made: ensuring that every schoolchild has a personal computer. Grove himself says this would be the most effective way to reboot education in America, yet he and others in the industry have been timid in enlisting in such a crusade.

In addition, though wage stagnation seems to be easing, workers' insecurity remains high. The layoffs that have accompanied technological change have been burned into their minds like code on a ROM chip. There are also more personal concerns. Computer networks allow information to be accessed, accumulated, and correlated in ways that threaten privacy as never before. Unseen eyes (of your boss, your neighbor, thousands of marketers) can track what you buy, the things you read and write, where you travel, and whom you call. Your kids can download pornographic pictures and chat with strangers.

But these challenges can be surmounted. Technology can even provide the tools to do so, if people supply the will. As Andy Grove says, technology is not inherently good or evil. It is only a tool for reflecting our values.

If the digital revolution is accompanied by ways to ensure that everyone has the chance to participate, then it could spark an unprecedented millennial boom, global in scope but empowering to each individual, marked not only by economic growth but also by a spread of knowledge and freedom and true community. That's a daunting task. But it shouldn't be much harder than figuring out how to etch more than seven million transistors on a sliver of silicon.

Our Century . . .
and the Next One

As the twentieth century neared its end, I looked for a way that we at Time *could fulfill Henry Luce's injunction to tell the history of our time through the people who made it. So we embarked on a project to profile the hundred most influential people of the century. We added an interesting biographical twist by picking important contemporary visionaries to write about each member of what we dubbed the* Time 100: *Tatyana Tolstaya on Gorbachev, Elie Wiesel on Hitler, Bill Gates on the Wright brothers, for example. In an attempt to put the project into a coherent historical framework, I wrote an essay that tried to look at the century's historical figures in relation to the great forces of the time. It appeared in the first of five issues of the* Time 100, *in April of 1998.*

As centuries go, this has been one of the most amazing: inspiring, at times horrifying, always fascinating. Sure, the fifteenth was pretty wild, with the Renaissance and Spanish Inquisition in full flower, Gutenberg building his printing press, Copernicus beginning to contemplate the solar system, and Columbus spreading the culture of Europe to the Americas. And of course there was the first century, which if only for the life and death of Jesus may have had the most impact of any. Socrates and Plato made the fifth century BC also rather remarkable. But we denizens of the twentieth can probably get away with the claim that ours has been one of the top four or five of recorded history.

Let's brag for a moment. To name just a few random things we accomplished in a hundred years: We split the atom, invented jazz and rock, launched airplanes and landed on the moon, concocted a general theory of relativity, devised the transistor and figured out how to etch millions of them on tiny microchips, discovered penicillin and the structure of DNA, fought down fascism and communism, bombed Guernica and painted the bombing of Guernica, developed cinema and television, built highways, and wired the world. Not to mention the peripherals these produced, such as sitcoms and cable channels, 800 numbers and Web sites, shopping malls and leisure time, existentialism and modernism, Oprah and Imus. Initials spread like graffiti. NATO, IBM, ABM, UN, WPA, NBA, NFL, CIA, CNN, PLO, IPO, IRA, IMF, TGIF. And against all odds we avoided blowing ourselves up.

All of this produced some memorable players. Look around. There's Lenin arriving at the Finland Station and Gandhi marching to the sea to make salt. Winston Churchill with his cigar, Louis Armstrong with his horn, Charlie Chaplin with his cane. Rosa Parks staying seated on her bus and a kid standing in front of a tank near Tiananmen Square. Einstein is in his study and the Beatles are on *The Ed Sullivan Show*.

Rarely does a century dawn so clearly and cleanly. In 1900, Freud published *The Interpretation of Dreams*, ending the Victorian era. Her Majesty, as if on cue, died the following January, after a sixty-three-year reign. Her empire included one-quarter of the earth's population, but the Boer War in South Africa was signaling the end of the colonial era. In China, the Boxer Rebellion heralded the awakening of a new giant. In America, cars were replacing horses, 42 percent of workers were in farming (today it's 3 percent), and the average life span was about fifty (today it's seventy-five).

The tape recorder was unveiled in 1900 at the Paris Exposition, to which visitors flocked to be scandalized by Rodin's non-Victorian statues, and Kodak introduced the Brownie camera, an apt symbol of a century in which technology would at first seem magical then become simple and cheap and personal. The Scholastic Aptitude Test was born that year, permitting a transition of power from an aristocracy to a meritocracy. The Wright brothers went to Kitty Hawk for the first time to try out their gliders. Lenin, thirty, published his first paper calling for revolution in Russia. Churchill, twenty-six, was elected to the House of Commons. J. P. Morgan, working with a young executive named Charles Schwab, bought out Andrew Carnegie and conglomerated U.S. Steel, by far the biggest business in the world. And the German physicist Max Planck made one of the discoveries that would shape the century: that atoms emit radiations of energy in bursts he called quanta.

From these seeds was born a century that can be summed up and labeled in a handful of ways:

The Century of Freedom. If you had to pick a two-word summation, it would be: Freedom won. It beat back the two totalitarian alternatives that arose to challenge it, fascism and communism. By the 1990s, the ideals developed by centuries of philosophers from Plato to Locke to Mill to Jefferson—individual rights, civil liberties, personal freedoms, and democratic participation in the choice of leaders—finally held sway over more than half of the world's population.

The Century of Capitalism. Democracy can exist without capitalism, and capitalism without democracy, but probably not for very long. Political and economic freedom tend to go together. Early in the century, Theodore Roosevelt laid the foundation for a government-guided free market, one that encouraged individual initiative while protecting people against cartels and the colder faces of capitalism. His cousin Franklin confronted capitalism's greatest challenge, the Great Depression, by following these principles. Half a world away, Lenin laid the ground for a command economy, and his successor Stalin showed how brutal it could be. They ended up on the ash heap of history. Although capitalism will continue to face challenges, internally and externally, it is now the economic structure for most societies around the world.

The Electronic Century. A defining event for the century occurred five years before it began: the discovery of the electron by British physicist J. J. Thomson. The subsequent understanding of the inner workings of the atom led to the first weapon of mass destruction, which helped hasten the end of World War II and became the defining reality of the cold war. Alan Turing helped harness electronics to devise the first digital computers. Five centuries earlier, Gutenberg's printing press had cut the cost of transmitting information by a factor of a thousand. That paved the way for the Reformation, by allowing individuals to have their own Bibles, and for the progress of individual liberties that became inevitable once information and ideas flowed freely. The invention of the transistor and the microchip has cut the cost of transmitting information by a factor of more than a million. The result has been a transition from an industrial age to an information age.

The Global Century. The basic unit of human society over the millennia has evolved from villages to city-states to empires to nation-states. In this century, everything became global. Much of the first half was dominated by the death spasms of an international order that for four hundred years had been based on the shifting alliances of European nation-states, but this time the resulting wars were world wars. Now, not only are military issues global, so are economic and even cultural ones. People everywhere are threatened by weapons anywhere, they produce and consume in a single networked economy, and increasingly they have access to the same movies and music and ideas.

The Mass Market Century. Yet another defining event of the century came in 1908, when Henry Ford opened his assembly line. Ordinary people could now afford a Model T (choice of color: black). Products became mass-produced and mass-marketed, with all of the centralization and conformity that entails. Television sets and toothpaste, magazines and movies, shows and shoes: They were distributed or broadcast, in cookie-cutter form, from central facilities to millions of people. In reaction, a modernist mix of anarchy, existential despair, and rebellion against conformity motivated art, music, literature, fashion, and even behavior for much of the century.

The Genocidal Century. Then there was the dark side. Amid the glories of the century lurked some of history's worst horrors: Stalin's collectivization, Hitler's Holocaust, Mao's Cultural Revolution, Pol Pot's killing fields, Idi Amin's rampages. We try to personalize the blame, as if it were the fault of just a few madmen, but in fact it was whole societies, including advanced ones like Germany, that embraced or tolerated madness. What they had in common was that they sought totalitarian solutions rather than freedom. Theologians have to answer the question of why God allows evil. Rationalists have one almost as difficult: Why doesn't progress make civilizations more civilized?

The American Century. That's what Henry Luce called it in a 1941 essay. He was using the phrase to exhort his compatriots to prepare for war, to engage in the struggle for freedom. They did, yet again. And they won. Some countries conduct their foreign policy based on realism or its Prussian-accented cousin realpolitik: a cold and careful calculation of strategic interests. America is unique in that it is equally motivated by idealism. Whether it be the fight against fascism or communism, or even misconceived interventions like Vietnam, America's mission is to further not only its interests but also its values. And that idealist streak is a source of its global influence, even more so than its battleships. As became clear when the iron curtain collapsed in 1989, America's clout in the world comes not just from its military might but from the power and appeal of its values. Which is why it did, indeed, turn out to be an American Century.

So what will the next century be? The reams of guesses made in the next two years are destined to be digitally retrieved decades hence and read with a smirk. But let's take that risk, peer into the haze, and slap a few labels on the postmillennial period:

In the digital realm, the Next Big Advance will be voice recognition. The rudiments are already here, but in primitive form. Ask a computer to "recognize speech," and it is likely to think you want it to "wreck a nice beach." But in a decade or so we'll be able to chat away as machines soak it all in. What will truly embed microchips into our lives is when we can talk to them. Not only to our computers; we'll also be able to chat to our automobile navigation systems, telephone consoles, browsers, thermostats, VCRs, microwaves, and any other device we want to boss around.

That will open the way to phase three of the digital age: artificial intelligence. By providing so many thoughts and preferences to our machines each day, they'll accumulate enough information about how we think that they'll be able to mimic our minds and act as our agents. Scary, huh? But potentially quite useful. At least until they decide they don't need us anymore and start building even smarter machines that they can boss around.

The law powering the digital age up to now has been Gordon Moore's: that microchips will double in power and halve in price every eighteen months or so. Bill Gates rules because early on he acted on the assumption that computing power—the capacity of microprocessors and memory chips—would become nearly free; his company kept churning out more and more lines of complex software to make use of this cheap bounty. The law that will power the next few decades is that bandwidth (the capacity of fiber-optic and other pipelines to carry digital communications) will become nearly free.

Along with the recent advances in digital switching and storage technologies, this means a future in which all forms of content—movies, music, shows, books, data, magazines, newspapers, your aunt's recipes, and home videos—will be instantly available anywhere on demand. Anyone can be a producer of any content; you'll be able to create a movie or magazine, make it available to the world, and charge for it, just like Time Warner!

The result will be a transition from a mass-market world to a personalized one. Instead of centralized factories and studios that distribute or broadcast the same product to millions, technology is already allowing products to be tailored to each user. You can subscribe to news sources that serve up only topics and opinions that fit your interests. Everything from shoes to steel can be customized to meet individual wishes. What does that mean for the modernist revolt against conformity that dominated art and literature? Postmodernism, with its sense of irony, is more amused by connections and historical hyperlinks.

The digital revolution that burns so brightly today is likely to pale in comparison to the biotechnology revolution that is just beginning. Physicist Stephen Hawking, speaking at the White House last month on science in the next millennium, pointed out that for the past ten thousand years there has been no significant change in our human DNA. But over the next hundred years, we will be able and tempted to tinker. No doubt we'll make some improvements and some mistakes. We'll encode our dreams and vanities and hubris. We'll clone ourselves, we'll custom-design our kids. By playing Dr. Frankenstein, we'll have the chance to make miracles or monsters. The challenges will not be scientific, but moral.

In the political realm, democratic capitalism, having defeated the twin foes of fascism and communism, is likely to face three others. The first is tribalism, as in Bosnia. This is, of course, nothing new. But democracies are often maladroit at dealing with minorities who seek group empowerment, and a global marketplace can antagonize groups that lack either the skills or desire to be integrated into it. The second challenge will be from fundamentalism. Capitalism can be cold, consumption-oriented, and spiritless, alienating those who feel repelled by its modernity and its materialist values. Finally, there is the radical environmentalism of the anti-growth green movements, which could start seeming less radical and more urgent if the quest for economic growth that is inherent in capitalism continues to threaten the health of the planet.

Among the few things certain about the next century are that it will be wired, networked, and global. Because national borders will be unable to block the flow of information and innovation, the societies that thrive will be those that are comfortable with openness and with the free flow of services, goods, and ideas.

By these standards, the United States is rather well positioned. Ever since the days of the colonial pamphleteers, we've been comfortable with the cacophony that comes from freedom of information. We're used to being multicultural, and though we're constantly struggling with the consequences, we don't balkanize because of it. Our disputes, such as over affirmative action, may be divisive, but we have political and constitutional structures to resolve them peacefully.

But like other nations, the United States will have to adapt to a new century. With a global economy that will be increasingly knowledge-based, we can no longer permit unequal educational opportunities. Schools need to be open to competition and subjected to standards so that we avoid creating a two-tiered society. We also must realize, as both Theodore and Franklin Roosevelt did, that capitalism can be efficient, but it can also be cold. America's social fabric is strong when it weaves together rewards for individual initiative with neighborly compassion for all members of the community. The ultimate goal of democracy and freedom, after all, is not to pursue material abundance but to nurture the dignity and values of each individual. That is the fundamental story of this century, and if we're lucky and wise it will be the story of the next one.

The Biotech Age

Even as the information technology revolution was under way, I felt that the coming century would be affected just as much by breakthroughs in biotechnology, as I noted in the previous essay. In January 1999, I wrote this piece for a special issue of Time *that looked at what medical advances might occur after the sequencing of the human genome.*

Ring farewell to the century of physics, the one in which we split the atom and turned silicon into computing power. It's time to ring in the century of biotechnology. Just as the discovery of the electron in 1897 was a seminal event for the twentieth century, the seeds for the twenty-first century were spawned in 1953, when James Watson sketched out to Francis Crick how four nucleic acids could pair to form the self-copying code of a DNA molecule. Now we're just a few years away from one of the most important breakthroughs of all time: deciphering the human genome, the twenty-five thousand genes encoded by three billion chemical pairs in our DNA.

Before this century, medicine consisted mainly of amputation saws, morphine, and crude remedies that were about as effective as bloodletting. The flu epidemic of 1918 killed as many people (more than twenty million) in just a few months as were killed in the four years of World War I. Since then, antibiotics and vaccines have allowed us to vanquish entire classes of diseases. As a result, life expectancy in the United States jumped from about fifty years at the beginning of the century to seventy-five now.

But twentieth-century medicine did little to increase the natural life span of healthy humans. The next medical revolution could change that, because genetic engineering has the potential to conquer cancer, grow new blood vessels in the heart, block the growth of blood vessels in tumors, create new organs from stem cells, and perhaps even reset the primeval genetic coding that causes cells to age.

Our children may be able (I hope, I fear) to choose their kids' traits: to select their gender and eye color; perhaps to tinker with their IQs, personalities, and athletic abilities. They could clone themselves, or one of their kids, or a celebrity they admire, or maybe even us after we've died.

In the five million years since we hominids separated from apes, our DNA has evolved less than 2 percent. But in the next century we'll be able to alter our DNA radically, encoding our visions and vanities while concocting new life-forms. When Dr. Frankenstein made his monster, he wrestled with the moral issue of whether he should allow it to reproduce: "Had I the right, for my own benefit, to inflict the curse upon everlasting generations?" Will such questions require us to develop new moral philosophies?

Probably not. Instead, we'll reach again for a time-tested moral notion: Treat each person as an individual rather than as a means to some end. Under this moral precept we should recoil at human cloning, because it inevitably entails using humans as means to other humans' ends—valuing them as copies of others we loved or as collections of body parts, not as individuals in their own right. We should also draw a line, however fuzzy, that would permit using genetic engineering to cure diseases and disabilities (cystic fibrosis, muscular dystrophy) but not to change the personal attributes that make someone an individual (IQ, physical appearance, gender, and sexuality).

The biotech age will also give us more reason to guard our personal privacy. Aldous Huxley, in *Brave New World,* got it wrong: Rather than centralizing power in the hands of the state, DNA technology has empowered individuals and families. But the state will have an important role, making sure that no one, including insurance companies, can look at our genetic data without our permission or use it to discriminate against us.

Then we can get ready for the breakthrough that could come at the end of the next century and is comparable to mapping our genes: mapping the 10 billion or more neurons of our brain. With that information we might someday be able to create artificial intelligences that think and experience consciousness in ways that are indistinguishable from a human brain. Eventually we might be able to replicate our own minds in a machine, so that we could live on without the "wetware" of a biological brain and body. The twentieth century's revolution in infotechnology will thereby merge with the twenty-first century's revolution in biotechnology.

Person of the Century

Time's project of profiling one hundred influential people of the twentieth century culminated on December 31, 1999, when we published our Person of the Century issue. Years earlier, those of us at the magazine had started discussing the options over drinks and dinners. It was more than just a parlor game, both for us and for our readers. Debating the relative influence of people in various fields forces us analyze which actions in this world have enduring importance, what leadership skills have a lasting impact, and who actually affects our lives in more than merely a transient way. I had always favored Einstein, and fortunately for him (and for me), I became editor and my vote carried more weight than it otherwise would have. I felt the need to justify the choice historically, so I wrote the following essay. In researching it, I also decided that I would someday write a biography of Einstein. In this piece, I reflect some of the ideas and descriptions of historical forces that I used in the essay launching the Time 100 *project, but I also simplified my assessment of the grand forces that shaped the century.*

What an amazing cast of characters! What a wealth of heroes and villains to choose from!

Some shook the world by arriving: Gandhi at the sea to make salt, Lenin at the Finland Station. Others by refusing to depart: Rosa Parks from her seat on the bus, that kid from the path of the tank near Tiananmen Square. There were magical folks who could make freedom radiate through the walls of a Birmingham jail, a South African prison, or a Gdansk shipyard.

Others made machines that could fly and machines that could think, discovered a mold that conquered infections and a molecule that formed the basis of life. There were people who could inspire us with a phrase:

fear itself, tears and sweat, ask not. Frighten us with a word: *Heil!* Or revise the universe with an equation: E=mc².

So how can we go about choosing the Person of the Century, the one who, for better or worse, personified our times and will be recorded by history as having the most lasting significance?

Let's begin by noting what our century will be remembered for. Out of the fog of proximity, three great themes emerge:

The grand struggle between totalitarianism and democracy.

The ability of courageous individuals to resist authority in order to secure their civil rights.

The explosion of scientific and technical knowledge that unveiled the mysteries of the universe and helped secure the triumph of freedom by unleashing the power of free minds and free markets.

The Century of Democracy

Some people, looking at the first of these themes, sorrowfully insist that the choice has to be Hitler, Führer of the Fascist genocides and refugee floods that plagued the century. He wrought the Holocaust that redefined evil and the war that reordered the world.

Competing with him for such devilish distinction is Lenin, who snatched from obscurity the nineteenth-century ideology of communism and devised the modern tools of totalitarian brutality. He begat not only Stalin and Mao but in some ways also Hitler, who was enchanted by the Soviets' terror tactics. Doesn't the presence of such evil—and the continued eruption of totalitarian brutality from Uganda to Kosovo—make a mockery of the rationalists' faith that progress makes civilizations more civilized? Isn't Hitler, alas, the person who most influenced and symbolized this most genocidal of centuries?

No. He lost. So did Lenin and Stalin. Along with the others in their evil pantheon, and the totalitarian ideologies they represented, they are destined for the ash heap of history. If you had to describe the century's geopolitics in one sentence, it could be a short one: Freedom won. Free minds and free markets prevailed over fascism and communism.

So a more suitable choice would be someone who embodied the struggle for freedom: Franklin Roosevelt, the only person to be *Time*'s Man of the Year thrice (for 1932, 1934, and 1941). He helped save capitalism from its most serious challenge, the Great Depression. And then he rallied the power of free people and free enterprise to defeat fascism.

Other great leaders were part of this process. Winston Churchill stood up to Hitler even earlier than Roosevelt did, when it took far more courage. Harry Truman, a plainspoken man with gut instincts for what was right, forcefully began the struggle against Soviet expansionism, a challenge that Roosevelt was too sanguine about. Ronald Reagan and Mikhail Gorbachev helped choreograph the conclusion of that sorry empire's strut upon the stage. So, too, did Pope John Paul II, a Pole with a passion for both faith and freedom. And if you were to pick a hero who embodied America's contribution to winning the fight for freedom, it would probably be not Roosevelt, but instead the American GI.

Nor is it proper to mythologize Roosevelt. The New Deal was at times a hodgepodge of conflicting economic ideas, marked more by enthusiasm than by coherence. It restored Americans' faith and hopes, saved them from fear itself, but never really managed to end the Depression. The war did that.

Nevertheless, Franklin Roosevelt stands out among the century's political leaders. With his first-class temperament, wily manipulations, and passion for experimentation, he's the jaunty face of democratic values. Thus we pick him as the foremost statesman and one of three finalists for Person of the Century. That may seem, to non-Americans, parochial. True, but this was, as our magazine's founder Henry Luce dubbed it in 1941, the American Century—politically, militarily, economically, and ideologically.

When Roosevelt took office at the beginning of 1933 (the same week that Hitler assumed emergency powers in Germany), unemployment in the United States had, in three years, jumped from four million to twelve million, at least a quarter of the workforce. Fathers of hungry kids were trying to sell apples on the street. FDR's bold experiments ("Above all, try something") included many that failed, but he brought hope to millions and some lasting contributions to the nation's foundation: Social Security, minimum wages, insured bank deposits, and the right to join unions. Henceforth the national government (in the United States and most everywhere else) took on the duty of managing the economy and providing capitalism with a social safety net.

By New Year's Day of 1941, the Depression still lingered, and the threat from Hitler was growing. Roosevelt went to his second-floor White House study to draft the address that would launch his unprecedented third term. There was a long silence, uncomfortably long, as his speechwriters waited for him to speak. Then he leaned forward and began dictating.

"We look forward to a world founded upon four essential human freedoms," he said. He proceeded to list them: freedom of expression, freedom of worship, freedom from want, freedom from fear. One of the great themes of this century was the progress made toward each of them.

Roosevelt made another great contribution: He escorted onto the century's stage a remarkable woman, his wife, Eleanor. She served as his counterpoint: Uncompromisingly moral, earnest rather than devious, she became an icon of feminism and social justice in a nation just discovering the need to grant rights to women, blacks, ordinary workers, and the poor. She discovered the depth of racial discrimination while touring New Deal programs (on a visit to Birmingham in 1938, she refused to sit in the white section of the auditorium), and subsequently peppered her husband with questions over dinner and memos at bedtime. Even after her husband's death, she remained one of the century's most powerful advocates for social fairness.

One political leader who rivals Roosevelt in embodying freedom's fight is Winston Churchill. Indeed, it's possible to imagine a president other than Roosevelt leading America through the war, but it's nearly impossible to imagine someone other than Churchill turning the world's darkest moments into Britain's finest hour.

He despised tyranny with such a passion that he, and by extension his nation, was willing to stand alone against Hitler when it was most critical. And unlike Roosevelt, he came early to the crusade against Soviet tyranny as well. His eloquent speeches strengthened the faith of all freedom-loving people in both the righteousness of their struggle and the inevitability of their cause.

So why is he not Person of the Century? He was, after all, *Time*'s Man of the Half-Century in 1950. Well, the passage of time can alter our perspective. A lot has happened since 1950. It has become clear that one of the great themes of the century has been the success of those who resisted authority in order to seek civil rights, decolonization, and an end to repression. Along with this came the setting of the sun on the great colonial empires.

In his approach to domestic issues, individual rights, and the liberties of colonial subjects, Churchill turned out to be a romantic refugee from a previous era who ended up on the wrong side of history. He did not become prime minister, he incorrectly proclaimed in 1942, "to preside over the liquidation of the British Empire," which then controlled a quarter of the globe's land. He bulldoggedly opposed the women's-rights movement, other civil rights crusades, and decolonization, and he called Mohandas Gandhi "nauseating" and a "half-naked fakir."

As it turned out, Churchill's tenacity was powerful enough to defy Hitler, but not as powerful as the resistance techniques of the half-naked fakir. Gandhi and others who fought for civil rights turned out to be part of a historic tide, one that Roosevelt and his wife, Eleanor, appreciated better than Churchill did.

Which brings us to:

The Century of Civil Rights

In a century marked by brutality, Gandhi perfected a different method of bringing about change, one that would turn out (surprisingly) to have more lasting impact. The words he used to describe it do not translate readily into English: *satyagraha* (holding firmly on to the deepest truth and soul-force) and *ahimsa* (the love that remains when all thoughts of violence are dispelled). They formed the basis for civil disobedience and nonviolent resistance. "Nonviolence is the greatest force at the disposal of mankind," he said. "It is mightier than the mightiest weapon of destruction devised by the ingenuity of man."

Part of his creed was that purifying society required purifying one's own soul. "The more you develop nonviolence in your own being, the more infectious it becomes." Or, more pithily: "We must become the change we seek."

He was, truth be told, rather weird at times. His own purification regimen involved inordinate attention to the bowel movements of himself and those around him, and he liked testing his powers of self-denial by sleeping naked with young women. Nevertheless, he became not just a political force but a spiritual guide for those repelled by the hate and greed that polluted this century. "Generations to come," said Albert Einstein, "will scarce believe that such a one as this ever in flesh and blood walked upon this earth."

Gandhi's life of civil disobedience began while he was a young lawyer in South Africa when, because he was a dark-skinned Indian, he was told to move to a third-class seat on a train even though he held a first-class ticket. He refused, and ended up spending the night on a desolate platform. It culminated in 1930, when he was sixty-one, and he and his followers marched 240 miles in twenty-four days to make their own salt from the sea in defiance of British colonial laws and taxes. By the time he reached the sea, several thousand had joined his march, and all along India's coast thousands more were doing the same. More than sixty thousand were eventually arrested, including Gandhi, but it was clear who would end up the victors.

Gandhi did not see the full realization of his dreams; India finally gained independence, but a civil war between Hindus and Muslims resulted, despite his efforts, in the bloody birth of Pakistan. He was killed, on his way to prayers, by a Hindu fanatic.

His spirit and philosophy, however, transformed the century. His most notable heir was Martin Luther King Jr. "If humanity is to progress," King once declared, "Gandhi is inescapable."

King, who began studying Gandhi in college, was initially skeptical

about the Mahatma's faith in nonviolence. But by the time of the Montgomery bus boycott, he later wrote, "I had come to see early that the
Christian doctrine of love operating through the Gandhian method of
nonviolence was one of the most potent weapons available to the Negro
in his struggle for freedom." The bus boycott, sit-ins, freedom rides,
and, above all, the Selma march with its bloody Sunday on the Edmund
Pettus Bridge showed how right he and Gandhi were.

Civil rights took a variety of forms this century. Women got the right
to vote, gained control over their reproductive life, and made strides
toward achieving equal status in the workplace. Gays and lesbians gained
the right to be proud of who they are.

Indeed, one defining aspect of our century has been the degree to
which it was shaped not just by powerful political leaders but also by
ordinary folks who civilly disobeyed: Nelson Mandela organizing a campaign in 1952 to defy South Africa's "pass laws" by entering white town-
ships, Rosa Parks refusing to give up her seat on a Montgomery bus just
as Gandhi had on the South African train, the unknown rebel blocking
the line of tanks rumbling toward Tiananmen Square, Lech Wałęsa
leading his fellow Polish workers out on strike, the British suffragist
Emmeline Pankhurst launching hunger strikes, American students pro-
testing the Vietnam War by burning their draft cards, and gays and
lesbians at Greenwich Village's Stonewall Inn resisting a police raid. In
the end, they changed the century as much as the men who commanded
armies.

The Century of Science and Technology

It is hard to compare the influence of statesmen with that of scientists.
Nevertheless, we can note that there are certain eras that were most
defined by their politics, others by their culture, and others by their scientific advances.

The eighteenth century, for example, was clearly one marked by statecraft: In 1776 alone there are Thomas Jefferson and Benjamin Franklin
writing the Declaration of Independence, Adam Smith publishing *The
Wealth of Nations,* and George Washington leading the Revolutionary

forces. The seventeenth century, on the other hand, despite such colorful leaders as Louis XIV and the château he left us, will be most remembered for its science: Galileo exploring gravity and the solar system, Descartes developing modern philosophy, and Newton discovering the laws of motion and calculus. And the sixteenth will be remembered for the flourishing of the arts and culture: Michelangelo and Leonardo and Shakespeare creating masterpieces, Elizabeth I creating the Elizabethan Age.

So how will the twentieth century be remembered? Yes, for democracy. And yes, for civil rights.

But the twentieth century will be most remembered, like the seventeenth, for its earthshaking advances in science and technology. In his massive history of the twentieth century, Paul Johnson declares, "The scientific genius impinges on humanity, for good or ill, far more than any statesman or warlord." Albert Einstein was more pithy: "Politics is for the moment. An equation is for eternity."

Just look at the year the century was born. The Paris Exposition in 1900 (fifty million visitors, more than the entire population of France) featured wireless telegraphs, X-rays, and tape recorders. "It is a new century, and what we call electricity is its God," wrote the romantic historian Henry Adams from Paris.

In 1900 we began to unlock the mysteries of the atom: Max Planck launched quantum physics by discovering that atoms emit bursts of radiation in packets. Also the mysteries of the mind: Sigmund Freud published *The Interpretation of Dreams* that year. Marconi was preparing to send radio signals across the Atlantic, the Wright brothers went to Kitty Hawk to work on their gliders, and an unpromising student named Albert Einstein finally graduated, after some difficulty, from college that year. So much for the boneheaded prediction made the year before by Charles Duell, director of the U.S. Patent Office: "Everything that can be invented has been invented."

So many fields of science made such great progress that each could produce its own contender for Person of the Century.

Let's start with medicine. In 1928 the young Scottish researcher Alexander Fleming sloppily left a lab dish growing bacteria on a bench when he went on vacation. It got contaminated with a *Penicillium* mold spore, and when he returned, he noticed that the mold seemed to stop the growth of the germs. His serendipitous discovery would eventually save more lives than were lost in all the century's wars combined.

Fleming serves well as a symbol of all the great medical researchers, such as Jonas Salk and David Ho, who fought disease. But he personally did little, after his initial eureka! moment, to develop penicillin. Nor has the fight against infectious diseases been so successful that it will stand as a defining achievement of the century.

The century's greater biological breakthrough was more basic. It was unceremoniously announced on February 28, 1953, when Francis Crick winged into the Eagle Pub in Cambridge, England, and declared that he and his partner, James Watson, had "found the secret of life."

Watson had sketched out how four chemical bases paired to create a self-copying code at the core of the double-helix-shaped DNA molecule. In the more formal announcement of their discovery, a one-page paper in the journal *Nature,* they noted the significance in a famously under-stated sentence: "It has not escaped our notice that the specific pairing we have postulated immediately suggests a possible copying mechanism for the genetic material." But they were less restrained when persuading Watson's sister to type up the paper for them. "We told her," Watson wrote in *The Double Helix,* "that she was participating in perhaps the most famous event in biology since Darwin's book."

DNA is likely to be the discovery made in the twentieth century that will be the most important to the twenty-first. The world is just a few years away from deciphering the entire sequence of more than a hundred thousand human genes encoded by the three billion chemical pairs of our DNA. That will open the way to new drugs, genetic engineering, and designer babies.

So should Watson and Crick be Persons of the Century? Perhaps. But two factors count against them. Their role, unlike that of Einstein or Churchill, would have been performed by others if they hadn't been around; indeed, competitor Linus Pauling was just months away from shouting the same eureka! In addition, although the next century may be, this did not turn out to be a century of genetic engineering.

What about the technologists?

There's Henry Ford, who perfected ways to mass-produce the horse-less carriages developed in Germany by Gottlieb Daimler and others. The car became the most influential consumer product of the century, bringing with it a host of effects good and bad: more personal freedom, residential sprawl, social mobility, highways and shopping malls, air pollution (though the end of the noxious pollution produced by horses), and mass markets for mass-produced goods.

Wilbur and Orville Wright also used the internal-combustion engine to free people from earthly bounds. Their twelve-second flight in 1903 transformed both war and peace. As Bill Gates said in these pages, "Their invention effectively became the World Wide Web of that era, bringing people, languages, ideas and values together." The result was a new era of globalization.

Even more central to this globalization were the electronic technologies that revolutionized the distribution of information, ideas, and entertainment. Five centuries ago, Gutenberg's advances in printing helped lead to the Reformation (by permitting people to own their own Bibles and religious tracts), the Renaissance (by permitting ideas to travel from village to village), and the rise of individual liberty (by allowing ordinary folks direct access to information). Likewise, the twentieth century was transformed by a string of inventions that, building on the telegraph and telephone of the nineteenth century, led to a new information age.

In 1927 Philo Farnsworth was able to electronically deconstruct a moving image and transmit it to another room. "There you are," he said, "electronic television." (In the heated historical debate, both *Time* and the U.S. Patent Office ended up giving him credit for the invention over his rival Vladimir Zworykin of RCA.)

In the 1930s Alan Turing first described the computer—a machine that could perform logical functions based on whatever instructions were fed to it—and then proceeded to help build one in the early 1940s that cracked the German wartime codes. His concepts were refined by other computer pioneers: John von Neumann, John Atanasoff, J. Presper Eckert, and John Mauchly.

Meanwhile, another group of scientists—including Enrico Fermi and

J. Robert Oppenheimer—was unlocking the power of the atom in a different way, one that led to the creation of a weapon that helped win the war and define the subsequent five decades of nervous peace that ensued.

In 1947 William Shockley and his team at Bell Labs invented the transistor, which had the ability to take an electric current and translate it into on-off binary data. Thus began the digital age. Robert Noyce and Jack Kilby, a decade later, came up with ways to etch many transistors— eventually millions—onto tiny silicon wafers that became known as microchips.

Many people—let's not pick on Al Gore here—deserve credit for creating the Internet, which began in 1969 as a network of university computers and began to take off in 1974 when Vint Cerf and Robert Kahn published a protocol that enabled any computer on the network to transmit to any other. A companion protocol devised by Tim Berners-Lee in 1990 created the World Wide Web, which simplified and popularized navigation on the Net. The idea that anyone in the world can publish information and have it instantly available to anyone else in the world created a revolution that will rank with Gutenberg's.

Together these triumphs of science and technology advanced the cause of freedom, in some ways more than any statesman or soldier did. In 1989 workers in Warsaw used faxes to spread the word of Solidarity, and schoolkids in Prague slipped into tourist hotels to watch CNN reports on the upheavals in Berlin. A decade later, dissidents in China set up e-mail chains, and Web-surfing students evaded clueless censors to break the government's monopoly on information. Just as the flow of ideas wrought by Gutenberg led to the rise of individual rights, so, too, did the unfetterable flow of ideas wrought by telephones, faxes, television, and the Internet serve as the surest foe of totalitarianism in this century.

Fleming, Watson and Crick, the Wright brothers, Farnsworth, Turing, Shockley, Fermi, Oppenheimer, Noyce—any of them could be, conceivably, a justifiable although somewhat narrow choice for Person of the Century. Fortunately, a narrow choice is not necessary.

Person of the Century

In a century that will be remembered foremost for its science and technology—in particular for our ability to understand and then harness the forces of the atom and the universe—one person stands out as both the greatest mind and paramount icon of our age: the kindly, absent-minded professor whose wild halo of hair, piercing eyes, engaging humanity, and extraordinary brilliance made his face a symbol and his name a synonym for genius—Albert Einstein.

Slow in learning to talk as a child, expelled by one headmaster and proclaimed by another unlikely to amount to anything, Einstein has become the patron saint of distracted schoolkids. But even at age five, he later recalled, he was puzzling over a toy compass and the mysteries of nature's forces.

During his spare time as a clerk in the Swiss patent office in 1905, he produced three papers that changed science forever. The first, for which he was later to win the Nobel Prize, described how light could behave not only like a wave but also like a stream of particles, called quanta or photons. This wave-particle duality became the foundation of quantum physics. It also provided theoretical underpinnings for such twentieth-century advances as television, lasers, and semiconductors.

The second paper confirmed the existence of molecules and atoms by statistically showing how their random collisions explained the jerky motion of tiny particles in water. Important as both these were, it was his third paper that truly upended the universe.

It was based, like much of Einstein's work, on a thought experiment: If you could travel at the speed of light, what would a light wave look like? If you were in a train that neared the speed of light, would you perceive time and space differently?

Einstein's conclusions became known as the special theory of relativity. No matter how fast one is moving toward or away from a source of light, the speed of that light beam will appear the same, a constant 186,000 miles per second. But space and time will be relative. As a train accelerates to near the speed of light, time on the train will slow down from the perspective of a stationary observer, and the train will get shorter and heavier. Okay, it's not obvious, but that's why we're no Einstein and he was.

Einstein went on to show that energy and matter were merely different faces of the same thing, their relationship described by the most famous equation in all of physics: Energy equals mass multiplied by the speed of light squared, $E=mc^2$. Although not exactly a recipe for an atomic bomb, it explained why one was possible. He also helped resolve smaller mysteries, such as why the sky is blue (it has to do with how the molecules of air diffuse sunlight).

His crowning glory, perhaps the most beautiful theory in all of science, was the general theory of relativity, published in 1916. Like the special theory, it was based on a thought experiment: Imagine being in an enclosed lab accelerating through space. The effects you'd feel would be no different from the experience of gravity. Gravity, he figured, is a warping of space-time. Just as Einstein's earlier work paved the way to harnessing the smallest subatomic forces, the general theory opened up an understanding of the largest of all things, from the formative big bang of the universe to its mysterious black holes.

It took three years for astronomers to test this theory by measuring how the sun shifted light coming from a star. The results were announced at a meeting of the Royal Society in London presided over by J. J. Thomson, who in 1897 had discovered the electron. After glancing up at the society's grand portrait of Sir Isaac Newton, Thomson told the assemblage, "Our conceptions of the fabric of the universe must be fundamentally altered." The headline in the next day's *Times* of London read "Revolution in Science ... Newtonian Ideas Overthrown." The *New York Times*, back when it knew how to write great headlines, was even more effusive two days later: "Lights All Askew in the Heavens/ Men of Science More or Less Agog Over Results of Eclipse Observations/ Einstein's Theory Triumphs."

Einstein, hitherto little known, became a global celebrity and was able to sell pictures of himself to journalists and send the money to a charity for war orphans. More than a hundred books were written about relativity within a year.

Einstein also continued his contributions to quantum physics by raising questions that are still playing a pivotal role in the modern development of the theory. Shortly after devising general relativity, he came up with a quantum theory of radiation explaining that all subatomic particles, including electrons, exhibit characteristics of both wave and particle.

This opened the way, alas, to the quantum theories of Werner Heisenberg and others who showed how the wave-particle duality implies a randomness or uncertainty in nature and that particles are affected simply by observing them. This made Einstein uncomfortable. As he famously and frequently insisted, "God does not play dice." (Retorted is friendly rival Niels Bohr: "Einstein, stop telling God what to do.") He spent his later years in a failed quest for a unified theory that would explain what appeared to be random or uncertain.

Does Einstein's discomfort with quantum theory make him less a candidate for Person of the Century? Not by much. His own work contributed greatly to quantum theory and to the semiconductor revolution it spawned. And his belief in the existence of a unified field theory could well be proved right in the new century.

More important, he serves as a symbol of all the scientists—such as Heisenberg, Bohr, Richard Feynman, and Stephen Hawking, even the ones he disagreed with—who built upon his work to decipher and harness the forces of the cosmos. As James Gleick wrote earlier this year in the *Time* 100 series, "The scientific touchstones of our age—the Bomb, space travel, electronics—all bear his fingerprints." Or, to quote a *Time* cover story from 1946 (produced by Whittaker Chambers):

> Among 20th-Century men, he blends to an extraordinary degree those highly distilled powers of intellect, intuition and imagination which are rarely combined in one mind, but which, when they do occur together, men call genius. It was all but inevitable that this genius should appear in the field of science, for 20th-Century civilization is first & foremost technological.

Einstein's theory of relativity not only upended physics, it also jangled the underpinnings of society. For nearly three centuries, the clockwork universe of Galileo and Newton—which was based on absolute laws and certainties—formed the psychological foundation for the Enlightenment, with its belief in causes and effects, order, rationalism, even duty.

Now came a view of the universe in which space and time were all relative. Indirectly, relativity paved the way for a new relativism in morality, arts, and politics. There was less faith in absolutes, not only of time and space but also of truth and morality. "It formed a knife," historian Paul Johnson says of relativity theory, "to help cut society adrift from its traditional moorings." Just as Darwinism became, a century ago, not just a biological theory but also a social theology, so, too, did relativity shape the social theology of the twentieth century.

The effect on the arts can be seen by looking at 1922, the year that Einstein won the Nobel Prize, James Joyce published *Ulysses*, and T. S. Eliot published *The Waste Land*. There was a famous party in May for the debut of the ballet *Renard*, composed by Stravinsky and staged by Diaghilev. They were both there, along with Picasso (who had designed the sets), Proust (who had been proclaimed Einstein's literary interpreter), and Joyce. The art of each, in its own way, reflected the breakdown of mechanical order and of the sense that space and time were absolutes.

In early 1933, as Hitler was taking power, Einstein immigrated to the United States, settling in Princeton as the world's first scientific supercelebrity. That year he help found a group to resettle refugees, the International Rescue Committee. Thus he became a symbol of another of the great themes of the century: how history was shaped by tides of immigrants, so many of them destined for greatness, who fled oppressive regimes for the freedom of democratic climes.

As a humanist and an internationalist, Einstein had spent most of his life espousing a gentle pacifism, and he became one of Gandhi's foremost admirers. But in 1939 he signed one of the century's most important letters, one that symbolizes the relationship between science and politics. "It may become possible to set up a nuclear chain reaction," he wrote President Roosevelt. "This new phenomenon would also lead to the construction of bombs." When Roosevelt read the letter, he crisply ordered, "This requires action."

Roosevelt, Gandhi, Einstein. Three inspiring characters, each representing a different force of history in the past century. They were about as different as any three men are likely to be. Yet each in his own way, both intentionally and not, taught us the century's most important lesson: the value of being both humble and humane.

Roosevelt, scarcely an exemplar of humility, nonetheless saved the possibility of governmental humility from the forces of utopian and dystopian arrogance. Totalitarian systems—whether Fascist or Communist—believe that those in charge know what's best for everyone else. But leaders who nurture democracy and freedom—who allow folks to make their own choices rather than dictating them from on high—are being laudably humble, an attitude that the twentieth century clearly rewarded and one that is necessary for creating humane societies.

Gandhi, unlike Roosevelt, was the earthly embodiment of humility, so much so that at times it threatened to become a conceit. He taught us that we should value the civil liberties and individual rights of other human beings, and he lived for (and was killed for) preaching tolerance and pluralism. By exhibiting these virtues, which the century has amply taught us are essential to civilization, we express the humility and humanity that come from respecting people who are different from us.

Einstein taught the greatest humility of all: that we are but a speck in an unfathomably large universe. The more we gain insight into its mysterious forces, cosmic and atomic, the more reason we have to be humble. And the more we harness the huge power of these forces, the more such humility becomes an imperative. "A spirit is manifest in the laws of the Universe," he once wrote, "in the face of which we, with our modest powers, must feel humble."

Einstein often invoked God, although his was a rather depersonalized deity. He believed, he said, in a "God who reveals Himself in the lawful harmony of all that exists." His faith in this divine harmony was what caused him to reject the view that the universe is subject to randomness and uncertainty. "Subtle is the Lord, but malicious he is not." Searching for God's design, he said, was "the source of all true art and science." Although this quest may be a cause for humility, it is also what gives meaning and dignity to our lives.

As the century's greatest thinker, as an immigrant who fled from oppression to freedom, as a political idealist, he best embodies what historians will regard as significant about the twentieth century. And as a philosopher with faith both in science and in the beauty of God's handiwork, he personifies the legacy that has been bequeathed to the next century.

In a hundred years, as we turn to another new century—nay, ten times a hundred years, when we turn to another new millennium—the name that will prove most enduring from our own amazing era will be that of Albert Einstein: genius, political refugee, humanitarian, locksmith of the mysteries of the atom and the universe.

7. JOURNALISM

———◆———

Luce's Values, Then and Now

The seventy-fifth anniversary of Time, *in 1998, provided me with an opportunity to reflect on the cofounder of the magazine. I had long admired Henry Luce's curiosity, unabashed love of informative middlebrow journalism, and belief that narratives about people can help us understand our world and the moral questions we face. For a history of the magazine written in 2009, I updated the piece a bit, but I didn't change the substance.*

When Henry Luce founded *Time* magazine with his friend Briton Hadden in 1923, he described a paradox: Folks were being bombarded with information but were nevertheless woefully underinformed. He set out to create a magazine that would sift through the clutter, synthesize what was important, and preach his cheeky prejudices.

Sound familiar? It was like a Web aggregator and blog for the age of print. By the time of Luce's death in 1967, television news had been added to the barrage of information hitting us each day, and in the years since, the world has become far more saturated with information than even Luce could have imagined: cable and talk radio, blogs and Web sites, RSS feeds and Twitter, all brimming with headlines and hype, news and sleaze, smart analysis and kooky opining.

Through it all, the basic mission and strategy that Luce developed endured. *Time* remains a way to help people cope with the clutter and sort out what's important and interesting. Although *Time* gradually moved away from providing a recap or digest of the previous week's news, it still tries to put events into context, anticipate trends, add new insights and facts, tell the behind-the-scene tales, and explore the questions others forgot to ask. It does this not only in print, but now also on the Web and in an ever-evolving variety of other electronic forms.

One aspect of Luce's original mission has been strengthened. The proliferation of magazines, channels, stations, blogs, Web sites, and services means that much of the media has become narrowly focused on special interests and niches. Yet *Time* continues to hold to the faith that intelligent people are curious about what's new in all sorts of fields, from politics to art, religion to technology. On the Internet, you can easily find nooks and crannies that focus on your special interests or cater to your ideological and political outlook. What *Time* tries to do, on both its pages and Web sites and blogs, is what Luce taught it to do: It exposes you to topics that expand your interests rather than narrow them, and it hits you with ideas and opinions that challenge your prejudices rather than merely reinforce them.

Each week *Time* still tries to follow Luce's injunction to bring together a mix of stories that conveys the excitement of our times in all its diversity. This mission helps us promote the rewards of serendipity, such as when a reader who is most interested in our Nation and World sections stumbles across something intriguing in Medicine or Music. It also helps us play a role that has become increasingly valuable in a world in which so many endeavors are hyperlinked: providing the common ground of information and knowledge that all informed folks should share and in fact enjoy sharing, whatever their specialized interests may be.

We also offer, or at least try to, a philosophical common ground. Since the great Left-Right struggles of the 1960s through the 1980s, the world has entered a millennial period in which common sense plays a greater role than knee-jerk ideological faiths. Although our stories often have a strong point of view, we try to make sure they are informed by open-minded reporting rather than partisan biases.

Yes, that represents a change from the days when Luce's global agendas infused these pages. The son of a Presbyterian missionary in China, Luce inherited a zeal to spread American values and Christianize the Communist world. He was very up front about his approach. In the prospectus that he wrote with Hadden, he noted that "complete neutrality . . . is probably as undesirable as it is impossible," and he proceeded to lay out a litany of what would be the new magazine's "prejudices."

As *Time* matured, it began to place more emphasis on reporting than on these prejudices. Nevertheless, there are certain prejudices—perhaps it's best to call them values—in the original prospectus that still inform *Time*'s journalism.

The foremost of these is the one Luce listed first: "A belief that the world is round." Luce was allergic to isolationism. In his famous 1941 essay, "The American Century," he urged the nation to engage in a global struggle on behalf of its values, most notably "a love of freedom, a feeling for the equality of opportunity, a tradition of self-reliance and independence and also of cooperation."

As the American Century draws to an end, these values are now ascendant. The main, albeit unfinished, story line of the century is the triumph of freedom (and its corollaries: democracy, individual liberty, and free markets) over totalitarianism and communism. When America has been willing to stand firm for its values, that willingness has proved to be, even more than its military might, the true source of its power in the world. *Time* thus remains rather prejudiced toward the values of free minds, free markets, free speech, and free choice. This reflects our faith that people are generally smart and sensible; the more choices and information they have, the better off things will be. To the extent that America remains an avatar of freedom, the Global Century about to dawn will be, in Luce's terminology, another American Century.

In a world that is not only round but also wired and networked, we remain committed to another prejudice in the original prospectus: "an interest in the new." The digital revolution, in particular, has the potential to change our world like nothing else since the invention of television.

Because we believe in the value of information, we have celebrated the explosion of sources that is the hallmark of the digital age. It is not only healthy for the public, it is also healthy for us. In a world of a thousand voices, people will gravitate to those they trust. That encourages us to stick to a formula that is clear yet demanding: good reporting, good writing, authoritative and fair analysis. We wouldn't be in this business if we didn't believe that more information and more opinions will eventually lead to more truth. That is why we were among the first journalists to go online and on the Web, and why we have pushed for open systems, like the Internet, that allow a diversity of voices to join the fray.

Time's emphasis on narrative storytelling as a way to put events into context is something that suits a weekly magazine. TV and the Internet are good for instant headlines and punditry. The Web is great for allowing people to explore links at their whim and drill down for raw data. But *Time* can play the storyteller who comes to your front porch with the color and insights that turn facts into coherent narratives. Part of the process is telling the news through the people who make it. As *Time*'s prospectus put it: "It is important to know what they drink. It is more important to know to what gods they pray and what kind of fights they love."

Through narrative and personality, analysis and synthesis, we try to make a complex world more coherent. The ultimate goal is to help make sure that the chaotic tumble of progress does not outpace our moral processing power.

A classic example came the week that World War II ended. *Time*'s cover stories, led by the writing of the great James Agee, focused on the dropping of the atomic bomb. Later in that issue, in a new section called Atomic Age, *Time* wrestled with the historic and moral implications of what passed for progress: "Man had been tossed into the vestibule of another millennium. It was wonderful to think of what the Atomic Age might be, if man was strong and honest. But at first it was a strange place, full of weird symbols and the smell of death."

The vestibule of this new millennium continues to have intruders that *Time* tries to wrestle into moral and historical context. The digital age, for example, has brought not only the excitement of more democratic forms of media but also the specter of invasions of our privacy and the spread of false information and poisonous ideas to every nook of a networked world. The impending biotech age promises not only the ability to engineer an end to diseases but also the weird prospects of cloning our bodies and tinkering with the genes of our children.

Nevertheless, the prejudice that we most firmly share with Luce and Hadden is a fundamental optimism. For them, optimism—a faith in progress—was not just a creed, it was a tactic for making things better. The challenges of a new millennium require that reporters be skeptical. But we must avoid the journalistic cynicism—as a pose, as a sophomoric attitude—that reigned in the '70s and '80s. Intelligent skepticism can, and should, be compatible with a belief in progress and a faith in humanity's capacity for common sense.

"As a journalist," Luce once said, "I am in command of a small sector in the very front trenches of this battle for freedom." Above all, we continue to share his belief that journalism can be, at its best, a noble endeavor. It can make people think—and make them think differently. It can be empowering and liberating. And, of course, it can be fun and exciting. That's what Luce sought to impart in his new magazine, and what we seek to impart in our new one each week.

Henry Grunwald

Henry Grunwald was the greatest intellectual to edit Time. *He made the magazine smarter and gave it more gravitas. He was not, however, completely attuned to American life. On a trip from Manhattan to Westchester County, he asked the driver to stop at a McDonald's so he could see what a Big Mac actually was. His clever, Dorothy Parker–like widow, Louise, asked me to give one of the eulogies at his memorial service when he died in 2005. I was slotted after Nora Ephron and Henry Kissinger, which made me feel like that guy who spun plates on a pole and had to follow the Beatles on* The Ed Sullivan Show.

Henry Grunwald had an unusual mix of intellectual rigor and personal grace, a combination that is rare in a human being, and perhaps even rarer among us journalists. His mark on American journalism, born of this rigor and grace, was likewise a rare one—so rare that it takes a moment to notice it and be surprised by it.

Here is what I think it was: When he took over *Time*, he transformed the magazine by aiming it upward rather than downward. He made it more intellectual rather than dumbing it down. He saved it by making it smarter, something that doesn't happen much in the media these days.

The process began when he joined *Time* as a twenty-two-year-old immigrant copy boy who was polishing his English by watching every movie that played on Forty-second Street. He wrote a memo to Harry Luce proposing a new magazine called *Ideas*. Content Peckham, the marvelously named boss of *Time*'s copy clerks, got hold of it. "Perhaps this guy belongs in the promotion department," she scribbled on it. "Or maybe on the moon."

As a copy clerk Henry famously fiddled with the pieces he was delivering, at one point completely rewriting a cover story he didn't like and then showing it to the original writer, who was not amused. One version has him hovering and commenting as a writer typed out a story until he suddenly saw the words: "Kid, if you don't cut this out, I'll break every bone in your body." As Henry backed out of the office, he muttered, "Cliché!"

As managing editor and then editor in chief, Henry displayed his intellectual rigor, if not always his personal grace, in the notes or memos he sent after reading each story. For me it began with the very first word I wrote in my first sentence in my first week at *Time*. I had begun the story, "Prior to his election as president, Jimmy Carter . . ."

The story came back from on high with an indecipherable Henry note across the top. I fancied it might be a few words of praise, or at least encouragement, for a new writer on his first piece. No one in the Nation section could read it. So the head of the copy desk, famed for her ability to read Henry's handwriting, was summoned. As we gathered around, she read the note in its entirety: "Prior," Henry had written, "is a god-awful word."

I have ever since recoiled when seeing the word.

Both in his life and in his *Time*, Henry displayed a mind that was deeply committed to old values and verities, yet also ever fascinated by new ideas. That made him both one of the most profoundly conservative and one of the most profoundly liberal people I have ever met. This outlook helped him move the magazine away from partisanship toward intellectual honesty.

From his father, the great Viennese operetta librettist Alfred Grunwald, he learned to appreciate both high and low culture, and seemed especially to embrace those who, like his father, thrived at the intersection of both: Norman Mailer, Jerzy Kosinski, Marilyn Monroe.

Even his worst ideas revealed his noble instincts. There was, for example, a dreadful series that Time Inc. publications did called "American Renewal" that was supposed to address every grand national challenge and come up with multipart proposals for solving them. It was an example of what Strobe Talbott once called Henry's penchant for solution-mongering. But it revealed in Henry a profound sense of moral mission that was rooted in a knowledge of evil.

In addition to the historic mark he made on journalism, Henry will be remembered for something else: He was one of the great exemplars, along with Henry Kissinger, of the amazing collection of Jewish refugees from fascism who arrived in the 1930s and transformed this nation with their intellect and profound patriotism. When the Nazis swamped Austria in 1938, the Grunwalds escaped to Czechoslovakia, then fled to France. In Biarritz he and his father bought a toy printing press to forge a visa, then he used his budding writing talent to write a petition to get them aboard the last freighter to Morocco.

Eventually they made it to New York Harbor on a very hot day, where young Henry was handed his first Coca-Cola. He took a sip. As he later recalled: "I hated it."

That, too, was emblematic. He loved his adopted country with the passion of a person who did not take its freedoms for granted. He may have loved it too much at times, for he despaired deeply about any of its lapses—its lapses in political will, and even more so its lapses of taste.

He capped his career in that quintessential American way, as his adopted country's ambassador to the country that he had been forced to flee. In 1989, I was denied entry into Romania, based on some perceived slight that had, long ago, appeared in *Time*. The authorities put me on the next plane out, which happened to be to Vienna. Unable to get hotel reservations, since it was the opening night of the opera season, I showed up to be Henry and Louise's guest at their ambassador's residence, under the assumption that whatever slight had so enraged the Romanians had probably been caused by one of Henry's closing-night memos.

My most vivid memory of Henry was of that evening, as he paced around in the living room where Kennedy had first met Khrushchev. He was putting on his white tie and tails for the opera while peppering me with questions—most of them rhetorical, thank goodness—about the future of Communist ideology and the Soviet hold on Eastern Europe.

This scene, almost out of an opéra bouffe by his father, might have seemed pompous. But Henry, even in white tie, rotund and orotund, always had a twinkle in his eye. It signaled his wry, self-aware wit, a wit that served to puncture any pomposity. Even after his eyes began to go dark on him, they were still able to twinkle, up until the very end.

Maynard Parker

Maynard Parker was my counterpart, the editor of Newsweek. *My admiration for him went from grudging to affectionate over the years. When he died in 1998, I wrote the following Milestone for* Time.

Both in person and in the pages he produced each week, *Newsweek* editor Maynard Parker had an edgy energy that was rooted in a passion for the news. Often tightly coiled and always ready to spring, he had the gleeful ability to rip up his magazine as it was going to press in order to make it more exciting.

Every Monday I felt the special kinship that comes from having tried to pull off the same feats: I could admire the smart way he had packaged a cover, spotted a trend, cropped a picture on a spread, or elicited a nugget of reporting. Maynard was one of the creative editors of the '80s and '90s who reinvented and revitalized newsmagazines, once considered news-rehashing dinosaurs. Although he had the hard-news instincts of a foreign correspondent, he developed a fingertip feel for the kind of cultural, social, family, and health trends that transcend last week's headlines and become next week's dinner-table conversations.

His competitive instincts caused him, like the rest of us, to make an occasional mistake, but his legendary intensity made him not merely a survivor but a person who prevailed in the struggle to keep journalism smart and relevant. I hope, and I suspect, that he would consider it a compliment and an accomplishment that he made all of us—not only his colleagues at *Newsweek* but his competitors at *Time*—better at what we do.

George Plimpton

George Plimpton was a delightful journalist. His words on paper matched his charm in person. Yet in a discomforting way, his life and death provided a cautionary tale. He had the preppy grace that led him to never look like, nor want to look like, he was trying too hard. He avoided being a striver. That made him a lot of fun to be around, but it also, I think, kept him from reaching his proper place in the literary pantheon. In 2009, I was asked to do a remembrance of him at Harvard's Memorial Church during an anniversary of the Lampoon. *Author Kurt Andersen was asked to do John Updike. Our pieces paired nicely, because Kurt explored how Updike's aversion to clubbiness and camaraderie allowed him to be a great writer, but it also made him into a writer who seemed a bit too inward at times. For the Harvard undergraduates, there were cautionary lessons, coupled like flip sides of a coin, in our respective eulogies.*

George Plimpton was the quintessential member of the *Harvard Lampoon*. Partly, that was because he was so very clubbable. He reveled in the lubricated camaraderie to be found in paneled rooms, and he was a master of the type of fraternal bonding that brushes up to, but never crosses, the edge of intimacy.

He also had a clever wit. In other words, he wasn't merely funny. He understood the essence of what was amusing about anecdotes and people. He once wore a piece of Japanese armor that hangs in the Lampoon Castle when playing in a baseball game against the *Harvard Crimson*. He also pulled with Farwell Smith the prank of sneaking into the Boston Marathon right near the end, while wearing *Harvard Lampoon* shirts, and trying to catch the leader at the finish.

He liked recalling the fake Harvard-Yale game program they published in which he wrote a story about "Why Harvard Will Not Go to the Rose Bowl This Year." One of the reasons, he noted, was that "California was in some kind of a time zone."

Later, that *Lampoon* style was reflected in *Not the New York Times*, an edition that Plimpton and friends put together in his apartment, published, and distributed during the 1978 newspaper strike. The lead story—done by Plimpton, Carl Bernstein, and Tony Hendra—read like a *Lampoon* parody of the *Crimson*. The top headline was "Pope Dies Yet Again; Reign Is Briefest Ever. Cardinals Return from Airport." It was about a pope from Liverpool named John Paul John Paul who served nineteen minutes. Amazingly, three weeks later, a new pope was actually elected and took the name John Paul II.

Plimpton also loved spectacle, hence his lifelong love of fireworks. He worked on the fireworks for the 1976 *Lampoon* Centennial, when he shot off the largest firework ever—known as Fat Man III—over the Charles.

He was also a master birdwatcher, and he applied that talent to humans as well. It was a joy to see him spot interesting people, charm them, and add them to his life list. Henceforth they would be found at his parties on 541 East Seventy-second Street, arrayed in his billiard room in their glory the way a lepidopterist might display a collection of butterflies.

When I was an undergraduate, Plimpton was very much in evidence after big football games, making his rounds to his various clubs. He instantly infused wherever he went with his sparkling mix of clubbiness and celebrity.

I ran into him once at the Yale game. He didn't know who I was, but I invited him to come to the party we were having afterward at the Signet, where he had been a member. He arrived with Gore Vidal in tow, and also William Styron, and a couple of minor literary lights and Kennedy cousins. After a few drinks, his entire entourage, with me now tagging along, swept over to the Lampoon Castle for more revelry.

A few years later, when I had just started working for *Time,* I shared a summer house in Sag Harbor and, on July 4, I was told that we were all going to the end of Town Line Road to George Plimpton's fireworks party. I protested that we hadn't been invited, but I was informed that our gang of softball players and junior journalists traditionally snuck onto the lawn, and if anyone asked, we were supposed to say we were friends of Wilfrid Sheed or something.

We sat in a dark recess of his great beachfront lawn and I watched him from afar as he readied the fireworks and wandered around with an aura that Gatsby would have envied. Then, to my horror, he wandered over to our group. I was about to stammer something about being a guest of the Sheeds when he said, "Hi, Walter, how are things at the *Lampoon*?"

He remembered everybody, and was always gracious. But there's something even more telling about this anecdote. It shows me trying to emulate Plimpton. He was the master of the anecdote that gave the pretense of being self-deprecating yet was also a bit name-dropping and self-inflating.

A good example was an event at Harvard where he was an after-dinner speaker, one of the many roles in life he mastered. He told of being invited to Camp David by the elder George Bush for a weekend. On the last afternoon, they were playing tennis and Plimpton recalled marveling that, with all the things going on in the world, the phone had never rung to interrupt the president. Then, suddenly, the phone at court-side rings. The president walks over, picks it up, nods, and then turns to Plimpton. "It's for you," he says. Plimpton told the tale with such self-effacing charm that only later did it sink in what a deft example of name- and place-dropping it was.

This style formed the basis for his signature books, the participatory journalism sports books, the most famous being *Paper Lion*, in which he tried out and briefly played for the Detroit Lions at age thirty-six. "I wore my helmet throughout the game, even though I spent most of it on the bench, because I had trouble getting it on and off," reported the real-life Walter Mitty with the deft self-deprecating ironic cadences of Mitty's own creator James Thurber.

His charm was that he knew how to share his Walter Mitty fantasies, which included not only being a Paper Lion but also being the character George Plimpton, which he played to the hilt.

My favorite tale of his involves Jerry Spinelli, who used most of his savings account, $425, to bid during a Philadelphia PBS station auction for a night on the town with Plimpton. When they arrive in New York,

Spinelli's wife confides that her husband wants to be a writer. Plimpton's heart sinks. But he decides to cancel his plan to take the Spinellis to see a play and eat at a midtown steakhouse, and instead takes the couple to Elaine's, where he knew his writer and publishing friends would be hanging out. Plimpton walked through the restaurant introducing all of his friends to "Jerry Spinelli, the writer from Philadelphia." There was Kurt Vonnegut and Jill Krementz at the first table with a bearded older man—Plimpton introduced him to Spinelli as the novelist James Farrell, even though he wasn't. They went through the restaurant, filled with the likes of Gay Talese, Irwin Shaw, Willie Morris. At each table, Plimpton introduced "the Philadelphia writer Jerry Spinelli." Finally they got to Woody Allen's table, where everyone knows you should never stop or intrude. But Plimpton, fulfilling his Mitty fantasy tour duty, interrupted to say, "Woody, forgive me, this is Jerry Spinelli, the writer from Philadelphia." Allen looked up slowly, stared a moment, and mysteriously replied, "Yes, I know." A few moments later, Spinelli's wife whispered to Plimpton, "He's going to be unbearable from now on." But what Plimpton understood—and was gracious enough to enable—was that people would love to share the name- and place-dropping participatory fantasies that he could weave.

His secret to success was that he conducted all aspects of his life as if he were playing the role of the master of ceremonies. Clubbable, puckish, witty, prank-loving—Jester, Ibis, Blot all rolled into one.

And his feel for fantasy, combined with his eye for people and ear for anecdotes, made him a very, very good writer. By taking Walter Mitty to a new level, and writing about the adventures so deftly, Plimpton came close to being a Thurber.

Close. But not quite. Herein lies the cautionary tale. Lean forward and listen up, for this could happen to you.

Near the end of his life, he began to seem a bit wistful and rueful. He had been offered a hefty advance to write a big book, a memoir of his life and times that—done right—could have, and should have, and maybe would have put him up there with James Thurber, perhaps even Henry Adams.

It brought home the questions that his friends sometimes asked: If he had cut back a bit on the evenings at the Brook Club and dinners at Elaine's and the book parties and even some of the *Paris Review* work, if he had been willing to look like he was trying hard, rather than floating merrily through life, might he be able to ascend into the literary pantheon? Or, as he sometimes self-deprecatingly put it, "I could have been a contender, right?"

I once ran into him at the Milan airport (how's that for Plimptonian name- and place-dropping?) and he graced me with the quasi-intimacy he could bestow in his clubbable manner by asking whether I thought he could, instead of writing his opus memoir, get away with writing a book about his ancestor Adelbert Ames, the youngest Union general during the Civil War, who became the governor of Mississippi during Reconstruction. He preferred the ironic detachment of a *Lampoon* editor to the reflection and introspection and sweat of a literary memoirist.

Like many very clubbable folks, I think he never wanted to be seen trying too hard, working up a sweat, striving. And thus he settled for being charming, and amusing, and at times brilliant and dazzling.

He gave the lie to Socrates' maxim that the unexamined life is not worth living.

He lit up the night, turned his world into a *Lampoon* party. And he grew comfortable with the fact that his literary work might seem, when compared to that of an Updike, a bit ephemeral—like some especially lovely fireworks blossoming in the night.

Indeed, perhaps the best final words in a eulogy about Plimpton are the final words of a eulogy that he gave for a friend named Jimmy Grucci, a Long Island fireworks manufacturer who was killed when his factory in Bellport exploded. "Artists," Plimpton said, "are perhaps fortunate in that they leave evidence of their greatness after they have gone—books, concertos, paintings, ballets. Who here in this church will not remember Jimmy Grucci when they see an especially lovely firework blossom in the night sky?" And who in this church will not remember George Plimpton whenever the night sky is merrily lit?

A Bold, Old Idea for
Saving Journalism

In the opening essay in this book, I concluded by saying that I worry about the future of journalism—and about the ability of those who need to pay a mortgage and put food on the table to make a living by writing, or by any other form of creation of intellectual property. In the digital age, we need to find ways to get people to pay for things that can be copied for free. That's difficult. In January 2009, I addressed this subject when I gave the Hays Press-Enterprise Lecture in San Diego, reprinted below, which was excerpted as a Time *cover story. My premise was that we should charge for some online content. Quite a few appalled pulpitarians of the blogosphere attacked the article, some very thoughtfully and sensibly. But subsequently there has been a gradual change in thinking: No longer is it axiomatic that all information has to be free. People came up with a variety of new ideas for funding journalism in the digital age. I do not think that my* Time *cover caused this change in attitude, any more than a rooster should think that his crowing caused the sun to rise. But like the rooster, I happened to squawk at the right time—just as it was becoming imperative to have some new thinking about the business models for journalism and all creative content.*

In this speech, one thing I suggested was creating an easy system for micropayments, which got some attention. It was one of many approaches I advocated, and I did not mean to suggest that micropayments would be the primary method for news organizations to charge for content. I think the subscription model will be the most common. But I believed then, and still do, that some easy micropayment system is needed for those Web surfers who want a specific article or issue of a paper but may not wish to subscribe. On gaming and social networking sites, where the users are younger and thus more adaptable than

the more conservative Web curates in their thirties and forties, we are
already seeing these easy-pay systems for small purchases catching on.
Jon Stewart on The Daily Show *advanced another approach: News*
organizations could license their content in bulk to various search
engines and aggregators. In addition, the mix of options should and
probably will include sites that depend on voluntary donations. And
finally, I believe that commodity news—the stories that people can get
from a wide variety of sources—will end up remaining free. My hope
is that the ability to charge for stories that are special will be an incen-
tive for journalists to focus on producing stories that are special, rather
than merely replicating what other organizations are doing. A mix of
all of these options will help us move back toward a model in which
the creators of cool, valuable intellectual property (stories, newspapers,
magazines, songs, pictures, videos, apps) have a right to benefit when
it is copied—in other words, a copyright system like we've had for three
hundred years.

During the past few months, the crisis in journalism has reached melt-
down proportions. It is now possible to contemplate a time in the near
future when major towns will no longer have a newspaper and when
magazines and network-news operations will employ no more than a
handful of reporters.

There is, however, a striking and somewhat odd fact about this crisis.
Newspapers now have more readers than ever. Their content, as well as
that of newsmagazines and other producers of traditional journalism, is
more popular than ever—even (in fact, especially) among young people.

The problem is that fewer of these consumers are paying. Instead, they
are reading it online, where news organizations are merrily giving away
their entire publications for free. Who can blame them? Even an old
print junkie like me has quit subscribing to the *New York Times,* because
I read it online for free.

This is not a business model that makes a lot of sense. Perhaps it
appeared to make sense when Web advertising was booming and every
half-sentient publisher could pretend to be among the clan who "got it"
by chanting the mantra that the ad-supported Web was "the future." But

when Web advertising declined in the fourth quarter of 2008, free felt like the future of journalism only in the sense that a steep cliff is the future for a herd of lemmings.

Newspapers and magazines traditionally have had three revenue sources: newsstand sales, subscriptions, and advertising. The new business model relies only on the last of these. That makes for a wobbly stool even when the one leg is strong. When it weakens, the stool is likely to fall.

Henry Luce, a cofounder of *Time,* disdained the notion of giveaway publications that relied solely on ad revenue. He called that formula "morally abhorrent" and also "economically self-defeating." That was because he believed that good journalism required that a publication's primary duty be to its readers, not to its advertisers. In an advertising-only revenue model, the incentive is perverse. It is also self-defeating, because eventually you will weaken your bond with your readers if you do not feel directly dependent upon them for your revenue.

When a man knows he is to be hanged in a fortnight, Dr. Johnson said, it concentrates his mind wonderfully. Journalism's fortnight is upon us, and I suspect that 2009 will be remembered as the year that newspapers, followed by magazines and other content creators, realize that further rounds of cost-cutting will not stave off the hangman. They will, instead, start exploring, as they should, new business models.

One option for survival being tried by some publications, such as the *Christian Science Monitor* and the Detroit *Free Press,* is to eliminate or drastically cut their print editions and focus on their free Web sites. For some, that makes sense. It will, and should, be one of the waves of the future.

That approach, however, still makes a publication totally dependent on ad dollars. So I am hoping that this year will see the dawn of another option that some news organizations might pursue. It's a bold, old idea: getting paid by users for some of the services and journalism they produce. If this happens, the advertising implosion of 2008 will have the benefit of birthing a business strategy that permits publications to become more beholden to their readers.

This notion of charging readers is an old idea not simply because newspapers and magazines have been doing it for nearly four centuries. It's also something that used to happen at the dawn of the online era in the early 1990s. Back then there were a passel of online service companies, such as Prodigy, CompuServe, Delphi, and AOL. They used to charge users for the minutes that they were online. It was in their interest to keep them online for as long as possible. As a result, good content was valued. When I was in charge of online media at *Time* back then, every year or so we would play off AOL and CompuServe. The bidding one year reached $1 million for our magazine and bulletin boards.

Then along came various tools that made it easier for publications and users to venture onto the open Internet rather than remain in the walled gardens created by the online services. There were various protocols for posting and finding content on the Internet. They had funny names, such as Gopher and Archie, and prosaic ones, such as file transfer protocol and the World Wide Web. I remember talking to Louis Rossetto, then the editor of *Wired,* in a lobby of New York's Waldorf-Astoria during the 1994 National Magazine Awards lunch. We discussed ways to put our respective magazines directly on the Internet, rather than on AOL or CompuServe, and we decided that the best way was to use the hypertext markup language and transfer protocols that defined the World Wide Web. *Wired* and *Time* both made the plunge onto the Web the same week in 1994, and within a year most other publications had done so as well.

We were inventing things such as banner ads, so we didn't try very hard to impose subscription fees. And thus we abandoned getting paid for our content.

One of history's ironies is that the concept of hypertext—an embedded Web link that refers you to another page or site—had been invented by Ted Nelson in the early 1960s with the potential for enabling micropayments for content. He wanted to make sure that the people who created good stuff were rewarded for it. In his vision, all links on a page would facilitate the accrual of small, automatic payments for whatever content was accessed.

Instead, the Web got caught up in the ethos that information wants to be free. Other folks smarter than we were had avoided that trap.

For example, when Bill Gates noticed in 1976 that hobbyists were freely sharing Altair BASIC, a code he and his colleagues had written, he sent an open letter to members of the Homebrew Computer Club telling them to stop. "One thing you do is prevent good software from being written," he railed. "Who can afford to do professional work for nothing?"

The easy Internet ad dollars of the late 1990s enticed newspapers and magazines to put all of their content, plus a whole lot of blogs and whistles, onto their Web sites for free. But much of the ad dollars ended up flowing to groups who did not actually create content, especially not journalistic reporting, but instead piggybacked on it: search engines, portals, and aggregators who compiled pages of links and pointers.

Another group also benefited from this system where content, reporting, and information were all posted for free: the Internet service providers, including the big telephone and cable companies. They get to charge customers $20 to $30 a month for access to this trove of free content and services. It was not in their interest to facilitate easy ways for newspapers and other media creators to charge for their content. Thus we have a world in which phone companies make it easy and expected for kids to pay up to 20 cents when they send a text message, but it seems technologically and psychologically difficult to get people to pay 10 cents for a magazine, newspaper, or newscast.

Currently a few newspapers—most notably the *Wall Street Journal*—charge for their online editions by requiring a monthly subscription. When Rupert Murdoch acquired the *Journal,* he ruminated publicly about dropping the fee. But Murdoch is, above all, a smart businessman. He took a look at the economics and decided it was lunacy to forgo the revenue—and that was even before the online ad market began contracting. Now his move looks really smart. Paid subscriptions for the *Journal*'s Web site were up 7 percent in a very gloomy 2008.

Subscriptions are likely to be the most prevalent method of charging for content, but I don't think that should be the *only* way to charge for content. A person who wants a copy of one day's edition of a newspaper or is enticed by a link to an interesting article is rarely going to go through the cost and hassle of signing up for a subscription under the current payment systems. Especially if it's a paper that he or she doesn't plan to read regularly. The key for attracting online revenue in such situations, I think, is coming up with an iTunes-easy, quick micropayment method. We need something like digital coins or an E-ZPass digital wallet—a one-click system that will permit impulse purchases of a newspaper, magazine, article, blog, application, or video for a nickel, dime, or whatever the creator chooses to charge.

Admittedly, the Internet has been littered for the past fifteen years by micropayment companies that have failed. Remember Flooz, Beenz, CyberCash, BitPass, Peppercoin, and DigiCash? Barely. Many tracts and blog entries have been written about why the concept can't work because of mental transaction costs and the like.

But things have changed. "With newspapers entering bankruptcy even as their audience grows, the threat is not just to the companies that own them, but also to the news itself," wrote the savvy *New York Times* columnist David Carr in a column endorsing the idea of paying for content. This creates a necessity that ought to be the mother of invention.

In addition, the two most creative digital innovators have shown that a pay-per-drink model can work when it's made easy enough: Steve Jobs got music consumers (of all people) comfortable with the concept of paying 99 cents for a tune instead of Napsterizing an entire industry, and Jeff Bezos with his Kindle showed that consumers would buy electronic versions of books, magazines, and newspapers if purchases could be done simply.

What Internet payment options are there today? PayPal is the most famous, but it's cumbersome and has transaction costs too high for impulse buys of less than a dollar. As usual, the denizens of social network sites such as Facebook and MySpace are leading the way by using systems such as Spare Change, which allows them to charge their PayPal accounts or credit cards to get digital currency that they can spend in small doses. Similar services include Bee-Tokens and Tipjoy. Twitter users have Twitpay, which is a micropayment service for the micromessaging set. Gamers have also been pioneers in purchasing digital currency that can be used for impulse buys during online role-playing games. The users of these gaming and social networking sites tend to be younger and thus more adaptable than the more conservative users in their thirties and forties, who tend to be more resistant to change.

The ideal micropayment system would be so easy to use that you'd hardly think about making an impulse purchase—akin to such gizmos as the E-ZPass, which somehow zaps out electronic change as you glide through a highway tollbooth, then replenishes itself when necessary by charging $25 to your credit card. I see no need for itemized accounting. Indeed, the lack of itemized bills floating around would make it particularly appealing to those who purchase things a bit more titillating than the *Wall Street Journal*.

Under a micropayment system, a newspaper might decide to charge a nickel for an article, or a dime for that day's full edition and Web site access, or $2 for a month's worth of editions and Web access. Some surfers would balk, but I suspect most would merrily click through if it were cheap and easy enough. Subscribers to the physical version of the paper could get the online version for free. Bundling free online access with paid subscriptions to the print product, as the *Wall Street Journal* does, could stem the erosion of print subscriptions that is currently being caused by folks like me who don't see the need to pay for a print publication if everything in it is online for free.

The system could be used for all forms of media: magazines and blogs, games and apps, TV newscasts and amateur videos, porn pictures and policy monographs, the reports of citizen journalists, recipes of great cooks, and songs of garage bands. This would offer a lifeline not just to traditional media outlets; it would also nourish and encourage all sorts of citizen journalism and blogging. Citizen journalists and bloggers have vastly enriched our realms of information and ideas. But most cannot make much money at it. As a result, they tend to do it for the ego kick or as a civic contribution, and they tend to be from the more privileged elite. A micropayment system would allow regular folks, the type who have to worry about feeding their families and paying their mortgages, to supplement their income by doing citizen journalism that is of value to their community.

Choosing to charge for content is merely one of many options that could play a role in sustaining a diverse media mix in this country. Many newspapers and magazines—and bloggers and citizen journalists—would decide to remain free, or rely on a tip jar for voluntary donations, or be subsidized by public-interest organizations or rich owners. That's fine. The more competing business models there are, the healthier the resulting media mix will be.

But a payment system would provide another option. Newspapers that felt their daily output was worth a dime—and whose readers felt that way—could end up charging a dime, and thus be more likely to survive and even thrive. The people at these papers would also wake up each morning with the worthy incentive to produce a paper that people thought was worth at least a dime.

By charging for their content—both through subscriptions and through single-copy micropayments—these newspapers would be in a position to make bundling or licensing deals with the big search engines and aggregators. For a modest licensing fee, the search engines that are willing to pay the newspaper could then in turn offer their users access to that newspaper without having to stop at a pay wall.

When I used to go fishing in the bayous of Louisiana as a young boy, my friend Thomas would sometimes steal ice from those machines outside gas stations. He had the theory that ice should be free. We didn't reflect much on who would make the ice if it were free, but fortunately, we grew out of that phase. Likewise, those who believe that all content should be free should reflect on who will open bureaus in Baghdad or be able to fly off as freelancers to report in Rwanda under such a system.

Over the past few weeks, for example, I've had a deep interest in what was happening in Gaza and how it might affect the status of Hamas. I've turned to the smart and nuanced reporting of Ethan Bronner of the *New York Times,* Griff Witte and Jonathan Finer of the *Washington Post,* and Ashraf Khalil of the *Los Angeles Times.* They are all deeply informed about the region. They are brave and industrious about getting to Gaza City and the various villages farther south. And it is valuable to me as a reader and, I think, to the world at large that their newspapers are willing—and able—to pay their salaries and expenses so that they can feed our desire for independent information.

So I hope that 2009 will be the year when a few good newspapers and other creators of valuable content start thinking about charging. I say this not because I am "evil," which is the description my daughter slings at those who want to charge for their content or music or applications on the Web. Instead, I say this because my daughter is very creative, and when she gets older and produces some really neat digital stuff, I want her to get paid for it rather than coming to me for money or deciding that it makes more sense to be an investment banker.

I say this, too, because I love journalism. I think it is valuable and should be valued by its consumers. That is why I want journalists to focus on producing things that people will pay for, rather than turning out the bland commodity news that people can find in a dozen other places. That way, journalists will again be beholden mainly to their readers, rather than catering increasingly to advertisers or other agendas. The need, even in the online realm, to be valued by readers—serving them first and foremost rather than relying only on advertising revenue—will allow the media once again to set their compass true to what journalism should always be about.

8. Interlude:
Woody Allen's Heart
Wants What It Wants

Sometimes in journalism, an interview subject is so revealing that you don't need to write a story or turn it into a profile. It speaks for itself. In the introduction to this book I mentioned my Woody Allen interview, which showed me again that journalism's secret is that people like to talk. Allow them to, and you have a story. This interview was done in August 1992, after the story broke about Allen's dispute with his former lover Mia Farrow over his relationship with her adopted daughter Soon-Yi Previn, and her allegations involving another of her daughters, Dylan. He invited me over to his Manhattan apartment. His final comment, "The heart wants what it wants," became a famous quote.

Q. How could you get involved with someone who was almost a daughter?

A. I am not Soon-Yi's father or stepfather. I've never even lived with Mia. I've never in my entire life slept at Mia's apartment, and I never even used to go over there until my children came along seven years ago. I never had any family dinners over there. I was not a father to her adopted kids in any sense of the word.

Q. But wasn't it breaking many bonds of trust to become involved with your lover's daughter?

A. There's no downside to it. The only thing unusual is that she's Mia's daughter. But she's an adopted daughter and a grown woman. I could have met her at a party or something.

Q. Were you still romantically involved with Mia when you became interested in Soon-Yi?

A. My relationship with Mia was simply a cordial one in the past four years, a dinner maybe once a week together. Our romantic relationship tapered off after the birth of Satchel, tapered off quickly.

Q. What was your relationship with Soon-Yi when you first started going over there to visit your children?

A. I never had a single extended conversation with her. As a matter of fact, I don't even think she liked me too much. The last thing I was interested in was the whole parcel of Mia's children.

Q. Why did you want to have children with Mia?

A. I didn't. She adopted Dylan, I didn't. But a month after she was there, I found myself bonding with her. She was just the greatest little girl. Suddenly I got tuned into the joys of parenthood. When Mia said it would be nice if she had someone else, I think I'll adopt another child, I said great. And coincidentally she got pregnant shortly after that. I was delighted.

Q. But then what happened to your relationship?

A. The relationship was starting to wane anyhow. Dylan's arrival sort of resuscitated it for a while; we had something in common, co-parenting the kids. But when Satchel came along, it drifted down to a polite and cordial end.

Q. But didn't you become a father surrogate to the children she had adopted with André Previn?

A. I was not involved with the other kids. They had their own father. I didn't spend much time with them, particularly the girls. I spent absolutely zero time with any of them. This was not some type of family unit in any remote way.

Q. Soon-Yi never treated you as a father figure?

A. Not remotely. She never said two words to me. For years I thought Soon-Yi was studying to be a nun. She was going to Sacred Heart, so I thought, well, I had no idea what she was doing. I was only interested in my own kids.

Q. Don't you worry about what the children might feel when their dad is sleeping with someone they consider a sister?

A. I don't think they think of "sleeping with." They only know what is constantly drummed into them. And I don't think my children feel any lack of affection or any rivalry. Soon-Yi and I will be very, very cognizant of their situation and feelings.

Q. Is Soon-Yi mentally handicapped in some way, as some have said?

A. No! Am I going to spend my time with a mental deficient? I mean, use your head. What would be the interest? She is not a mental deficient in any remote way. She goes to college, she is a psychology major, she has a B average.

Q. No learning disability?

A. Yes, a learning disability. I don't know what. She came here when she was seven and didn't know the language.

Q. How did your relationship with her begin?

A. One night, just fortuitously, I was over at Mia's, and I had no one to go to the basketball game with. And Soon-Yi said, I'll go. And so I took her, and I found her interested and delightful. This was a couple of years ago. Mia had encouraged me to get to know her. She would say, Take a walk with Soon-Yi, do something with her. Try and make friends with her. She's not really as hostile to you as you might think. Mia thought it was fine I took her to the game.

Q. So then you started secretly dating her?

A. No. I took her to a game again, maybe a month later. And this happened on a few occasions. And we struck up a relationship. It was strictly—I don't want to say an intellectual relationship, because I'm not saying we were discussing Kant or anything, but we chatted about different things.

Q. Did you talk about Mia?

A. Well, yes, I'm not sure I want to get into that too deeply, but she told me things that were surprising to me about the family, and that it was not exactly as happy as I thought it was. She and the other kids had problems with their mother. Soon-Yi did not have a good relationship with her, and we spoke about that. She said her mother had been very cruel to her.

Q. Physically?

A. Physically, and mentally. Mia was very impatient with her. She had hit her with a brush. She had written English words on her hand because she couldn't learn them, and made her go to school with them on her hand, and that humiliated her. I believe also she threatened to put Soon-Yi into an institution because she was impatient with her for having trouble learning the language. There were many other things. But I don't want to say, because I don't want to get anybody in trouble. But if I do have to say them someday, I will.

Q. But she may have been telling you these things because she was interested in you or trying to get back at her mother. How do you know they were true?

A. Because when I made it my business to check about it, I found out. She was worse to Soon-Yi because she stood up to her. And there was a definite difference in the way she treated the adopted children and her own children.

Q. How did your sexual relationship with Soon-Yi come about?

A. We'd chat when I came over to Mia's house. It started to become hotter and heavier late last year, very late. We had a number of conversations, saw a couple of movies, and you know it just—well, I can't say there was any cataclysmic moment.

Q. But you fell in love with her?

A. Yes, yes. My flair for drama. What can I say?

Q. She fell in love with you at the same time?

A. That's hard to say. My guess is after. She returned my feelings.

Q. But didn't it occur to you, worry you, that her feelings had something to do with her resentment of her mother?

A. I did not think that. I never think of those things. When you're having a nice time, you don't look for those motivations.

Q. Weren't you worried that the emotions and motivations were too complex for a young girl?

A. No. Because if you knew her, you'd know that's not true. She's a sharp, grown-up person. She's probably more mature than I am. I really mean that.

Q. Your movies always explore these types of emotions and motives. You must have sat up one night and thought about the problems you might cause dating the daughter of a previous lover, a mother she doesn't like?

A. I didn't think about her not liking Mia. I did think that, well, she is the adoptive daughter of my previous girlfriend, but that didn't mean anything to me. It didn't manifest itself in any significant way. She was a grown, sophisticated person. She was raised in New York.

Q. You're a guy who can find moral dilemmas in a broken DON'T WALK sign. Didn't you see some here?

A. I didn't find any moral dilemmas whatsoever. I didn't feel that just because she was Mia's daughter, there was any great moral dilemma. It was a fact, but not one with any great import. It wasn't like she was my daughter.

Q. Did you ever discuss with her, "What is Mom going to think of this?"

A. Mom would have thought more or less the same thing if it had been my secretary or an actress.

Q. Come on!

A. There is a different psychodynamic here, without any question, but the difference is one of small degree. If I had said to "Mom"—it was actually "Mia" that she called her—I'm in love with my secretary, there would have been some version of the same thing.

Q. But you didn't tell Mia before it blew up, right?

A. I wanted to make sure this thing was going to take off. For all I knew I might have just been a little footnote in Soon-Yi's life, and then she would later say, Well, I had a little flirtation with my mother's boyfriend at the end of their relationship.

Q. Did you talk to your analyst about how this would affect a child?

A. It wasn't so complex. It doesn't have that quality to it that you think.

Q. What about how it would affect her siblings?

A. These people are a collection of kids, they are not blood sisters or anything. If Mia did not keep them whipped up and enraged these days, telling them how to react, I don't think they would have cared two seconds.

Q. Did you really take nude pictures of Soon-Yi?

A. Yes. Soon-Yi had talked about being a model and said to me would I take some pictures of her without her clothes on. At this time we had an intimate relationship, so I said sure, and I did. It was just a lark of a moment.

Q. What did Mia do when she found them?

A. She hit the ceiling. I said, Look, our relationship has been over for some time. We should go our separate ways. The important thing is that we do what is right for our children. She was too angry. She instantly brought all the kids in on it, told all of them. This was January 13. It was a dreadful thing to do. She phoned people saying I had molested her daughter, raped her daughter.

Q. What did she do with Soon-Yi?

A. She locked Soon-Yi in the bedroom in her apartment—there's a lot of corroboration of this—beat her on numerous occasions, smashed her with a chair, kicked her, raised black-and-blue marks so the kids at school said, Where did you get those? Finally, through the intervention of, I believe, a doctor, she got out of the house and went to live up in the college dormitory.

Q. Did you talk to Soon-Yi while this was happening?

A. She called me once when she could get to a phone and told me she was fine, that her mother would say she was suicidal, but it's untrue. I love you, and I don't regret a minute of this.

Q. Why did the whole thing become public?

A. Suddenly I got a memo from her lawyers saying no more visits at all. Something had taken place. When I called Mia, she just slammed down the phone. And then I was told by my lawyers she was accusing me of child molestation. I thought this was so crazy and so sick that I cannot in all conscience leave those kids in that atmosphere. So I said, I realize this is going to be rough, but I'm going to sue for custody of the children.

Q. Did you molest your daughter?

A. I have not molested my daughter, nor would I ever.

Q. What did happen in the house?

A. It was a Wednesday two weeks ago. I came in the midafternoon for a visit. Allegedly, I took her in the attic, according to what the child-protection agency told me was the allegation, and did unspeakable things to her. But nothing at all happened. Nothing. In light-years I wouldn't go into an attic, I wouldn't even know how to find Mia's attic. I'm a famous claustrophobic. And I would not molest my daughter.

Q. Were you ever with her alone?

A. I may have been with her alone for a second, a moment or something, but I wasn't really alone with her. I am not going to, on the eve of hammering out a separation agreement, drive to Connecticut and in Mia's house, an open house, where there are two babysitters and people are always walking in and out, I'm not going to take her and molest her.

Q. Mia was there?

A. Of course she was there.

Q. There must have been some incident, some basis for this charge?

A. No, nothing. I was never in a private room with Dylan. I slept downstairs that night in the guest bedroom. The next morning when I was about to leave, the kids ran downstairs and were jumping all over me and playing with me. And Dylan gave me some brochure from a toy store and she had checked off some toys she wanted me to get for her. Everything was wonderful.

Q. Have you seen Dylan's videotape?

A. No. And don't you think that's strange, that Mia made a videotape?

Q. Was there any other evidence?

A. She brought the kid to the doctor, and there is no physical evidence of anything.

Q. Then why do you think Mia and Dylan made the allegation?

A. The atmosphere up there in Connecticut is so rife with rage against me. So it's possible this emerged from that. But it also could have been made up intentionally.

Q. Have you talked to Mia recently?

A. Yes, in fact she called me five times today.

Q. What do you say to each other?

A. She said, Can we stop this grotesque publicity circus? And I said, You have hired a lawyer, you're parading relatives and the kids on television, you leaked this videotape of Dylan unconscionably. She said, Can't we negotiate this? And I said, First you must clear my name unequivocally. And if you do that and we can agree to give Dylan some real therapy to get over the dreadful scars of this thing, and I am part supervisor of that therapy, then okay, we can see if there's a way of toning things down.

Q. Do you use your movies to work through dilemmas you're facing in life?

A. No, people always confuse my movies and my life.

Q. But don't you confuse your movies and your life?

A. No. Movies are fiction. The plots of my movies don't have any relationship to my life. My next movie is a murder mystery.

Q. Who's going to get murdered?

A. Oh, some stranger.

Q. Inappropriate love with younger women seems to be a theme in your movies and in your life, right?

A. It's not a theme in my life. I've been married twice, both times to women practically my age. My two other relationships—Diane Keaton and Mia Farrow—they're not really much younger women.

Q. Will your relationship with Soon-Yi continue?

A. Yes. I'm in love with her. As soon as the reporters go away, we'll do the things we like to do. We'll walk and eat out and go to the movies and basketball games.

Q. What's your emotional bond, since it's not intellectual?

A. It's fully dimensional. I would not be interested in someone who's not interesting.

Q. Do you consider it a healthy, equal relationship?

A. Well, who knows? It's perfectly healthy. But I don't think equal is necessarily a desideratum. Sometimes equality in a relationship is great, sometimes inequality makes it work. But it's an equal-opportunity relationship. I mean, I'm not equal to her in certain ways.

The heart wants what it wants. There's no logic to those things. You meet someone and you fall in love and that's that.

9. NEW ORLEANS, MON AMOUR

Green Trees

The school I went to in New Orleans celebrated its centennial in 2003, and I was asked, along with other alumni, to reflect on a particular memory of it. Such invitations run the risk of inducing you to sound like a Robert Fulghum homily, but I realized that, clichéd as the concept might be, there were some lessons from kindergarten that resonate years later.

My most vivid memory from my schooldays at Newman is of a patch of land, just outside our kindergarten classroom, that was called Green Trees. It was no more than a tiny grove, but to our even tinier eyes it was an enchanted forest. "Once upon a time Newman children played under a stand of beautiful trees near this spot" reads the apologetic plaque on the building that replaced our verdant temple.

Although we did not know it then, Green Trees contained more lessons than all the classrooms of all the teachers we would have over thirteen years, no matter how great each and every Miss LaFrantz and Mrs. Grout turned out to be. It was the first place where we were permitted to venture out on our own, and there we learned to be little explorers in a world teeming with wonders. To paraphrase that Robert Fulghum book of a few years back, which highlighted these lessons of kindergarten, almost all we really needed to know we could learn in Green Trees.

There were plants large and small, each struggling to reach the sun, and even some that we had sowed ourselves in plastic trays on Miss LaFrantz's windowsill and then transplanted into the worm-rich soil. And we learned that as they grew taller, their roots grew equally deeper, and that both processes were important to their well-being, the growing up and the deepening of roots.

There were also the inchworms that climbed the tree trunks. They seemed always heading upward. Hunching their backs, then extending themselves, they would bend and stretch and reach for the sky, inch by inch, as they made their mysterious pilgrimage up the bark of the trees. If and when something happened and they fell to the ground, they would resume their journey unfazed, along the same path, inch by inch.

There were very few rules, but they were important ones. Find a buddy. Take turns. No whining. Those turned out to be important for the real world as well. We also learned another lesson there, and I can still hear its singsong chant: *Sticks and stones may break your bones, but words will never hurt you.* That one turned out to be wrong, as we would later discover, but it was useful to learn that not every lesson turns out to be right.

And there were Justin and Robby and Steffi and Billy and Alan and Allan and Rusty and Chip and at least two Lindas, each with their own lessons to teach. When it was time to leave each day, we would all gather under the metal and plastic awning on Loyola Street to wait for our car-pools, and the kindly old janitor would help us into the car and we would remember to say, "Thank you, Brown," until Billy's father, who was a rabbi, taught us another little lesson, and thenceforth we would remember to call him "Mr. Brown."

Eventually we learned the lessons—hold hands, look both ways— that allowed us to cross the street to Zara's Food Store and, figuring out the value of a dime and a dollar, buy a Barq's root beer or, in those days before Doritos, a bag of Lay's barbecue chips. And once we had learned to read, we could look at the sign in the window of the Laundromat on Jefferson Avenue that said WHITES ONLY and learn to wonder why.

Even after we became third-graders, and thus very sophisticated, we would still go back to Green Trees occasionally. And being by then a bit more mischievous, we would sometimes knock the inchworms off the trees and onto the ground. But they would still resume their journey to their mysterious high destinations, inch by inch by inch.

I sometimes yearn to go back to Green Trees, where we spent such wondrous days, to paraphrase James Agee, so successfully disguised to ourselves as children. But Green Trees exists now only in memory, and I guess that may be its final lesson for us. Nothing remains the same, except for a few timeless lessons that are as valid in Act III as they were in Act I. Remember your roots: They should deepen as you grow. Remember the inchworms. And because there are still a few streets left to cross, remember to hold hands and look both ways.

How to Bring the Magic Back

My favorite poem is T. S. Eliot's Four Quartets. *In the second of them, he notes, "Home is where one starts from. As we grow older / The world becomes stranger, the pattern more complicated." And in the last of the quartets, he concludes, "We shall not cease from exploration / And the end of all our exploring / Will be to arrive where we started / And know the place for the first time." I started this book by invoking New Orleans, and every year I go back to my hometown two or three times and feel that I know it always and also know it for the first time. I was in Italy when Katrina struck in 2005. On my way back home, I wrote this piece for* Time *discussing why New Orleans would come back, why the recovery would happen slowly, and why that slow pace was not a bad thing. I've not always been right in my journalism, but this time I think I was. New Orleans is irrepressible, and it has come back. Slowly, but with its soul intact.*

All of us from New Orleans have savored that Proust-bites-into-the-madeleine moment when a stray taste, sound, smell, or sight brings remembrances of things past. It happens whenever I hear the badly rhymed but beautifully mournful—now even more so—first few bars of "Do you know what it means to miss New Orleans?" It can even happen with a single chord. A friend gave me a CD of a local band called Jonas Rising, and at the sound of the very first Neville Brothers–inspired piano chord, I was back inside Tipitina's, where Napoleon Avenue meets the Mississippi, listening to Professor Longhair.

The taste of a particularly pungent garlic sauce can evoke similar remembrances. What makes New Orleans eating so joyous is not just classic restaurants like Antoine's or Commander's Palace. It's the neighborhood places like those just up Napoleon Avenue from Tipitina's: the pan-roasted oysters at Manale's and the fried ones at Casamento's, nestled between a costume store and a building-ornament supply shop.

My family home was, and I hope still is, on Napoleon Avenue as well. It's a raised West Indian cottage, at merely a hundred years old not historic by local standards, yet part of the distinctive mix that makes even the uncelebrated neighborhoods of New Orleans so seductive. It was in neighborhoods such as these, more than the famous ones, where people lost their lives and cherished communities were washed away. I glimpsed on CNN our avenue underwater and felt like crying.

I was just in Venice, a city of masks and decadent grace that New Orleanians are genetically encoded to find enchanting. Because it's a world treasure, there is an international Save Venice movement. I hope New Orleans will evoke the same response.

But saving New Orleans will require not merely re-creating the French Quarter. It will involve nurturing back to health the genuine and distinctive neighborhoods that serve as an incubator for the city's music and food and funkiness. A friend of mine, Stephanie Bruno, has run an organization that restores old shotgun cottages, the long and narrow houses built of old barge planks that dominate in the older areas. A New Orleans rebuilt with tract homes rather than shotguns would no longer have the same soul.

The best writers to have lived in New Orleans were William Faulkner and Tennessee Williams. But my other favorites were two who knew the neighborhoods better. Walker Percy wrote about the savory malaise emanating from middle-class enclaves such as Gentilly and Elysian Fields. And Lillian Hellman recalled wandering up Esplanade Avenue below the French Quarter.

Hellman titled her second book of memoirs *Pentimento,* meaning the brushstrokes and old images that struggle to emerge from a repainted canvas. You see that a lot in New Orleans: advertisements for defunct brands of beer and coffee poking through the fading paint of old brick buildings. Indeed, it has always been a city of masks and painted faces, with past mysteries and glories lurking faintly visible underneath.

After disasters such as last week's storm, it's commonplace to extol the fierce determination of the afflicted as they rise like a phoenix. But indomitable energy is not what earned New Orleans the sobriquet the Big Easy, and it has never been a phoenix in any sense. The evacuees I know talked about wandering to visit far-flung friends for a few months before heading home.

It's probably not in the nature of most New Orleanians to roll up their sleeves and quickly build a grander city. They're better at making things akin to Creole gumbo and Cajun jambalaya—which involve a variety of ingredients and spices that are blended slowly. You start by making a roux, the mix of hot oil and flour that can hold the tastes together, a process that ought not be rushed.

This easygoing lethargy might actually serve New Orleans well as it rebuilds. The city needs to restore itself authentically rather than produce a theme-park re-creation. It needs shotguns, not cold condos. Its talented preservation and community-planning experts should be offered the chance to devise an approach that revives charming old neighborhood patterns rather than producing alienating cul-de-sacs or artificial quaintness. It has the opportunity to rebuild itself in a way that emerges from its rich heritage while guarding against any projects that would sap its soul.

Like a pentimento, New Orleans has long been a canvas repeatedly repainted. Paint well, my artistic homeboys and -girls, and carefully. Preserve the previous layers, and let them guide your brushwork. One false stroke, and the magic could disappear.

The Future Restored

The last time that I saw Walker Percy, we talked about hurricanes. It was August 1988, the start of storm season, and I was down in New Orleans because the Republicans were holding their convention there. He let me know, gently, that his health was declining and I should come visit. So I snuck away from the *Time* magazine workspace at the convention and drove the causeway across Lake Pontchartrain on a Tuesday morning, when no news was supposed to happen.

He had a theory, which we discussed over a lunch of hog's head cheese and bourbon, that people are at their happiest when a hurricane is about to hit. When you're mired in the everydayness of ordinary life, he explained, you're likely to be afflicted by what he called "the malaise," a free-floating despair associated with the feeling that you're not a part of the world or connected to the people in it. You are alienated, detached. But not when a hurricane is about to hit! Everyone is focused, connected, engaged. We know what we're supposed to do, and we do it. It's only after the waters recede and the earth begins to heal that the malaise and alienation creep back.

It was midafternoon before I headed back. As I got on the causeway, I turned on the radio to discover that George Bush had picked Dan Quayle as his running mate. Both the choice and the timing were a surprise. Since I was the national editor of *Time,* my colleagues had been searching for me, but this was in the days before we had cell phones. I ended up being in serious trouble for disappearing without letting my bosses know where I was, but I had no regrets. It was the last time I was to see Walker Percy.

Hurricane Katrina in 2005 was, I think, an exception to Percy's theory. It wrought such destruction that, even years after the waters receded, the alienation and malaise have not returned. Instead, Katrina continues to keep people in New Orleans engaged and connected to one another. There's an edgy creativity that comes from the shared aftertaste of danger, and there's a sense of community that comes from being in the same boat. The city remains rife with enticing challenges that attract young people from around the country seeking to avoid the malaise and the everydayness of ordinary life.

I grew up on Napoleon Avenue in a racially diverse neighborhood called Broadmoor, right in the heart of the city. It was integrated in a way that was common in parts of New Orleans: Blacks and whites lived on the same blocks, but in the evening they went to separate corner bars, often across the street from each other. The black bars had a big Jax Beer sign out front, and the white bars advertised Dixie Beer. In other places where I've spent time—such as Boston, Atlanta, Washington, and Philadelphia—the upper-crust folks tend to think of themselves as racially enlightened, which they generally are, but their neighborhoods tend to be more segregated by race and class. The older core of New Orleans is one of the few places that offers the frictions and the friendships of mixed neighborhoods.

I remember the first time I became aware of the concept of race. I was six at the time and walking in Audubon Park with my cousin Allan, his family's black housekeeper, and her son. Allan announced he wanted to go on the big indoor merry-go-round. Suddenly, I recalled a sign that was on the door of that facility. It said WHITE ONLY. I had never focused on what that meant, but now it became clear to me. I tried to convince everyone that we didn't want to go on the merry-go-round, to no avail. When we got there and saw the sign, we paused for a while as everyone figured out that we couldn't go in. The pain of that moment still haunts me.

I came to believe that the cultural and ethnic interplay produced by the town's diversity—and especially the electricity that was generated by its integrated neighborhoods, such as Broadmoor, Tremé, Central City, Marigny, and the Irish Channel—was a source of its creativity. Valence Street near my house was the home of a private club called Valencia, where teenage white preppies hung out, and it was also the street where many old-line blacks and Creoles of color lived, including the Neville

Brothers, who named a New Orleans funk song after it. When we got old enough to graduate from Valencia to real bars, we moved a few blocks away to Tipitina's, on Napoleon Avenue at the river, which was a temple of New Orleans funk masters such as the Nevilles, Dr. John, Professor Longhair, and Allen Toussaint.

We also used to hang out at F&M Patio, around the corner on Tchoupitoulas Street. One night, we paid a princely sum to hear the queen of local soul, Irma Thomas. It was a great New Orleans crowd, racially mixed and exuding funky energy. Somewhere into the second song, my friend Stephanie Bruno whispered to me, "That's not Irma Thomas." I ignored her. A moment or two later, Stephanie made her assertion more loudly. I edged away. Soon Stephanie was making this announcement to everyone around her. There was a murmur. "That white girl's right," someone in the crowd shouted. "It's *not* Irma." Suddenly the singer was whisked offstage. It had been a scam by someone who had rented the place. We never got our money back.

I played clarinet growing up. Though I was never a star, I loved jazz. I used to sit at the feet of Willie Humphrey when he and his brother Percy played Preservation Hall, then I would go home and practice their versions of "Muskrat Ramble" and "The Saints." Later, I became friends with Tom Sancton, who went to college and worked at *Time* with me. He played clarinet far, far better than I did, and was such a close protégé of the great George Lewis that he played in his funeral parade. Tom once lured Willie and Percy Humphrey's band, when they were on tour in New York, to my loft in lower Manhattan for a jam session.

One thing that made my Napoleon Avenue neighborhood feel particularly integrated was the vibrant black bars and honky-tonks that were happy to let in white kids and didn't enforce the eighteen-year-old drinking age. There was Mason's Motel Americana on Claiborne Avenue, a concoction of motel rooms and lounges, the classiest of which, the VIP Room, featured Germaine Bazzle and the Gentlemen of Jazz. Slightly sultrier was Sylvia's on Freret Street; at 3 a.m., the great clarinetist and saxophonist James Rivers would show up for his set. There was also the street music. On Mardi Gras, we would get up early to scout out the marching clubs of black musicians who would parade as Indians—the

Neville Brothers' family tribe was called the Wild Tchoupitoulas—and then catch the meandering Zulu parade, an exultation of racial joy, signifying, and poking fun at stereotypes.

Although the old neighborhoods like ours remained integrated, the parents of some of my friends moved to the suburbs when we were growing up. During the 1950s and '60s, when new highways and mortgage programs promoted suburban homebuilding, New Orleans began to develop neighborhoods on its periphery that were mostly white, such as Lakeview, or mostly black, such as parts of the Lower Ninth Ward and New Orleans East. These tended to be on lower ground, in some cases below sea level. This was no mere happenstance. Back in the nineteenth century, people were smart enough to build on the higher areas. By the 1950s, it was mainly the low-lying areas that were yet to be developed. Thus, these were the neighborhoods that flooded when the levees failed during Hurricane Katrina.

A few weeks after the storm, I got a call from the governor asking me to be the vice-chairman of the Louisiana Recovery Authority. I didn't know her, and I was surprised by the offer. I pointed out that, even though I consider New Orleans home, I now live in Washington, D.C. But she said that someone living in Washington would be useful, so I accepted. I flew right down to Baton Rouge, and on the lawn of the governor's mansion we boarded a National Guard Chinook helicopter to tour New Orleans and the flooded parishes. The devastation was so bad that I was unsure if people would ever come home.

But by my next visit, a few weeks later, a few intrepid restaurants had reappeared, like crocuses. They were filled with people who wanted to see kindred intrepid spirits who had returned. The atmosphere was as energized and unalienated as the pre-hurricane parties that used to amuse Walker Percy. I went to Upperline, where the owner, JoAnn Clevenger, was holding court. There was Stephanie Bruno, my friend from kindergarten onward who was now running "Operation Comeback" for the Preservation Resource Center, and the writer Julia Read, whose bourbon-cured voice and Tallulah Bankhead personality were able to make even a disaster seem rather amusing. That night, over many Sazeracs, we plotted ways to entice others back. The method we settled upon, this being New Orleans, was to throw a party. We enlisted Wynton Marsalis to join the cause, and we chose to hold it on Martin Luther King weekend that upcoming January, part of a series of events that would culminate with the official reopening of Tulane University.

Wynton said he would be coming down after a performance at Carnegie Hall that Friday. I didn't know that he hated to fly. It wasn't until Saturday, when he called from the highway just north of Atlanta, that I realized he was being driven down in his band's tour bus. The party and related events were jammed, since everyone was eager to catch up and swap tales. It culminated with an amazing speech by Wynton, which he punctuated with riffs on his horn. "It's good to be home," he said. "It's especially good to be home in a time of crisis, because tough times force us to return to fundamentals. And there is nothing more fundamental than home."

The Tulane freshmen in the audience impressed me. They had been dispersed around the country for five months, and now they embodied the spirit of those eager to return to a challenge. After the September 11 attacks, I was struck by the folks whose instincts were to run toward the burning buildings to help, rather than to flee. The students who chose to be at Tulane after Katrina were a similar breed, the type who relish challenges and serving others, rather than going to more comfortable colleges in quiet enclaves. In my biographies, I've tried to reflect on the elements of good leadership. After Katrina, one person stood out: Scott Cowen, Tulane's president. He was steadfast, cool, and never lost his humor or optimism. Some others in town flinched, even fled. Cowen saw the crisis as an opportunity. Tulane became the primary engine of the town's revival, and in the process transformed itself into a unique institution in a unique place. In 2009, close to forty thousand students applied for admission, the greatest number ever, and it produced an incoming class with the highest test scores—and, no doubt, the greatest amount of spunk and drive and cool personalities—in Tulane's history. I'm not sure how good he'd look on a rearing stallion waving a hat, but we should build some kind of statue of Scott Cowen as a companion to the one we have of Andrew Jackson, who saved the city back in 1815.

On that helicopter tour when I first returned after the storm, I sat next to a volunteer, Sarah Usdin, who had previously been with Teach for America. She had tears in her eyes, but it was clear that she wasn't going to flee from this crisis. In addition to creating a corps of young teachers, Teach for America has become a wellspring of leadership talent; its alumni go on to become education entrepreneurs, administrators, and activists. Sarah was an example. In the months after our helicopter ride, she formed an organization called New Schools for New Orleans, to support school leaders who wanted to come to New Orleans to open charters or pioneer new educational opportunities.

Sarah's work was supported by the New Schools Venture Fund, started by Kim Smith as her project when she was a Henry Crown Fellow at the Aspen Institute, where I work. Each summer, the Fund convenes a meeting in Aspen of educational entrepreneurs, and at its July 2006 gathering they decided that they would help to reinvent the New Orleans system. Some initially worried that the task would be too daunting; I argued, perhaps too fervently, that if they were not willing to take on such a challenge they should find an easier line of work, such as managing a hedge fund.

The attendees decided that they needed a "harbormaster" in New Orleans, someone who could help bring in organizations, funders, and school operators. So one of the group, Matt Candler, was recruited to go down. Matt already had a great job helping charter-school operators in New York City, and he and his wife had just had their first child. So I thought it would be a hard sell. But when we talked, I realized that he was eager to move down. New Orleans was already becoming a magnet for the school reform movement. It offered the chance to invent a city school system from the ground up. For anyone infected with the spirit of the cause, to pass up the opportunity to go there was like missing the chance to fight beside Henry V at Agincourt. That desire to surge into the breach likewise infected another participant at the meeting, Jon Schnur, the head of New Leaders for New Schools, which seeks to recruit and train principals to work in inner-city schools. Jon, cheery and tenacious, moved from New York along with his pregnant wife and their two-year-old son. Like Teach for America, which has now quadrupled its corps size in New Orleans from 126 teachers to 500, Schnur's organization became a brain magnet in a town that had once suffered from a brain drain. In their first week of recruiting, they had two hundred applicants for ten openings.

These reformers have created a new type of school system, one that the writer Paul Tough described in the *New York Times* as "an educational landscape unlike any other, a radical experiment in reform." More than 60 percent of the students are in charter schools, all of which have open enrollment (they can't cherry-pick the best kids). The schools get to hire and fire teachers based on their performance. Parents get to choose which of the schools they want for their kids. The money follows the student, so schools that are bad attract fewer kids and end up shrinking or closing. Many of the charters have lengthened the school day to more than eight hours and the school year to more than ten months, two obvious ways to produce better outcomes; as a result, the noncharter schools, in order to compete, have lengthened their hours. Partly because of this, test scores in every grade and every subject have gone up significantly over the past three years. In fourth-grade English, there has been an eleven-point gain; in eighth-grade English, a sixteen-point gain.

The chairman of the Louisiana Recovery Authority was Norman Francis, the president of Xavier, a historically black Catholic university located near my family home. I had gotten to know Norman when I covered city hall for the *Times-Picayune;* he chaired a municipal board, and used to give me a ride home after work. I once ran into him on a street in Rome, and he invited me to a beatification ceremony that Pope John Paul II was conducting for a nun who had helped launch schools such as Xavier. From a back pew, I marveled at how much Norman reminded me of that pope: Decency and humility exude from every pore.

Although born to a relatively poor family, Norman had long ago become part of the city's black and Creole aristocracy. Many of the things we had to deal with in the Recovery Authority involved race, and Norman did a good job of protecting me. Most notable was the issue of rebuilding the devastated Lower Ninth Ward, which had been populated mainly by blacks. I felt it was wrong to send people back to a place that was below sea level and where the levees might not be ready until 2012.

We developed a plan that would buy up property in that area and offer "Road Home" incentives to resettle the former residents in a safer part of town. At one of our meetings, a group of white community organizers staged a noisy protest along with some of the blacks from the Lower Ninth. I was about to say something when Norman touched my arm. "Let me handle this," he said. He gave a very moving speech about the need for everyone to come back home, but he said that didn't mean we should rebuild where it was unsafe. Donna Brazile, my old source from my newspaper days in the 1970s, was also on our commission. She put it more bluntly. Looking at the white organizers, she said: You can move your families into the Lower Ninth, but don't you go trying to send my family back there.

As it turned out, a resolution evolved over time that made sense. The parts of the Lower Ninth that are above sea level, mainly the Holy Cross area near the river, have been built back nicely. College students from around the country have come to clean and restore the old shotgun houses there. Just above the Holy Cross area, along the industrial canal, there are a sprinkling of new houses—astonishing and delightful—built by Brad Pitt's Make It Right Foundation and the creative architects he lured to town. But the lower parts of the neighborhood have been allowed to go back to park and wetland, with the residents getting incentives to move into safer parts of the city. Practicality and individual common sense trumped political theatrics, as Benjamin Franklin would have hoped.

I realized better what some Lower Ninth Ward residents felt when one of the citywide planning proposals suggested that my neighborhood of Broadmoor, which had flooded badly during the storm, might be turned into parkland. The residents of Broadmoor, black and white, rallied together. Years ago, my parents had helped start the Broadmoor Improvement Association, with the goal of having a racially balanced organization that would work to keep the neighborhood mixed, rather than tipping white or black. Now the association had a critical new mission: Save the neighborhood from tipping into oblivion. Any racial differences were put aside. A rally, replete with jazz bands and food stalls, was held in the yard of our family home, and it spilled out into Napoleon

Avenue. The former mayor Moon Landrieu, a neighbor, was there, along with LaToya Cantrell, a cheerfully intense black woman who became the leader of the association.

Not only was the neighborhood saved, it became a model of rebuilding. Shortly after the storm, Doug Ahlers, a senior fellow at Harvard's Kennedy School, came to visit my house in Washington, D.C. He suggested that Harvard could hold a series of meetings to impart its expertise to those engaged in the recovery. I replied, I fear rather curtly, that the Harvard folks could do more good by coming to New Orleans and actually becoming engaged in the recovery, rather than merely dispensing expertise from afar. To my sweet surprise, Doug and an entire Harvard team indeed moved down, and (with some prodding from me) picked Broadmoor as their neighborhood to adopt. They were soon joined by a contingent of students from Bard College, who were as joyful in their spirit of service as their president who had encouraged them, Leon Botstein.

It was on my trip back to New Orleans around New Year's 2009, perhaps my twentieth return since the storm, that I finally quit worrying about whether the town would fully revive. My wife and I stayed in an apartment we use on Jackson Square, with a balcony overlooking the river and the levee where I proposed to her. I noticed that the traditional traits of the town—the old sounds and smells and tastes—had mostly been restored. The port, which for two centuries has made New Orleans a cosmopolitan crossroads, was back in full swing. All day and night I could hear the horns of the pushboats passing one another as they rounded Algiers Point, one long blast from the descending vessel to signal a port-to-port pass, two short blasts for a starboard-to-starboard one. The French Quarter was packed, Galatoire's filled with old friends and familiar waiters. The irrepressible James Carville and Mary Matalin had moved down to a gracious home near Tulane and become cheerleaders and intellectual dynamos for the town. At the Fair Grounds racetrack, the restored clubhouse looked a little too clean, but I was confident that would be rectified. On Napoleon Avenue, Tipitina's was back and honoring the legacy of Professor Longhair, while Manale's and Casamento's were back and honoring oysters. Further up Napoleon, our family home had been restored by my brother and his wife, who left intact, as the storm's only legacy, the spray-painted FEMA cross by our front door that noted which National Guard unit had first arrived there (California 5th) and how many dead they found inside (none).

These were the old neighborhoods of New Orleans, faithfully being restored in the manner I had hoped for in my *Time* essay "How to Bring the Magic Back," reprinted earlier in this collection. But what surprised me was not the restoration of the old but the advent of the new: the influx of innovators and entrepreneurs and creative young people who were painting, like a pentimento, fresh brushstrokes onto the canvas of New Orleans. Michael Lewis, who grew up in New Orleans and surpassed me as the most successful writer from Newman High School when he wrote *Liar's Poker,* told me that New Orleans after Katrina had the opportunity to recapture the entrepreneurial spirit it had in the late nineteenth century, when its young business leaders were creating the New Orleans Cotton Exchange and Edgar Degas was painting it. I thought he was crazy. He turned out to be right. Nowadays, a few blocks from the cotton and coffee exchanges that dominated New Orleans business a century ago is a building, dubbed the Intellectual Property, that has been taken over and rehabbed by start-up firms, led by Tim Williamson of the Idea Village. It houses small companies started by entrepreneurs who have moved to New Orleans from around the world.

The diversity of New Orleans is even greater now. Both blacks and whites have moved back, and there has also been a welcome influx of Vietnamese and Hispanics. My old Broadmoor neighborhood still has an equal share of white and black families, but it is now also graced by a couple of new seafood shops run by Vietnamese families.

In the wake of the storm, I began looking for a way to explore the creativity of New Orleans and celebrate its roots in the diversity of the local culture. As always, I felt it would be best done through a biographical narrative. The subject was an easy choice: Louis Armstrong, one of the greatest creative geniuses in American history. He grew up in my old neighborhood half a century before I did, but he led a very different life. He hustled nickels on streetcorners by selling the afternoon newspaper that I later wrote for. He was abandoned by his father, his mother was a struggling prostitute, and as a young boy he was arrested for shooting off a gun. A judge sentenced him to the Colored Waifs' Home. When we were working to help rebuild the school in our neighborhood, none of us—including the people at the school board—knew anything about the person it was named for, Andrew Wilson. But when I was reading in the archives about Armstrong's arrest, my head snapped when I noticed the name of the judge who sentenced him: Andrew Wilson. He was a white judge who helped to create schools for black youths, and he was the one who sent young Armstrong to the Waifs' Home, where he ended up learning to play the cornet.

All of the elements of New Orleans music a century ago flowed into making Armstrong who he was: the marching brass bands, the funeral parades, the rhythms that still echoed from the drummers of Congo Square, the gospel of his mother's sanctified church, the sophisticated orchestras led by Creoles of color, the ragtime piano playing in the brothels of Storyville, the nascent jazz sounds of Buddy Bolden at corner honky-tonks, the blues from the plantation field hands who had moved to town, and even the arrival of military bands from the Spanish-American War who came back to New Orleans and either played or hocked their horns. Plus, he learned Russian lullabies from a Jewish family that took him under their wing as a kid. What a rich combination! Armstrong embodies the cultural mix and creativity of New Orleans a century ago, and I hope that he can serve as the patron saint of those concepts today. Despite the hardships of his heritage, he always loved to please people, saw no harm in being an entertainer as well as an artist, and deeply believed that this is a wonderful world. He stands as a rebuke to the great scourge of history and of our world today: the tribalism that pits people of different religions, races, and ethnicities against one another.

Technology and media have the potential either to exacerbate this tribalism or to ameliorate it. With so many new sources for information, some people fall prey to the tendency to self-segregate into their own ideological bunkers with like-minded souls. They hunker down on their preferred end of the talk radio dial, seek out the cable news hosts who reinforce their biases, and lurk in the corners of the blogosphere shared by their ideological cronies. On the other hand, good narrative storytelling can bind us together, provoke shared sentiments, and evoke our common underlying values. Simply diagnosing our bouts of detachment and alienation, as Dr. Percy did, can help cure them. Narrative storytelling and journalism can also provide us with (as one of my early heroes, J. Anthony Lukas, entitled his book on the Boston desegregation battles) common ground—just as our nation's first towns had a commons where people of all backgrounds rubbed elbows and shared ideas.

Benjamin Franklin's greatest contribution to our nation was his emphasis on the importance of transcending tribalism and exalting the glory of pluralism. He ran away from the exclusionary fundamentalism of Puritan Boston—where questioning the prevailing orthodoxy meant having to move away and go establish Rhode Island or something—to the town of Philadelphia, where people of all sorts of religions and ethnic backgrounds were learning to live together. During his lifetime, he donated to the building fund of each and every church there. When they were building a new hall for visiting preachers, he wrote a fund-raising document that declared, "Even if the Mufti of Constantinople were to send a missionary to preach Mohammedanism to us, he would find a pulpit at his service." And on his deathbed, he was the largest individual contributor to the first synagogue in Philadelphia. When he died, instead of his minister accompanying his casket to the grave, all of Philadelphia's thirty-five preachers, priests, and ministers joined arms with the rabbi of the Jews to lead his funeral procession. Louis Armstrong likewise celebrated, through his music, the delightfully diverse variety of creative influences that enrich our society. The emotions and sentiments that are part of our shared narratives are evoked in his songs, whether it be "West End Blues" or "What a Wonderful World."

Transcending tribalism and strengthening the weave of multiethnic societies is one of our great challenges today, as it has been throughout history. In this struggle, I think that there is still a place for those who pursue the so-called writing life, and I hope there will always be. Good narrative reporting and writing, I believe, can bring us in touch with our shared humanity by telling tales about people—tales we can all relate to, ones that evoke values and sentiments we can all share. It can also, at its best, help us find common ground, both by encouraging us to be open to the joy of different ideas, as Franklin did, and by striking chords that resonate in us all, as Armstrong did.

Acknowledgments

I want to thank John Huey and Rick Stengel at Time Inc. for facilitating this book and for being fun friends and colleagues over the years. I also owe a lot of thanks to the other personal friends I worked with at *Time*, most notably Norman Pearlstine, Jim Kelly, Priscilla Painton, Nancy Gibbs, Josh Tyrangiel, Romesh Ratnesar, Joe Klein, Michael Elliott, and Joel Stein. I was edited by an array of great bosses over the years at *Time*, and instead of trying to single them all out, I would like to honor the memory of four who are no longer with us: Otto Friedrich, Ron Kriss, John Elson, and Henry Grunwald.

Alice Mayhew, who has been my editor at Simon & Schuster for almost thirty years and is mentioned in the first essay, drove this project, with the encouragement of Amanda Urban, who has been my agent for just as long. I also want to thank David Rosenthal at Simon & Schuster. I am also deeply grateful to my smart, fun, and astonishingly competent colleague at the Aspen Institute, Patricia Zindulka, who keeps everything under control. My greatest thanks, as usual, goes to my wife, Cathy, and our daughter, Betsy. They are delightful in all ways.

About the Author

Walter Isaacson is the president and CEO of the Aspen Institute. He has been chairman and CEO of CNN and managing editor at *Time* magazine. He is the author of *Einstein: His Life and Universe, Benjamin Franklin: An American Life, Kissinger: A Biography,* and he is the coauthor with Evan Thomas of *The Wise Men: Six Friends and the World They Made.* He lives with his wife and daughter in Washington, D.C.